THE FIVE DOLLAR DAY

SUNY Series in American Social History
Elizabeth Pleck and Charles Stephenson, Editors

THE
FIVE
DOLLAR
DAY

Labor Management and
Social Control in the
Ford Motor Company
1908–1921

STEPHEN MEYER III

State University of New York Press

ALBANY

Published by
State University of New York Press, Albany

Printed in the United States of America

For information, address State University of New York
Press, State University Plaza, Albany, N.Y., 12246

Library of Congress Cataloging in Publication Data

Meyer, Stephen, 1942–
  The Five Dollar Day

  (American social history)
  Bibliography: p. 229
  Includes index.
    1. Automobile industry workers—Michigan—Highland
Park—History. 2. Ford Motor Company—History.
3. Machinery in industry—Michigan—Highland Park—
History. 4. Automobile industry and trade—Michigan—
Highland Park—Personnel management—History.
5. Automobile industry and trade—Michigan—Highland
Park—Technological innovations—Social aspects—
History. I. Title. II. Series.
HD6331.18.A8M49   338.7'6292'0977433   80–22795
ISBN 0–87395–508–0
ISBN 0–87395–509–9 (pbk.)

TO MY PARENTS

Contents

Tables

Acknowledgments

The research for this book had its beginnings as a doctoral dissertation at Rutgers University. I especially want to thank the graduate students and faculty associated with the Comparative Labor History Program who made Rutgers an exciting place to study labor and social history. I particularly want to thank Warren Susman and Danny Walkowitz for allowing me the autonomy to pursue a fascinating topic. Peter Stearns, Rudy Bell, Norman Markowitz, Ron Grele, Dick Wasson, and many others established a positive intellectual environment for the study of how the other half lived. Many have read all or part of the original manuscript, notably Peter Stearns, Daniel Nelson, Margo Conk, David Noble, David Montgomery, Jim Cronin, Nathan Miller, David Brody, and Carl Torgoff. I sincerely want to thank them for their comments and suggestions.

I also want to express my appreciation to the staff members of the libraries and archives which provided the research materials for this book. The Ford Motor Company Archives, the Archives of Labor History and Urban Affairs at Wayne State University, the New York Public Library, the Rutgers University Library, the National Archives, the Burton Historical Collection of the Detroit Public Library, the Wisconsin State Historical Society, the Fromkin Collection at the University of Wisconsin-Milwaukee, and the Milwaukee Public Library provided invaluable aid and assistance. I especially want to thank the dozens of anonymous persons in the back rooms and basements of the libraries and archives who found, delivered, and copied the necessary materials.

In different forms, parts of this book have been presented at the 1977 MARHO Conference on History and Culture, the 1978 meeting of the American Historical Association, and the Interface '80 Humanities and Technology Conference. An earlier version of Chapter VII appeared in the *Journal of Social History*.

I also want to thank Marie Mayer and Jessica Myers who typed the manuscript on short notice.

And, finally, I want to express my deepest appreciation and gratitude to Margo, who gave her considerable intellectual and emotional support, and to Jennifer, Rachel, Stephen, and Eric, who constantly reminded me that the world is more than books.

1. Introduction

In the popular mind, Henry Ford and his Ford Motor Company have assumed mythic proportions within the framework of American consciousness. Ford was the archtype of the rags-to-riches myth—the poor farm boy who through spunk, discipline, and hard work moved up the social ladder to become skilled mechanic, engineer, and finally billionaire industrialist. He was the tinkerer-craftsman who produced one of many horseless carriages. In 1903, he founded the Ford Motor Company in a small Detroit workshop. In 1908, he introduced the Model T Ford and met with extraordinary commercial success. Between 1910 and 1914, the technical genius developed mass production and made the conveyor a symbol of the auto-industrial age. In 1914, Ford outraged financiers and industrialists and stunned trade unionists and socialists with his announcement of the then-outrageous Five Dollar Day. He immediately acquired the reputation of humanitarian, philanthropist, and social reformer. And, the Ford legend survived his repressive anti-labor policies in the 1920s and 1930s. In 1940, a Roper survey of American workers revealed that Ford ranked first as the political, industrial, or business leader most "helpful to labor."[1]

To be sure, the Ford myth took different forms with various interpretations. To the venerable John D. Rockefeller, the Ford Highland Park factory was "the industrial miracle of the ᴗge." To many others, Ford propounded a new religious cult and he was "the industrial high priest" or "the high priest of efficiency." To Charlie Chaplin, Ford brought on "Modern Times," with workers condemned to perpetual involuntary motions. To Ford workers, he brought on a new disease, Forditis, whose symptoms included "a nervous stomach and all parts of your body breaking down." To Aldous Huxley, Ford mass production inaugurated the "brave new world" which began in "the year of our Ford" with the birth of the Model T.[2]

Of course, the Ford legend contained much substance. The period from 1908 to 1921 was important for the development of the Ford

Motor Company, the automobile industry, and the American industrial economy. These developments took place in the Highland Park factory. In this period, the Ford Motor Company was a remarkable industrial and financial success. It rapidly increased the size of its workforce, the number of automobiles produced, and the amount of its net income. In 1903, it employed 125 workers who manufactured 1,700 automobiles. In 1908, 450 workmen produced 10,607 automobiles. In 1914, 12,880 workers produced 248,307 automobiles. And, in 1921, 32,679 persons manufactured 933,720 automobiles. This was a phenomenal growth in the size of the workforce and in the number of automobiles manufactured. For the same period, the company's net income also increased substantially. It grew from about $246,000 in the first year, to about $3,000,000 in 1909, to about $25,000,000 in 1914, and to almost $78,000,000 in 1921. And, the small Ford plant began as one of hundreds of small automobile manufacturers in 1903. Yet, in 1908, its share of the automobile market was 9.4 percent. In 1914, it reached 48 percent. Indeed, the period from 1908 to 1914 was one of spectacular organizational and technical innovation as workers and machines strained to satisfy the considerable popular demand for the Model T Ford.[3]

As a result, the legend and the success have generated countless articles and books on Henry Ford and his Ford Motor Company. The principal works are Allan Nevins and Frank Hill's multivolume *Ford* and Keith Sward's *The Legend of Henry Ford*. Sward, a psychologist who published his work first, has dismantled adequately the Ford myth. He thoroughly surveyed the primary and secondary literature, but he never had access to the Ford Archives. Later, Nevins and Hill compiled their truly massive and comprehensive history of Ford and his enterprise. But contained by the entrepreneurial spirit of the fifties, they did not view Ford and his industrial system with a sufficiently critical eye. They only too readily glossed and glided over the immense social and personal impact of the Ford industrial system on Ford workers. Recently, others have written in depth about Ford's influence on grass-roots America, his public image, and his psychological profile as a business leader. Nonetheless, Ford and his company require a new and substantive re-evaluation and reinterpretation. Recent trends in the history of technology, labor, and management force the relocation of Ford's place in the evolution of the American social and economic system. Such a reinterpretation is the purpose of this book.[4]

In the past, the history of technology has tended to emphasize the principal inventors, the internal history of technical innovations, and their entrepreneurial exploitation. It has divorced technology from the social relationships of the real industrial world. It has failed to address critically the profound social impact of technology on the world of work. And, this failure has resulted in misinformation on, and misinterpretations of, our social past and present. Recently, historians of technology have begun to chart new directions toward our understanding of the technological past. Merritt Roe Smith's work on the Harpers Ferry armory details the technical development of small arms manufacture with a sensitivity to the influence of technology on the work process. More significantly, David Noble's work on the engineering profession demonstrates how science and technology evolved to serve corporate interests in the late nineteenth and early twentieth centuries. And, his work on the numerical control of machine tools suggests the influence of social decisions and choices on the design of a modern generation of machine tools. Possibly, a "new" history of technology will stand beside the "new" labor and social histories.[5]

Within this context, the Ford Motor Company offers a critically important example of the social impact of technology on work processes. Uniquely situated in the historical evolution of industrial technology, the Ford Highland Park factory represented full realization of the American system of production and the maturation of the modern industrial age. And, the Ford experience suggests that the conscious control of labor and labor processes was an essential feature of the development of Ford industrial technologies. The Ford industrial technology did not emerge in a social vacuum, but in an environment of social and economic decisions and chioces about the nature of workers and work processes. Most important, the Highland Park plant transcended craft techniques in the metal and the carriage and wagon trades and moved toward the sophisticated, capital-intensive technologies of the auto-industrial age.

In this sense, the history of Ford industrial technology moves over to the terrain of the history of Ford labor. In recent years, the "new" labor history has examined and emphasized the worker rather than his institutions. It has studied "history from the bottom up" in order to uncover the richer and more complex textures of working-class life. The "new" labor history has followed the lead of Edward P. Thompson and Eric Hobsbawm in Great Britain and David Brody, Herbert Gutman, and David Montgomery in the United States. It has been far more sensitive to the questions of class, ethnicity, culture, family and community life, work processes, and work discipline. It truly has transformed our understanding of the role of labor in the American past.[6]

In spite of their considerable importance to American social and economic development, the history of Ford workers never really has been written. Of course, Nevins and Sward have touched on some aspects of the lives of Ford workers, but they consistently have focused on Ford or his company. Particularly in the early years, the Ford community of producers has remained in the background of the historical past. They did not conduct a successful great strike and did not create a formidable labor institution. Instead, their history has resided in the anonymous corners of the shops and departments of the Highland Park plant. Their history has involved changed work processes, diluted skills, degraded work, and transformed social relations between managers and workers and among workers themselves. It also has involved a persistent pattern of resistances and struggles against the disciplines and controls imposed from above.

So, the history of Ford labor is inextricably interconnected with the history of Ford management. Labor history must consider "history from the top down." Despite the prevailing American opinion that labor and management are bound together with common interests, they do have antagonistic interests in certain realms of their relationship. A bottom line is wages and profits. Here, both sides make the impossible demand for more, more, more. Another area is control over work and work processes with its mutual incompatible interests. Managers strive for discipline and productivity; workers demand autonomy and a reasonable pace of work.

The history of management also has been transformed in recent years. Alfred D. Chandler, the dean of American business historians, has produced a definitive work on the development of the modern managerial tradition. However, he basically has been silent on the impact of modern forms of management on workers and their work processes. Nonetheless, others have addressed these important questions. Daniel Nelson has written a survey on the origins of the "new factory system" from 1880 to 1920. Moreover, he included workers in this important aspect of American industrial development. And, David Montgomery has detailed the struggles between managers and workers over the control of labor and labor processes in the late nineteenth and early twentieth centuries. And, all three have indicated that the early twentieth century was critical for the evolution of modern management.[7]

In this respect, the Ford Motor Company emerged in the midst of the genesis of modern management. It stood at the transition from traditional and crude forms of labor management to modern and sophisticated ones. It combined the traditions of scientific management, welfare work, and personnel management. Moreover, for a brief period, the Ford Motor Company experimented with a unique and sophisticated set of social controls which presaged the social science approach of the Hawthorne experiments in the 1920s. The Ford experiment reflected the contradictory mood of the Progressive Era and contained a deep-seated paternalism towards Ford workers. In the end, it failed because it did not meet a fundamental managerial need—the discipline and control of the Ford labor force.

Against this backdrop, the basic theme of this book is the transformation of the industrial technology and the subsequent changes in the social and cultural framework of the modern factory. In other words, this book explores the development of a new industrial technology, the personal and social reaction of workers to that technology, and the managerial efforts to overcome worker resistance to the new form of production. In order to accomplish this, it draws together various strands from the discipline of history—the history of technology, social and labor history, cultural history, and business history.

This book begins with an examination of the introduction of the Model T Ford in 1908 and the evolution of mass production in the Ford Highland Park factory from 1910 to 1914. It pays particular attention to the adoption of new and advanced machine-tool technologies, the reoganization of work, and the development of the concepts of progressive production and progressive assembly. It explores the impact of these innovations on craft forms of production, skill, and the character of work. It then examines changes in the structure of the workforce within the factory. The emergence of the new form of specialized worker—the "deskilled" specialist—resulted in the influx of large numbers of new workers to the Ford factory. Not possessing the industrial skills and discipline that came from the traditional craft system, former peasants and former farmers created special problems for Ford factory managers.

Whereas the Ford Motor Company created the most sophisticated and efficient industrial technology of the time, serious social and psychological limitations to the new technology emerged. Low rates of productivity resulted from problems in which industrial managers labelled the "human element of production." These problems included preindustrial immigrant attitudes and forms of behavior,

worker lateness and absenteeism, high rates of labor turnover, soldiering and output restriction, and craft and industrial unionism. In
late 1913, as the coordinated and synchronized industrial processes
neared completion, the company selected John R. Lee to update and
upgrade its labor policies. Lee inaugurated a series of reforms which
followed the Progressive Era's pattern of welfare capitalism. He established an employment department and instituted a "skill-wages"
job classification system. This system it created a "job ladder" based
upon productivity and sought to connect industrial discipline with
the desire for upward mobility. He also instituted an Employees' Savings and Loan Association to ameliorate the economic insecurities of
immigrant working-class life.

Nevertheless, the Lee reforms did not solve the Ford labor problems. Consequently, in January 1914, the company went further and
announced its famous Five Dollar Day. More than simply a high-
wage policy, the Five Dollar Day attempted to solve attitudinal and
behavioral problems with an effort to change the worker's domestic
environment. The company divided the worker's income into approximately equal parts of wages and profits. Each worker received
his wages. However, the worker received his profits, and hence the
Five Dollar Day, only when he met specific standards of efficiency
and home life. The implementation of this labor policy required the
formation of a Sociological Department and its staff of investigators
to examine the Ford worker's domestic life and advise him how to
live in order to obtain profits. The company attempted to change an
immigrant worker's life and culture to its preconceived ideal of an
"American standard of living," which it felt was the basis for industrial efficiency. It even instituted an English School to teach the English language, American values and customs, and the proper habits
of work to foreign factory operatives.

However, the Ford industrial experiment proved short-lived. The
First World War undermined the unique Ford Profit-sharing Plan,
war-induced inflation eroded the financial incentive of the Five Dollar Day, the war-time labor market brought back labor problems,
and the national mood became more authoritarian and repressive.
During the war, Ford labor policies shifted from social uplift to industrial espionage. The American Protective League maintained a
network of spies within the Ford factory. It was connected to the
Sociological Department and to local, federal, and military authorities. It maintained reports on the anti-patriotism, trade
unionism, and inefficient habits of recalcitrant or dissident workers.

In 1919, the Automobile Workers' Union conducted a strike against a major Ford body supplier. In the face of labor insurgency in Detroit, the company resorted to factory spies to discover and eliminate inefficiency, trade unionists, and socialists from the Ford plant. From this point on, tougher labor policies forced the acceptance of more regimented work routines in the Ford factories.

In the end, the unique and short-lived Ford program did not succeed. Yet, its significance goes beyond the boundaries of success or failure. It marked an early managerial strategy to match working-class culture to the requirements of the modern factory. It sought to transform personal and social attitudes and behavior through the home and the community, but the root of Ford problems lay in the factory.

The primary perspective of this study is that of the automobile worker. Its purpose has been to detail the crucial events and circumstances that created modern line production in the automobile industry, as well as the reactions and responses of automobile workers to the new work processes. For this reason, the study has boundaries relative to time, place, and subject matter. First, the period from 1908 to 1921 has been emphasized because it contains important technical and managerial innovations in the Ford enterprise. It saw the introduction of the Model T Ford, the technical transformation of industrial processes, the experimentation with novel social controls, and the return to conventional management. Second, this study only examines developments in the Highland Park factory. To be sure, the Ford empire included numerous, but relatively small, branch assembly plants in this period. And, the huge River Rouge plant came into being at the end of this period. Nevertheless, the Highland Park plant was the location of Ford technological innovation and social experimentation. It employed the overwhelming majority of the Ford workforce with tens of thousands of workers. Third, this study does not focus on the biographical profile of the leading figures of the Ford Motor Company. From the perspective of Ford workers, Ford officials, engineers, and factory managers are important for what they did to industrial processes and how they thought about workers. Again, this is the story of automobile workers, a chapter in the larger history of labor and work in modern America.

2. The Evolution of the New Industrial Technology

I have heard it said, in fact I believe that it's quite a current thought, that we have taken skill out of work. We have not. We have put a higher skill into planning, management, and tool building, and the results of that skill are enjoyed by the man who is not skilled.[1]—Henry Ford, 1922

The dominant American attitude toward technology has been contained in the metaphor of "Prometheus unbound." Until recently, technology has been viewed generally as a powerful, positive, and autonomous force which, once unleashed, has provided greater and greater levels of material comfort for the Western world. To be sure, Marxists and humanists have criticized the prevailing mood, but they generally have been unheeded. Historians of technology have tended to emphasize the lives of great inventors, their creations, and their entrepreneurial development. Usually, the social context of innovation and change has concerned the social environment of the inventor or its industrial and commercial exploitation. Frequently, when historians have addressed the subject of industrial technology, they have stressed the achievements of the captains of industry, the innovations in factory methods and techniques, and the satisfaction of consumer desires. Too often, they have isolated industrial technology from the objects of technical change and have neglected its impact on workers. To date, historians have not integrated fully the fields of social history and the history of technology.[2]

Within this context, the experience of the Ford Motor Company represents an important case study for the integration of the history of technology and social history. For the early twentieth century, it provides an example for the detailed examination of the inter-relationship between industrial technology and work. Undoubtedly, automotive production technology established the pattern for technical change in the modern mass production industries through the twentieth century. In the matter of a few years, a single industrial establishment demonstrated the transition from traditional craft

9

forms of work to modern industrial ones. Additionally, in the popular mind, Henry Ford and the Ford Motor Company gave the world mass production with its modern dilemma of work and its discontents. While this popular view was only a partial truth, technical and organizational innovation in the Highland Park factory did represent, as Alfred Chandler noted, "the culimination of earlier developments in the metal working industries." Here, "the new technology was most fully applied" and "brought an enormously swift expansion in the output and productivity of a single factory." If the concept of mass production did not exactly originate in the Ford factory, Ford innovations nevertheless allowed the nearly universal extension of the American system of production and the general adoption of its principles. Through the 1920s, Fordization and Fordism characterized by true standardization and interchangeability of parts, work rationalization, and line production methods, became the label for modern industrial techniques in Detroit, the United States, and the entire world in industry after industry.[3]

Generally, American advances in industrial technology have been attributed to a shortage of skilled labor. Most certainly, such was the case for the Ford factory. Technical change was the result of a phenomenal growth in the volume of Model T production and the concommitant expansion of Ford labor force. In 1908, the Ford Motor Company employed an estimated 450 persons. By 1913, it grew to more than 14,000 workers. This growth created a monumental labor problem—a severe shortage of skilled mechanics who could machine and assemble parts for the popular Model T Ford. Consequently, the company hired large numbers of less-skilled and non-skilled American and immigrant workers. Prior to the rapid expansion in the workforce, Ford production workers were predominantly skilled American and German craftsmen. By 1914, three-quarters of the workforce was foreign-born and slightly more than half of the workforce came from southern and eastern Europe. Indeed, the workforce lacked traditional industrial skills. So, in the design of machines, the rationalization of work tasks and routines, and the rearrangement and integration of work processes, Ford managers and engineers found their technical solution to a social and economic problem. With advanced machine-tool technology, the division and subdivision of labor, and the novel techniques of line production and assembly, they relied on the traditional American solution to labor shortages. Technical and organizational innovation displaced skill. It permitted unskilled labor to perform work of high quality and in large quantities.[4]

Specifically, Ford managers and engineers redesigned what they labelled the "mechanical element" of production. The "human element" had to conform to its new work tasks and routines. The result was the destruction of traditional patterns of work and discipline and the overall deterioration of conditions of work in the newly mechanized factory. In order to produce their incredibly popular automobile and to overcome their shortage of skilled labor, Ford managers and engineers brought together and implemented a number of interconnected technical and managerial innovations. In the end, they revolutionized automobile production and factory production in the modern world.

The specific components for the new Ford industrial system were not entirely new. Yet, taken together and systematically applied, they completely transformed factory production. First, Ford managers and engineers standardized the design of their product. This enabled them to specialize and routinize machine and work processes throughout the Ford plant. Second, they used the most recent advances in machine-tool technology. The new machines "transferred" skill into the design of sophisticated and complicated machines. Third, they analyzed, rationalized, and reorganized work tasks and routines. In effect, they "Taylorized" work processes and eliminated wasteful moments and motions in the performance of work. In other words, they followed the proposals of Frederick W. Taylor, the originator of scientific management. Finally, they developed and extended the unique concepts of progressive production and progressive assembly. And, ultimately, they created an integrated industrial system. The result was a complete change in tasks and routines, a new occupational structure, and new forms of control in the various shops and departments of the Ford factory.

Founded in 1903, the Ford Motor Company followed the pattern of development of other early automobile manufacturers. Generally, the evolution of Ford manufacturing processes mirrored the pattern of growth for the industry. Automobile manufacture was a complicated process—first, the foundry production of castings and their machine production into individual parts; second, the assembly of these individual parts into components, such as a magneto or an engine; and, finally, the assembly of thousands of parts and components into the motor vehicle. The manufacture of parts and components often involved a substantial capital expenditure. At the same time, the infant automobile industry suffered from a volatile and fluctuating demand for its luxury product. Consequently, the Ford enterprise, like other early automobile manufacturers, reduced its financial risk through its concentration on the final assembly of automobiles. The company subcontracted the manufacture of various parts and components to outside machine shops and foundries. Gradually, as the company grew, it began to produce more and more of its own parts and components, such as engines, axles, transmissions, chassis, bodies, and so forth. By the 1920s, most automobile manufacturers produced all of their major parts and components and left the minor small ones to outside shops and factories. In the Ford Motor Company, the subsumption of part and component manufacture began in 1906 and rapidly accelerated with the manufacture of the popular Model T in 1908 and with the construction of the Highland Park plant in 1910.[5]

Against this background, from the early years until the arrival of assembly lines in 1914, the Ford shops relied on customary craft methods for the organization of production. To be sure, a long tradition of innovation and change existed in American workshops and factories. But, at the same time, a strong craft tradition delineated the boundaries for change in machines, work routines, and shop organization.

As David Montgomery and Daniel Nelson have noted, the late nineteenth- and early twentieth-century shop regimen relied on the work patterns of the "autonomous craftsman" and on the social relations of the "inside contract" and "helper" systems. "The functional autonomy of the craftsman," Montgomery wrote, "rested on both their superior knowledge, which made them self-directing at their tasks, and the supervision which they gave to one or more helpers." Many skilled workers, and sometimes even machine tenders and operators and journeymen machinists and fitters, "exercised broad discretion in the direction of their own work and that of their helpers. They often hired and fired their own helpers and paid the latter some fixed proportion of their earnings." Accordingly, Montgomery noted that custom and tradition ruled the shop in the form of output quotas and a "manly" bearing toward the boss and among fellow workers. Moreover, union work rules and the workers' ethic of mutual support were social and cultural manifestations of shop customs and traditions. As Nelson noted, the inside contract and helper systems centered around the contractor or skilled craftsman who directed small and relatively autonomous work groups. These skilled workers controlled their colleagues and assigned work tasks within their particular craft.[6]

For the craftsman, the skilled worker, or the contractor, their skill and knowledge translated into power. Craft skills and knowledge meant status, authority, and control over the performance of tasks within work groups. Indeed, from the 1890s to the 1920s, the development of systematic and scientific forms of management and control represented an effort to break the hold of the autonomous craftsman on the work force and on work procedures.

These customs and traditions formed the backdrop for the work patterns in the early automobile shops and factories. And, most certainly, they contained and restrained technical innovation in the Ford shops. For example, as late as 1912, Ford assembly procedures seemed rather routine. A photograph of the Ford engine assembly room showed a large room with row upon row of assembly benches. At the center of each bench was an engine block, on the side a vise, and behind the block bins of parts. H. L. Arnold, an industrial journalist, described traditional assembly operations in the Ford plant:

> Ordinary shop practice stations the principal component in a convenient place on the shop floor . . . and proceeds with the assembly by bringing other components to the principal component and applying or fixing them to the principal component which remains in place until the assembly is completed.

Even in June 1913, Fred H. Colvin, another industrial journalist, described traditional assembly procedures for the engine:

> Here motors in all stages of completion, the one in front simply having its valves in position, while the one behind it having its crankshaft put in place. The convenient arrangement of the assembling benches will be noted, the bins containing the parts to bring in the center of the benches so as to be easily reached by the assemblers on either side of the benches.

These three fragments of evidence suggested the customary Ford assembly procedures, work routines, and relationships among workers.[7]

At the assembly bench, the skilled worker occupied a central place. He began with a bare motor block, utilized a wide range of mental and manual skills, and attached part after part. Not only did he assemble parts, but he also "fitted" them. If two parts did not go together, he placed them in his vise and filed them to fit. The work routines contained variations in tasks and required considerable amounts of skill and judgment. Additionally, unskilled truckers served the skilled assemblers. When an assembler completed his engine, a trucker carried it away and provided a new motor block. The laborer also kept the assembler supplied with an adequate number of parts and components. Here, the division of labor was relatively primitive—essentially, the skilled and the unskilled. Under normal conditions, a Ford motor assembler needed almost a full day of work to complete a single engine.[8]

The Ford foundry also relied on traditional shop practices. In this period, the foundry relied on the skill and knowledge of the molder. Usually, the molder prepared a sand mold which accepted the molten metal and which hardened to form a rough casting. The coremaker, another highly skilled worker, prepared the core for the hollow part of the casting. Generally, the molder prepared the mold and poured the molten metal from his ladle, but sometimes he had the aid of helpers. Flaskers made the container to hold the mold, rammers forced the sand around the pattern for the mold, pourers poured the molten metal, skimmers removed impurities from the metal, and shakers shook the sand from the casting. Henry Ford described his early foundry:

> Our foundry used to be like other foundries. When we cast our first 'Model T' cylinders in 1910, everything in the place was done by hand; shovels and wheelbarrows abounded. The work was skilled or unskilled; we had moulders and we had laborers.

In this instance, the term molder referred to one of the many skilled specialties within the craft. Nonetheless, skilled molders surely exercised supervisory authority over their less-skilled helpers and laborers.[9]

In the Ford machine shops, the social relationships were much more dynamic and much less certain. From the 1880s on, factory managers and engineers devoted considerable attention to the productive efficiency of the machine shop. Yet, despite the efforts of Taylor and other systematic and scientific managers, craft customs and traditions, technological limitations, and market considerations hindered the efforts to manage and control independent machinists. For in spite of an increasing division of labor and an increasing technical sophistication, machinists still retained sufficient skill and knowledge to maintain some degree of functional autonomy.

By the turn of the century, technical and organizational innovation narrowed the range of the traditional machinist's skill. Both work tasks and basic machine tools became more specialized. But, the machinist still needed practical knowledge and manual ability. By this time, the division of labor progressed along the line of specialized work within the craft or the operation of specialized machine tools. For example, general workman, vise hand, die sinker, and tool maker represented specialities of the trade, lathe, planer, and milling machine operator represented specialized machine occupations. Nevertheless, even the specialized machinist exercised considerable intellectual and manual skills within a narrower range.

In 1900, while attempting to categorize the impact of machine-tool technology on work, United States Census officials first formulated the idea of three grades of factory workers on the basis of "experience" and "judgment." This was a forerunner to the contemporary classification of skilled, semi-skilled, and unskilled workers. In addition to foremen and "all-around" workmen, the "first class of skill" also included the "specialist, who, though he operates one kind of high grade machine, does important work with this to a high degree of perfection." In its definition of a competent workman, an International Association of Machinists' contract noted that the worker "shall be able to take any piece of work, pertaining to his class, with drawings and blue prints, and prosecute the work to completion within a reasonable time." The worker also had either to serve an apprenticeship or to work at the trade for four years. To be sure, machine hands and tenders operated some highly specialized and partially automatic machines. The trade was in a considerable state of flux. But, machinists who first entered the Ford shops in the early 1900s possessed the sophisticated intellectual and manual skills which translated blue prints into first-rate pieces of work.[10]

Until the full mechanization of the Ford factory, which began around 1910, assemblers, molders, machinists, and many other production workers were skilled craftsmen. Additionally, large numbers of less-skilled and unskilled workers—helpers, assistants, laborers, truckers, and so forth—complemented and assisted this highly skilled workforce. Indeed, until its technological and organizational transformation, the early Ford factory was "a congeries of craftsmen's shops rather than an integrated plant."[11]

The popular and practical design of the Model T Ford facilitated the technological and administrative transformation of the Ford factory. Gradually, as Model T sales increased and as production schedules stabilized, Ford and his engineers and managers began to realize the profound impact of product design on their factory operations. The standard design of the Model T influenced machine selection, work and task organization, and the integration of the entire plant. It facilitated the division of labor through the simplification of work routines. This, in turn, meant that some operations could be designed into machines. Finally, the systematic analysis of work and machines logically resulted in an equally systematic examination of the interconnected operations of the entire plant. To this end, the standard design proved a catalyst for innovation and for the integration of the entire Ford industrial system.

Henry Ford's personal contribution to this process was his dogged determination to realize his imaginative concept for the Model T Ford. "I will build," he proclaimed:

> a motor car for the great multitude. It will be large enough for the family, but small enough for the individual to care for. It will be constructed of the best materials, by the best men to be hired, after the simplest designs that modern engineering can devise.

In another instance, he suggested a relationship between design and production methods:

> The way to make automobiles is to make one automobile just like another automobile, to make them all alike, to make them come through the factory alike—just like one pin is like another pin when it comes from the pin factory, or one match is like another match when it comes from the match factory.

Indeed, Ford had a deceptively simple idea—"a motor car for the great multitude," a complicated product for a mass market, with "the simplest designs." He wanted to produce a standardized automobile that could be manufactured like a pin or a match.[12]

A stream of industrial journalists, engineers and others who visited the Ford plant testified to the advantage of standard design as the foundation of the remarkable technical and commercial success of the Ford enterprise. In 1914, H. L. Arnold noted the technological merits of a single and standard product: "The Ford car holds so closely to one unchanged model that it becomes commercially possible to equip the shops with every special tool, great or small, simple or complex, cheap or costly, which can be made to reduce production-labor costs." H. F. Porter elaborated on the varied economic and engineering benefits of Model T design. With the production of a single model, he noted that managers and engineers devoted their complete attention to the handling of men, machines, materials, and work routines. The Model T's "unlimited run" resulted in "a free hand in the selecting and developing machinery, special tools, dies, and men." Engineers and tool makers directed "their attention to changes in equipment and methods that will effect further cost reductions or increase the output per unit of floor space." Furthermore, supervisors and inspectors became more specialized and experienced in their work. Hence, the quality of the work improved and the amount of waste declined. Additionally, workers became more specialized and experienced in their repeated tasks and routines. Machine operators, he observed, "engaged regularly in repetitive work become highly proficient. The entire organization, in fact, becomes a body of specialized experts."[13]

Finally, Porter described how product design influenced work patterns and integrated industrial processes. "Nothing," he wrote:

> is quite so demoralizing to the smooth commercial operation of a factory as incessant changes in design. Even small changes at the beginning of the season occasion much confusion for weeks or months; meanwhile, production is curtailed and costs go skyward.

The problem involved the interaction of workers and machines. Both needed adjustments to the new conditions of changed product design. Workers had to change their tasks and routines. Machines required redesign.[14]

Porter cited an instance where "minor changes" in the design of the Model T sharply reduced worker productivity. Ford engineers changed the metallic composition of some parts and the appearance of the hood and fenders. "The first month," Porter noted, "saw production curtailed by fifty per cent; and it was nearly three months before the entire organization could be geared up for the stipulated work." A changed product meant alterations in machines and work tasks. Managers and workers had to rediscover the most efficient way to produce or assemble the different part or component.[15]

Once initiated, the process of standardization had its own inexorable inner logic. It influenced each routine and operation throughout the entire plant. In 1916, John R. Lee, a Ford factory manager described this process:

> For the past eight years, the plan of the company has been steadfastly toward standardization. A single model chassis with a very limited number of bodies have been built in large quantities with the exercise of exacting thought and care in the development of mechanism and material which are especially adapted to the product.

Consequently, the factory became an integrated industrial system. As Porter observed, the flow of materials to and through the plant had to be balanced perfectly. "Lapses," he related:

> . . . would, if given any leeway here, cause untold havoc. Thorough standardization in one department, therefore, entails equally thorough standardization in all other interdependent departments.

As in the eighteenth century textile mills, innovation in one area of production necessitated innovation in others. Technical advance in one shop created bottlenecks in other shops. And, these bottlenecks spurred innovation in technologically backward departments.[16]

For Porter, the standardized product was "Ford's great lesson for other manufacturers." He continued:

> let standardization begin with the design of the product itself. Ford believes in spending plenty of time to perfect the model in the first place. Thereafter, he tolerates no changes that are not justified fully by economic considerations.

Within this context, Ford had a sound economic logic in his oft-repeated statement that the customer could choose any color so long as it was black. Another color meant a deviation from a standard design and from standardized production procedures.[17]

In the development of their novel methods and techniques of production, Ford managers and engineers worked within a rapidly evolving tradition of American technological innovation. In 1912, a special subcommittee of the American Society of Mechanical Engineers (ASME) detailed this tradition in its survey of "the present state of the art of industrial management." In this study, American mechanical engineers attempted to synthesize the new industrial ideas and practices which bore the general label, "scientific management." The subcommittee wanted to amalgamate the ideas of Taylor and his followers and successors. In the process, it developed the notion of "labor-saving management." And, it concluded that the new art of management emphasized two older principles, the division of labor and the transference of skill, and a more recent one, the new "mental attitude" on the part of industrial engineers and managers.[18]

Indeed, the elements of this technical and managerial tradition provided the basis for innovation and change in the Ford factory. First, the ASME subcommittee cited the classical political economists, Adam Smith and Charles Babbage, for their definition of the division of labor. Smith and Babbage also provided examples on how the division and subdivision of work tasks and routines resulted in higher productivity. Second, the subcommittee pointed to Henry Maudsley's eighteenth-century invention of the lathe slide rest as an early and important illustration of the transference of skill from worker to machine. In its design, the survey noted, this mechanical device "substituted for the skillful control of hand tools." Finally, the ASME subcommittee noted a new attitude on the part of engineers:

an attitude of questioning, of research, of careful investigation of everything affecting the problems in hand, of seeking for exact knowledge and then shaping action on the discovered facts.

This new mental attitude brought the method of science to industry. The result was "to extend the principle of the transference of skill to production, so that it completely embraces every activity in manufacture." Ultimately, each principle related to the skill of workers: the division of labor simplified skills, the transfer of skill shifted it to the machine, and the new mental attitude uncovered its fundamental elements, and relocated skills in the design of work tasks and routines, of machines, and of the entire integrated industrial system.[19]

The new "scientific" division of labor was an important element in the evolution of mass production in the Ford factory. While Ford denied that "scientific management" or "Taylorism" formed the basis of his new industrial methods, most surely some elements of the new managerial tradition influenced the reorganization of work tasks and routines in the Highland Park plant. In 1912, the ASME also issued a report on "modern shop practice." It noted:

> One of the noteworthy improvements in modern shop practice is the application of the principles of scientific management. . . . Undoubtedly the fundamental principles are coming to be more thoroughly understood and are being quite generally applied.

Ford managers and engineers may not have followed a specific program, but they surely followed general principles. The new ideas on industrial management readily diffused through the community of factory owners, managers, engineers, superintendents, and foremen in the nation's more modern factories and particularly in Detroit's automobile plants.[20]

In fact, Taylor himself visited Detroit several times. In 1914, he addressed an assemblage of Detroit factory managers, superintendents, and foremen. Here, he commented favorably on the application and, in some instances, the autonomous development of his principles in the automobile industry. This industry, he said, was "the first instance in which a group of manufacturers had undertaken to install the principles of scientific management without the aid of experts." In Detroit, the practical men in automobile shops and factories independently developed and expanded on Taylor's general principles. And, Ford and his managers and skilled workers were at the forefront of technical innovation and change.[21]

In 1913, Fred H. Colvin, an industrial journalist, described Ford methods for the assembly of rear axles. The procedure, he related, "is one of the interesting propositions which show that motion study has been carefully looked into, whether it is called by that name or not." The assembly stands, he added, were "simply made" and "convenient for the man putting the axles together." Trays for parts and other materials were "arranged as conveniently as possible that the workman need reach but a short distance to find everything that he needs in making the complete assembly." Here, Ford managers and engineers paid considerable attention to the design of the work station. Yet, the work routine still required a skilled assembler.[22]

In 1914, H. L. Arnold commented on the Ford plant's "highly original and wonderfully effective cost-reducing methods." He then listed the basic principles for the Ford reorganization of work tasks and routines:

(1) A broad survey of the field of effort with a wholly free and unfettered mind.
(2) The careful examination of existing conditions.
(3) The elimination of every needless muscular movement and expenditure of energy.

In effect, Ford managers and engineers Taylorized work tasks and routines in their modern automobile factory. They followed Taylor's idea that intellectual activity should be separated from manual work and should be located in a planning department. As Taylor noted: "the cost of production is lowered by separating the work of planning and the brain work as much as possible from the manual labor." Through their accurate and methodical studies of work tasks and routines, Ford managers and engineers—the brain workers— eliminated nonproductive moments and motions from the work routines.[22]

Henry Ford detailed how the division of labor through time study changed the assembly procedures for pistons and rods. The "old plan" of assembly, he related, was:

... a very simple operation. The workman pushed the pin out of the piston, oiled the pin, slipped the rod in place, put the pin through the rod and piston, tightened on screw, and opened another screw. That was the whole operation. The foreman, examining the operation, could not discover why it should take as much as three minutes. He analyzed the motions with a stopwatch. He found that four hours of a nine-hour day were spent walking. The assembler did not go off anywhere, but he did shift his feet to gather in his materials and to push away his finished piece. In the whole task, each man performed six operations. The foreman devised a new plan; he split the operation into three divisions, put a slide on the bench and three men on each side of it, and an inspector at the end. Instead of one man performing the whole operation, one man then performed only one-third of the operation—he performed only as much as he could do without shifting his feet.

The reorganization of work resulted in a phenomenal increase in worker productivity. Under the old method, twenty-eight men assembled 175 pistons and rods in a nine-hour day; under the new one, seven men assembled 2,600 in an eight-hour day.[24]

Arnold reported on the division of labor for hand and automatic machine work throughout the entire Ford plant. Managers and engineers possessed "actual stop-watch time" for thousands of operations. "Minute division of labor," he concluded:

> is effective in labor-cost reducing in two ways: first by making the workman extremely skilled, so that he does his part with no needless motions, and secondly by training him to perform his operation with the least expenditure of will-power, and hence with the least brain fatigue.

In this instance, Arnold revealed an important aspect of the managerial attitude about technical and organizational achievements. Needless to say, his concept of skill differed considerably from that of the craftsman. Moreover, his ideal worker was the mindless automaton who applied himself constantly and consistently with little thought.[25]

In other instances, Ford managers and engineers established specific tasks and standards for machine and assembly operations. As early as 1908, William A. Klann, a machinist who became general foreman of motor assembly, related: "I was setting work standards. They didn't call it the Time Study Department then. It was work standards." In 1912, O. J. Abell, the Midwestern correspondent for *Iron Age*, noted that machine ratings for individual machines determined the work standards for Ford workers. The engineers determined the most efficient "possible rate of production and then made an allowance of perhaps 10 per cent for time when the operator was not at the machine. . . ." In other words, each machine operation had a predetermined output which the worker had to meet. The same was true for assembly operations. Surely, Taylor's "task idea" prevailed in the Ford shops. In both cases, the specific task determined the amount of a worker's effort.[26]

Next, improvements in machine-tool technology constituted a powerful force for the transformation of work routines and factory procedures. In fact, Ford industrial expansion occurred at the same time that machine tools underwent notable improvements in their design and construction. Until the early twentieth century, the general-purpose machine tool, which relied on the varied and complex skills of the machinist, prevailed in American workshops and factories. To be sure, some nineteenth-century industries developed their specialized machines for the volume production of nearly identical parts. Indeed, the automatic screw machine was a classic nineteenth-century example of the automatic and special-purpose machine. Additionally, the small arms, sewing machine, agricultural implement, and bicycle industries all made important contributions in the design of specialized machines for the manufacture of nearly identical parts. Nonetheless, due to technical limitations of the machines, these parts were not truly interchangeable, because they often required skilled mechanics to file and to "fit" the parts together. Undoubtedly, the new automobile industry sparked a most intense phase in the design and specialization of machine tools in the first decades of the twentieth century. As the new machine-tool technology acquired technical sophistication, the volume production of duplicate parts required little, if any, skill. Furthermore, assembly operations no longer needed skilled machinists. And, Ford engineers and tool makers were in the forefront of technical innovation in machine shop practices.[27]

In the short period from 1905 to 1912, the American Society of Mechanical Engineers reported on the significant advances in the design of industrial machinery. The basic principle was the transfer of skill from the worker to the machine. The special committee on machine shop practice reported:

> . . . 'The transference of skill" by the machine designer from the operators to the machines has embodied in the latter much of the accumulated experience of many mechanics working on simpler and more primitive tools; . . . much of the improvement in machine shop practice has appeared in the improvement of machine tools themselves in one way or another.

In the same year, the report on the art of industrial management also noted the significance of the transfer of skill. The committee reported:

> After the traditional skill of a trade, or the peculiar skill of a designer or inventor, has been transferred to a machine, an operator with little or no previously acquired skill can learn to handle it and turn off the product.

The transfer of skill involved an accumulation of small innovations and changes in the design and construction of machine tools.[28]

In its report, the ASME machine shop practice committee detailed some of these innovations and changes. In the short seven-year period, the traditional machine tools, such as drilling machines, lathes, milling machines, planers, boring machines, grinding machines, and gear-making machines, acquired new features. The new generation of machine tools became larger and more powerful. At the same time, they became more sophisticated and more specialized. New features made them semiautomatic, or even automatic, especially when used for high-volume production. The new machines gained special controls to change and to reverse speeds. They had special jigs and fixtures, improved clamps and chucks, and multiple spindles to hold the tool or work. All of these features simplified the "set up" and controlled the tolerances of the work. These new machines produced only a single part and enabled the production of large numbers of identical parts by unskilled workmen. In the end, the new specialized machines established the need for a new generation of specialized machine operators. These new workers had no skills and simply placed a piece in and removed it from the machine.[29]

From 1910 to 1914, Ford engineers and tool makers fully utilized and further developed this new machine-tool technology. For plant superintendent Charles Sorensen reported that the move to Highland Park in 1910 "was followed by a tremendous expansion in equipment." He continued:

> Until then, our production had been carried on with standard equipment; we had little experience with special tools or machinery for multiple operation. . . . But we soon made up for lost time and knowledge. After moving to Highland Park, we began developing special-type machines, multiple spindled drills, milling machines with multiple heads at different angles. Whenever I approached Mr. Ford on the possibility of new types of machine tools, he never hesitated for a moment.

Indeed, the company invested staggering amounts of capital for the purchase and construction of specialized machines for the manufacture of th- Model T Ford. By 1914, it spent $3.6 million for "plant, buildings, tanks and fixtures" and $2.8 million for "machine-tool equipment." For the manufacture of a single part, Ford engineers purchased the very best machines available. If a required machine did not exist on the market, they designed and built their own in the factory tool room. The company relied so thoroughly on the new productive technology that in 1914 the Highland Park plant had more than 15,000 machines and fewer than 13,000 workers. "The policy of the company," Allan Nevins wrote, "was to scrap old machines ruthlessly in favor of better types—even if 'old' meant a month's use."[30]

In addition to the purchase and construction of the most modern machine tools, Ford engineers designed and constructed special attachments, such as jigs, fixtures, and other mechanical devices, which transformed multipurpose machines into single-purpose ones. Not only engineers, but also skilled tool makers, experimental room hands, draftsmen, and metal pattern makers, developed and manufactured the novel machines and devices. In an era where craft skills and traditions still survived, little delineated the tasks of the college-educated engineer and the shop-bred mechanic. Both proved invaluable and essential for technical innovation in the Ford plant. The practical skilled workers, Arnold observed, "constitute the aristocracy of every shop." Moreover, they had to be good, experienced, and highly paid. "Nothing," he concluded, "is scamped or hurried in Ford's tool-making . . . , because economy in tool-making is rank extravagance." In the tool-making department, engineers and mechanics transferred skill from human to mechanical form in the design of machines and their attachments.[31]

In 1915, F. L. Faurote described the technical innovations and accomplishments of the tool designing department. "During the course of the last three years," he wrote:

over 140 special machines and several thousand special dies, tools, jigs and fixtures have been made. Fifty machines and 2,500 to 3,000 jigs and fixtures are not considered an unusual output for the 55 men employed in this department.

In June 1914, Arnold noted that the tool-making department employed 59 draftsmen and 472 toolmakers. At this time, a total of 871 skilled workers—draftsmen, patternmakers, toolmakers, and others—designed, constructed, and arranged the Ford plant's industrial equipment. "Improvements," Faurote noted:

are constantly being introduced. Hardly a week passes when

some radical change is not made in the various departments. The less efficient machine is displaced by the more efficient one. Not only the Ford engineers, but the men in the shops, are constantly trying to do things in an easier and better way.[32]

Jigs and fixtures were work-holding devices which adapted multi- and special-purpose machines for the high volume production of identical parts. Technically, a jig held work but was not fastened to the machine. A fixture also held work but was fastened to the table or the bed of the machine. In 1912, the ASME Machine Shop Committee reported: "The development of jigs and fixtures for interchangeable manufacturing has been remarkable." These new mechanical devices, it added, insured "interchangeability, low production costs, and systematic production." Generally, engineers and machinists referred to fixtures as "furniture" or "appliances" since they were additions to the table or the base of the machine. Ford managers, engineers, and skilled workers called these devices "farmers' tools" because they allowed green farm hands to produce large amounts of high-quality work.[33]

The design of jigs and particularly fixtures facilitated the transfer of skill from worker to machine tool. With these attachments, "practically unskilled labor" performed the work of "expert machinists and tool workers" in automobile shops and plants. Franklin D. Jones reported that proper design and correct construction allowed "equally good, or, in some cases, even better results to be obtained by a cheaper class of labor. . . ." Sterling H. Bunnell, a critic of American reliance on jigs and fixtures, also noted their impact on the productive skill of workers. "Evidently," he concluded:

> the jig equipment should be the minimum which will meet the requirements. This minimum will be set by the maximum of the trade workers' skill which can be obtained at a minimum price. Cheap men need expensive jigs, highly skilled men need little outside of their tool chests.

Detroit had an abundance of cheap men. The rapidly expanding automobile industry made a tight labor market for employers, and tens of thousands of unskilled American and immigrant workers swarmed to the city. As a result, Ford engineers and toolmakers attempted to select, design, and construct machine tools and attachments to match the skill level of the labor force.[34]

Several examples of the new Ford machines illustrated changes in the work routines. Many of these machines exhibited the very latest advances in design of the increasingly sophisticated American machine-tool technology. Throughout the Ford plant, examples abounded. The Foote-Burt Company manufactured a special drilling machine for the Ford Motor Company. It drilled holes for the Model T cylinder. This multiple drilling machine, Abel reported:

> is arranged to drill four sides of the cylinder, finishing 45 holes simultaneously. The cylinder is jigged into position, the operator throws the starting lever, the machine is equipped with automatic stop and reverse, the operator takes the cylinder out and the work is done.

This specialized machine was the pride of the Ford shops.[35]

In this instance, the special-purpose machine tool combined forty-five separate operations. In order to save labor costs, the specialized machine had to perform the greatest number of operations on a single piece of work. As Arnold noted: "in automatic machine work . . . time is saved by combining operations at one setting or chucking of the work." As human work became more routine, machine work became more varied. The worker placed and removed the piece; the machine performed a variety of different operations on it. The ideal was to minimize the cost of the machine and to maximize the machine's work on the piece.[36]

Another specialized Foote-Burt machine faced the top of the piston and cut grooves for the piston rings. The fixture which held the piston was a temporary connecting rod. "These machines," Colvin reported:

> are entirely automatic, except for placing the casting on the inverted spindle and starting the tools at work. . . . The top is faced off at the same time that the outside diameter is being turned, and the three grooving tools are automatically fed to the required depth. The feed is tripped automatically, and the cutters return to their original position, making it necessary for the operator only to release the star wheel clamp by which the pistons are held in position, slip out the pins and put another piston in position to return.

Two models of the machine existed—a roughing machine partially finished the work and a finishing machine completed it. The former processed four pistons; the latter two. The different capacities took into account the speed of the machines and the time it took operators to place and remove the pieces.[37]

Although hundreds of different special-purpose machine tools operated in the Ford shops, thousands of novel and innovative jigs and fixtures held work on these machines and also specialized the operations of standard machine tools. In 1912, Abel noticed a group of 100 "upright and sensitive drilling machines." In other words, the machines operated vertically and contained automatic control features. "All of the work for these machines," he continued, "is jigged and the same pieces go to the same machines and operators continuously." In addition, some fixtures were huge holding devices. Abel described an Ingersoll milling machine with a fixture that held six cylinders. The fixture moved the cylinder past the cutting tools which surfaced them. Abel noted: ". . . the operation is continuous, the operator setting up pieces at one end while those at the opposite end are being finished." In 1913, Colvin saw a larger fixture on the same machine. He related that "the entire 15 cylinders are carried on one fixture. . . . having a heavy base plate fastened to the base of the miller table, the base of the miller table, the base of the fixture carrying all of the necessary bolts and clamps so as to be self-contained in every way." Another large fixture carried thirty cylinder heads for milling in a similar manner.[38]

The Ford fixtures and machine tools also demonstrated new and higher levels of technical complexity. In 1913, Colvin detailed "the extremely interesting application of a Blanchard verticle spindle grinder. . . ." The fixture was a large circular magazine for holding valve lifters. A "magnetic chuck" held the magazine to the bed of the machine while the tool ground each valve lifter. Colvin reported:

> These holding rings are made in duplicate so that one ring can be loaded by a helper on a bench which stands conveniently near the grinder. This avoids practically all loss of time of the machine itself, after a ring is once loaded; for as soon as the work has been completed, the table is run forward. . . . the chucks demagnetized, the ring, with its 104 valve lifters, removed, and the freshly loaded spring put into place.

In 1915, Arnold described another multiple-operation machine with a complicated fixture. This New Britain Machine Tool Company creation drilled, bored, and reamed the piston-pin hole. "In this adequate and well designed machine," Arnold commented, "which is automatic save for fixing and removing pistons on the four arms of the work carrier, this fixture is automatically indexed by revolving the fixture on a horizontal axis. . . ." This magazine-style fixture rotated the piston through four stations: first, removal of old and placement of new piston; second, drilling; third, boring; and, finally, reaming. The workman simply unloaded and loaded pistons; the fixtures carried the work to the three different cutting tools.[39]

Finally, progressive production and progressive assembly involved the arrangement of men and machines and the coordination and synchronization of productive operations. They were the next logical step from the division of labor and the advanced and specialized machine tools. Assembly lines and conveyors were central images of Ford mass production. But, they represented only one aspect of the new innovation in the industrial process. As Ford engineers labeled it, the fundamental notion was "progressive" or "continuous" production. Following this idea, Ford managers and engineers arranged sequentially all industrial operations to manufacture and to assemble automobile parts, components, and the final product. "Progressive production," Arnold related, was:

> . . . the scheme of placing both machine and hand work in straight-line sequence of operations, so that the component in progress will travel the shortest road from start to finish, with no avoidable handling whatsoever.

Progressive production originated in the machine shops which produced finished metal parts around 1912 to 1913 and then gradually moved to assembly operations from 1913 to 1914.[40]

Continuous forms of production were not entirely new ideas and had a long history of evolution. In the past, successful manufacturers subdivided work processes, utilized advanced machinery, and even sequentially organized various phases of the industrial process. Nevertheless, the machine shop presented technical difficulties for this form of organization. In machine shops, custom located various machines—drillpresses, lathes, milling machines, etc.—in generic groups in different sections or departments of the factory. The technical problem was the connection of belts to overhead driveshafts to provide power for the individual machines, since similar machines could be connected readily to similar drive-shafts at the same locations. Under this system, managers and engineers attempted to move materials from department to department in a logical sequence. Nevertheless, this practice proved expensive. In order to perform the different machine operations on castings, a large corps of laborers carted them from machine operation to machine operation.[41]

At the time of the move to Highland Park, the factory community in general began to express more interest and concern about the location and arrangement of their machinery. Managers and engineers even began to experiment with the sequential placement of their machines. In 1912, the ASME reported:

> More attention is given to the relative location of tools in the shop in order that all machining operations can be performed with no unnecessary handling of the work, the aim being to finish the parts by advancing them from one tool to another in a direct line without any seesawing or useless movements.

Ford managers and engineers rapidly moved to the forefront of this experimentation and innovation.[42]

Charles Sorenson, a Ford production manager, described the plans for the move to the Highland Park plant. He related:

> A room was set aside for my assistants. We set up a layout board on which we worked the production lines and the placement of machines to scale. Numbered brass plates were attached to all the machines in the Piquette plant with corresponding tags on the layout boards so that every machine would be set up in its assigned place when the move to Highland Park was made.

Nonetheless, the rearrangement of the new plant was not quite as complete or as systematic as Sorensen implied. When Abel visited Highland Park in 1912, he commented on the sequential arrangement of a group of drill presses. But, the traditional group plan of machine arrangement seemed to prevail. "In keeping with the remarkable economy of floor space," he wrote, "the orderly arrangement, in groups, of the principal machining operations, is the most interesting features of the shop layout." The sequential arrangement of machines was within groups of machines. And machining departments were in the most logical proximity to each other.[43]

In 1913, Fred H. Colvin discovered an entirely different machine shop. In spite of a maze of belting, machines followed the logic of productive operations. "So thoroughly," he reported, "is the sequence of operations followed that we not only find drilling machines sandwiched in between heavy millers and even punch presses, but also carbonizing furnaces and babbitting equipment in the midst of the machines." The basis of factory departments shifted from class of machine operation performed to type of product produced. Porter added that "the plan of manufacture carries the parts along from machine to machine, with comparatively little labor; far less labor than would be necessary if the departments were arranged by operations instead of work." Within a single year, true progressive or continuous production, not simply the orderly flow of material from machine to machine or department to department, became a reality.[44]

Oscar Bornholt, a Ford mechanical engineer, calculated the economic advantages of sequential production. He noted that in the orthodox shop with generic groups of machines, the Model T cylinder casting would be trucked twelve times to perform the necessary machining operations. This included a trip back and forth to one department. He further estimated that trucking would require a workforce of about twenty-four men to handle 1,000 cylinders each day. Truckers, he noted, were "expensive" and their labor was "nonproductive." He then described another advantage:

When machines are placed according to sequence of operation, there is no trucking of parts after the first operation is started, as each operator lays the part down in such a manner as to allow the next operator to pick it up and perform his operation, and so on. When finished, the part goes either to the finished stock room or assembling department.

With sequential operations, workers moved parts through their departments. The rearrangement of machines eliminated the need for twenty-four costly truckers.[45]

As a consequence of this innovation, materials handling became a central concern of Ford managers and engineers. Progressive production meant the constant and continuous movement of raw materials, parts, and components to and through the Highland Park factory. To facilitate this movement, Ford engineers developed a number of new devices, such as gravity work-slides and rollways to move work by hand, and endless chains and endless conveyor belts to transport parts and materials from location to location. Overhead craneways carried the heavier and bulkier items or batches of parts to and from storage. The Ford engineers believed that "anything in the way of a work conveyor which keeps the work in progress off the shop floor, will be found to effect a large saving in direct labor costs, and to increase the factory maximum productive capacity." In other words, the mechanical movement of materials further eliminated the need for costly truckers and increased the amount of floor space for productive men and machines.[46]

Visitors to the Highland Park plant described the impact of these new methods on work in the Ford machine shops. Arnold commented: "the Ford engineers have taxed the convolutions of their brains to shorten lines of natural work-travel on the shop floors. . . ." Machines were much closer than customary shop practice dictated. So close, in fact, that "there is but barely room for the workman to make his needful movements." E. A. Rumley observed that "the men stand elbow to elbow, like a line of soldiers." Moreover, as it moved from hand to hand, each part of the Model T had "its predetermined path through the machine shop."[47]

From 1913 to 1914, Ford managers and engineers further refined their notion of progressive or continuous production with the creation of moving lines for the assembly of parts into automobile components and for the final assembly of parts and components into the Model T Ford. As late as 1913, Colvin described rather traditional methods and techniques for the assembly of engines, axles, and the final product. To be sure, some experimentation was under way. For automobile assembly, the work-process was divided and subdivided and workers performed specialized operations. At first, teams of workmen moved from car to car and attached their part or component. However, materials did not move in the same manner as in the machine shops. Two examples illustrated the evolution and the advantages of the Ford assembly lines. One was the magneto assembly line, the first to develop; and the other was the chassis assembly line, the most difficult to implement, into which all other parts and components flowed.[48]

The flywheel magneto provided the electrical charge to ignite the fuel of the Ford automobile. It was the first component to be assembled on a moving assembly line. Prior to May 1913, one Ford worker put together approximately 35 to 40 magnetos in a nine-hour day. A skilled assembler constructed the entire component. "The work was done by experienced men," H. L. Arnold noted, "but was not so uniformly satisfactory as was desired, and was costly . . . as all one-man assembly must of necessity be forever." In May 1913, Ford managers and engineers analyzed the work and subdivided it into twenty-nine separate operations. As in existing progressive machining operations, the assemblers passed the component from worker to worker by hand. The managers and engineers continued to redesign and to restructure the work and the assembly processes. They added a chain-driven conveyor to move the component from one worker to another. And, after March 1914, productivity dramatically increased—fourteen workers assembled 1,335 magnetos in an eight-hour day. Even though the working day was reduced by one hour, the assemblers more than doubled their average productivity and produced an average of 95 magnetos per person each day.[49]

Ford engineers duplicated this procedure with varying degrees of difficulty in other assembly departments throughout the Highland Park factory from the late summer of 1913 through 1914. They created a coordinated and synchronized industrial system as a result of their efforts to provide for the progressive machine production of parts and the progressive assembly of these parts into components and finally the Model T Ford. As Sorensen recalled:

What was worked at Ford was the practice of moving work from one quarter to another until it became a complete unit, then arranging the flow of these units at the right time and the right place to a moving assembly line from which came a finished product.

According to Sorensen, Clarence Avery tackled the problem of the coordination and synchronization of the newly mechanized plant. Trained over a period of eight months in each department, Avery:

worked out the timing schedules necessary before the installation of conveyor assembly systems to motors, fenders, magnetos, and transmissions. One by one those operations were revamped and continuously moving conveyors delivered assembled parts to the final assembly floor. Savings in labor time were enormous; some parts were put together six times as fast.

Hands, rollways, gravity slides, chain and belt conveyors, and overhead cranes moved materials from location to location. Men, machines and materials became an intricately interconnected mechanical organism.[50]

Eventually, everything flowed to the chassis assembly line, where "from 1,000 to 4,000 separate pieces of each chassis component" streamed "daily, infallibly, and constantly." Begun in the late summer of 1913 and completed in the late spring of 1914, chassis assembly lines presented the greatest difficulty to Ford engineers. Until August 1913, Ford workers assembled the Model T chassis as a single location. H. L. Arnold described the early method for chassis assembly:

> First, the front and rear axles were laid on the floor, then the chassis frame with springs in place was assembled with the axles, next the wheels were placed on the axles, and the remaining components were successively added to complete the chassis. All the components needed to make the chassis had to be brought by hand to each chassis assembly location.

At the time, 250 skilled assemblers with the assistance of 80 "component carriers" assembled 6,182 chassis in the course of one month. Colvin reported that the assemblers moved from chassis to chassis to attach their pieces or component. It required an average of 12½ hours of one workman's time to put together a single chassis.[51]

In August 1913, Ford managers and engineers began to analyze, experiment with, and systematize their procedures for chassis assembly. In September 1913, they connected the Model T chassis to a "rope and windlass" device and pulled it along a row of parts and components. Six assemblers and their helpers walked along with the chassis and attached the necessary parts and components as they went down the line. This resulted in a dramatic reduction of the assembly time for each chassis. It fell to an average of five hours and fifty minutes of a workman's time—a reduction of 50 percent. Next, in October, the mechanical device pulled the chassis along a line of 140 stationary assemblers. They stood at stations near supplies of parts and components and attached them as the chassis passed. The assembly time now averaged slightly less than three hours per worker. Additional changes in the length of the line and the number of stations further reduced the chassis assembly time. In January 1914, the engineers developed an "endless chain-driven" conveyor to pull the chassis along the line. In April 1914, they created a "man high" line to eliminate unnecessary and unproductive movements on the part of the workers. In the end, these experiments reduced chassis assembly time from 12½ hours to one hour and thirty-three minutes.[52]

By June 1914, Ford managers and engineers perfected the new chassis assembly line to their satisfaction and introduced it as a part of the normal industrial operations of the new mechanized Highland Park plant. Eighteen workmen performed the first two operations which set the chassis frames on two assembly lines. On these lines, unskilled assemblers performed the remaining forty-three operations to put together the Model T chassis. Mechanical conveyors delivered the parts and components to their stations. One hundred and forty-two workers assembled an average of 600 chassis in an eight-hour day. The average assembly time for each chassis under normal, as opposed to experimental, conditions was slightly under two hours of a worker's time. This was approximately one-sixth of the time that traditional methods and techniques of assembly required.[53]

The chassis assembly line capped the Ford system of mass production. A commonplace fact of our industrial world, Ford industrial processes fascinated and overwhelmed contemporary observers in 1914. They even impressed H. L. Arnold, a man thoroughly familiar with the very latest and most advanced industrial systems of this time. The Ford assembly lines, he said, afforded "a highly impressive spectacle." He described:

> Long lines of slowly moving assemblies in progress, busy troups of successive operators, the rapid growth of the chassis as component after component is added from overhead sources of supply, and, finally the instant start into self-moving power.

The main assembly line, he continued, excited "the liveliest interest and imagination" as "the varied elements" came together and formed "the new and seemingly vivified creation."[54]

In a few brief years, modern mass production became a reality in the Ford Highland factory. Within an extremely short period of time, Ford engineers and skilled workers transformed traditional industrial process and broke ground for modern forms of integrated and synchronized production. Although difficult, the technical and organizational problems were not insurmountable. Nevertheless, the new industrial technology was a mixed social blessing, perhaps even a curse. It promised a material cornucopia for all. Yet, at the same time, it contained incredible social costs. The world of work would never be the same again. The new industrial technology made the worker's daily routine more monotonous and more repetitive. It dramatically altered the social structure of the shop, the factory, and, in fact, modern industrial society. And, it possessed or required new patterns of authority and control over the workforce. Indeed, the new industrial technology had a profound impact on modern social existence.

3. The Social Impact of the New Technology at the Workplace

... Improvements in machinery and methods, and the specializing of operations are constantly reducing the necessity of skilled labor. It is up to us to change our plan of organization to meet these changed conditions or sink in the mire of degradation and become mere slaves.[1]—Detroit Metal Trades Council, *Circular for Industrial Unionism*, 1914

Equipment obviously sets the pace in the Ford shops. That is why Ford needs no highly refined method of wage payment to furnish an incentive for output. They must very nearly do a standard day's production whether they wish to or not. . . . The average Ford employee, like Barkus, is usually quite 'willing.'[2]—H. F. Porter, Industrial Journalist, 1916

The new Ford industrial technology had a dramatic impact on the character of work and on the social relations at the workplace. First, it completely transformed the tasks and routines in the various shops and departments of the Highland Park plant. In the past, highly skilled and relatively autonomous craftsmen performed the direct productive operation in the metal industries. In some instances, less-skilled specialists, who nonetheless had clearly identifiable on-the-job skills, operated specialized (but not automatic) machines or performed partially subdivided assembly operations. Now, however, Ford managers and engineers completely removed the traditional notion of skill from a workman's tasks and routines.

Second, the new industrial technology and the new tasks and routines altered the traditional social relationships in the Ford shops and departments. The "deskilled specialist" became the principal occupational group in the Ford plant. In addition, other occupational groups became more important in order to provide more direct and closer supervision over the less skilled workforce. Foremen, sub-foremen, "straw bosses," clerks, and inspectors increased in numbers and oversaw both the quantity and the quality of production.

Finally, the new technical system possessed new forms of control over the unskilled productive workforce. While office and shop supervision persisted, new technical and social forms of control evolved in the Ford shops. The design of machines, the arrangement of men and machines, the new forms of record keeping and inspection, and the new means of mechanical conveyance all controlled the pace, the intensity, and the quality of production.

The Ford technical and organizational innovations made work in the mechanized Highland Park factory more specialized, more repetitive, and more automatic. Indeed, the new technology and the minute subdivision of labor restructured work tasks and work routines to their most basic and fundamental elements. In machining operations, the design of machine tools made all work basically similar. The worker inserted a piece in the machine, threw a switch, and removed it. The work task and routine involved little thought or judgment, simply the rapid repetition of the same operation. Moreover, if he changed machines, he might have to relearn how to locate a piece, but his routine quickly would become monotonous. In assembly operations, the subdivision of labor and the mechanical movement of materials created similar conditions. In both instances, work lost its mental content and became a purely manual activity. The traditional notion of skill contained an intellectual component. The worker needed thought and judgment to perform his varied tasks. Now, skill in work required only physical attributes.[3]

To be sure, the image of work in the Highland Park factory varied with the eyes of the beholder. In 1914, a *New York Times* reporter observed that the Ford plant gave "the impression of bustle and confusion." Nevertheless, he continued, "if one picked out a single workman . . . as a rule that workman's duty was to make four or five continuous motions—nothing more." The worker did not appear to work hard. And, of course, his work was monotonous and routinized. "Indeed," the reporter concluded, "when you watched closely, nobody seemed to be hurrying. He performed the new motions his work required him to make, and that was all. There was no haste. It was all-clockwork!" The middle-class reporter did not consider the personal and social impact of the worker as part of a clock-like mechanical system.[4]

On the other hand, in the same year, John A. Fitch, a more sympathetic Progressive journalist, expressed the more typical reaction to Ford's system or continuous production. He related:

Fifteen thousand men work in gangs on the track system. Each gang, and each man on each gang has just one small thing to do—and do over and over again. It's push and bustle and go. The man behind you may shove his work at you at any moment—you must not hold back at any moment the man in front of you may be ready for another piece to work on—he must not be kept waiting.

Fitch also detailed the extent of the division of labor in the Ford plant. Each worker performed only a small fragment of a complete operation. In the motor assembly department:

One man fits the parts together so that the bolt holes come right. The next man fits the bolts into place. The next has a pan of nuts before him and all day he scoops them up and with his fingers starts them on the thread of the bolts. The next man has a wrench and he gives them the final twist that makes them tight.

Fitch marveled at the wonderful efficiency of the system, but he also considered how the workers felt. "It may be fine," he noted, "to see an automobile come through that door every twenty seconds—but you don't see them if your job is to start the nuts on the threads. You haven't time. There are always more bolts to be capped."[5]

Another more colorful journalist, Julian Street, found the Ford factory "a Gargantuan lunatic asylum where fifteen thousand raving, tearing maniacs had been given full authority to go ahead and do their damnedest." To be sure, he recognized the need for "relentless system" and "terrible efficiency" in the Ford machine shop. But, he continued:

to my mind unaccustomed to such things, the whole room, with its interminable aisles, its whirling shafts and wheels, its forest of roof-supporting posts and flapping, flying, leather belting, its endless rows of writhing machinery, its schrieking, hammering, and clatter, its smell of oil, its autumn haze of smoke, its savage-looking foreign population—to my mind it expressed but one thing, and that thing was delirium.

Only at the end of the process did he find "one complete lucid spot." Here, at the final assembly line, he discovered the reason and the ultimate logic for the system and efficiency. For outsiders, who stood and viewed from a distance, the Ford plant possessed a clock-like mechanical quality and conveyed a sense of activity, excitement, and accomplishment.[6]

On the other hand, workers, who were themselves parts of the intricate mechanical system, had quite different attitudes about, and reactions to, work in the Ford plant. In 1917, William A. Logan, president of the Automobile Workers' Union, wrote:

> The skilled mechanics may be in the factories, but they get little or no chance to use their skill. The work in each department is split up into many operations and instead of carrying a piece of work from start to finish they do only a small part, over and over, and thus an army of specialists is created.

In 1923, Logan recalled the impressions of some Ford workers. They said that "their grind is tedious and nerve-wrecking." Moreover, he related the words of one Ford worker: "If I keep putting on Nut No. 86 for about 86 more days, I will be Nut No. 86 in the Pontiac bughouse." On the assembly line, the image of the asylum was a real condition, rather than a metaphor.[7]

Other workers emphasized the monotony of repetitive tasks and routines and its impact on their mental and physical well-being. One worker was struck:

> by the way in which Henry has reduced the complexity of life to a definite number of jerks, twists, and turns. Once a Ford employee has learned the special spasm expected from him he can go through life without a single thought or emotion. When the whistle blows he starts to jerk and when the whistle blows again he stops jerking, and if that isn't the simple life, what is?

On another occasion, a ten-year Ford veteran recalled: "in that time, I was continuously honored with increased production until today the best of my life has been sapped out." Furthermore, he related:

> ... workers cease to be human beings as soon as they enter the gates of the shop. They become automatons and cease to think. They move their arms spontaneously to and fro, stopping long enough to eat in order to keep the human machinery in working order for the next four hours of exploitation. ... Many

healthy workers have gone to work for Ford and have come out human wrecks.

No wonder Ford workers labeled a nervous condition that accompanied their work "Forditis."[8]

In the mid-1920s, a number of Yale students worked in the various shops and departments of the Ford factory for the summer months. As part of an "industrial experiment" with the Sheffield Scientific School, their experiences detailed the new forms of work in the mechanized plant. One reported that 90 percent of the Ford jobs did not require any formal training. "Division of labor," he noted,

> has been carried on to such a point that an overwhelming majority of the jobs consist of a very few simple operations. In most cases a complete mastery of the movements does not take more than from five to ten minutes. All the training that a man receives in connection with his job consists of one or two demonstrations by the foreman, or the workman who has been doing that job. After these demonstrations he is considered a fully qualified 'production man.' All that he has to do now is to automatize these few operations so that speed may rapidly be increased.

Another student described his adjustment to work at an assembly line: "This was a fast line and every operation was simple. I was 100% efficient one minute after I started."

A third student relayed the words of a Ford worker:

> You've got to work like hell in Ford's. From the time you become a number in the morning until the bell rings for quitting time you have to keep at it. You can't let up. You've got to get out the production (a word, by the way which no Ford worker ever slurs over or mispronounces) and if you can't get it out, you get out.

A fourth student told about a woman who requested that her husband be transferred to a "lighter job because when he comes home at night, 'he's too tired to make babies.' Other cases of a similar nature could be cited."[9]

At one point, Ford and his managers experimented with the transfer of workmen from one machine or assembly operation to another. Similar to modern theories of job-enlargement or job-enrichment, they hoped that the transfers would eliminate the monotony of routine operations and would permit workers to gain a better sense of the total industrial enterprise. At first, one observer reported: "All were enthusiastic. The second change was not greeted too favorably. A storm of opposition came with the third change and when time came for the fourth change it was made optional and only 18% wished to change." For Ford and his managers, this reluctance to transfer jobs was an indication of worker satisfaction with their jobs, or perhaps a dull-witted contentment with monotonous work. However, for auto workers, their initial response to the transfer policy was enthusiastic. Nevertheless, when they discovered that one job was just like another, they simply preferred to remain with a familiar routing rather than fumble over an unfamiliar one.[10]

In 1920, Myron W. Watkins, a political economist who worked in Detroit's automobile factories, reflected on the social impact of technical and organizational changes in the automobile industry. He concluded: "The consequence of the rigid application of standarization in production has been the standardization of labor. Along with the interchangeability of parts goes the interchangeability of producers." Indeed, automotive factory managers and production engineers went far beyond the mere dilution of skills in the metalworking shops and departments of their factories. They homogenized skills to the point where it became impossible to differentiate one set of skills from another. Moreover, a new definition of skill came into existence. It emphasized the attributes of dexterity and speed and found application in diverse machine and assembly operations.[11]

Historians have paid considerable attention to broad changes in the American occupational structure in their efforts to understand the nature of social mobility. Nonetheless, few have studied the impact of technical and organizational innovations in different industries or individual factories. For the late nineteenth and early twentieth centuries, existing studies and fragmentary evidence suggest that the structure of work relationships in the carriage and wagon shops, small automobile factories, and machine and metal-working shops retained an essentially artisanal character. For the most part, skilled mechanics directed the labor process and performed the principal productive operations in the workshop or factory. These skilled workers often supervised unskilled laborers and/or helpers, who assisted them and who did the more strenuous tasks in the shop. Even in technologically advanced shops and factories, the fundamental division of the workforce was between the skilled "mechanic" and the unskilled "laborer." (Late nineteenth and early twentieth century photographs of workers frequently showed skilled workers wearing white shirts and ties at their machines and unskilled workers wearing the more conventional blue collar or traditional immigrant clothes.)

Nevertheless, as mechanization advanced through the late nineteenth century, the "specialist" began to emerge as an important figure in the shop or factory. But, the nineteenth-century specialist still retained significant productive skills. While the division of labor may have narrowed the range of the specialist's skills, or the number of machines operated, he still retained the crucial combination of mental and manual skills which characterized the skilled worker's routines. In the machine shop, the mechanic might operate a full range of machine tools and do "bench work" and the specialist might operate a single machine tool and also do bench work. The machine tool required skill and judgment for its operation. Bench work required a skilled hand and eye for filing and fitting.[12]

In 1903, Frederick W. Taylor, intimately familiar with conventional shop practice, referred to the skilled worker in the machine shop as a "mechanic." The mechanic's work, Taylor reported, involved" . . . especial skill or brains, coupled with close application but without severe bodily exertion, such as the more difficult and delicate machinist's work." A census report on job classifications described his work more precisely: "machinist, in its highest application, means a skilled worker who thoroughly understands the use of metal-working machinery, as well as fitting and work at the bench with other tools." In the classic sense of the term, the machinist was a "jack-of-all-trades," and did a full range of very different tasks. He was an aristocrat in the shop. He utilized his numerous and varied skills in his work routine. Additionally, he learned and acquired these skills throughout many years of apprenticeship and experience.[13]

In contrast, the laborer possessed no identifiable "productive" skills. In this period, manufacturers did not even consider his labor productive, because the laborer did not fashion raw materials into a finished part or product. According to Taylor, the work of the laborer, or "ordinary day labor," required "little brains or special skill, but call[ed] for strength, severe bodily exertion and fatigue." Indeed, the laborer was no more than a human beast of burden. The census report described the laborer's work as "manual labor that requires little or no experience or judgment, such as shovelers, loaders, carriers, and general laborers." In the shop or factory, the laborer performed the more physical and burdensome chores and usually carted or trucked materials from place to place. He truly earned his livelihood from his sweat and toil. Moreover, the skilled worker's helper was a glorified laborer. At the beck and call of the mechanic, the helper was the skilled worker's servant who fetched and carried materials to and from his work station or machine.[14]

The development of American craft or trade unionism reflected this basic division between the skilled, and usually American, mechanic and the unskilled immigrant laborer. This division touched on questions about the structure of the American working class and on issues of status and culture within the American working class. Craft unionism mirrored the skilled mechanic's contempt and disdain for the unskilled laborer. Taylor, although from a wealthy family, worked in the shops and expressed similar views. He "firmly" believed that it was "possible to train an intelligent gorilla so as to become a more efficient pig iron handler [i.e., laborer] than any man can be." Frequently, the gap between mechanic and laborer bore ethnic and racial overtones about the character of immigrant workers. In 1900, *Iron Age*, a manufacturer's trade journal, reported: "The vast majority of foreigners in this country are employed at manual labor, which requires a trained back and not a trained head. The skilled mechanic in every large industry is the born and bred American."[15]

At the turn of the century, a third category—the specialist—was an important segment of the workforce in American shops and factories. Indeed, he was the classic semi-skilled worker. Holding an anomalous position between the skilled mechanic and the unskilled laborer, the specialist was a skilled worker who possessed only one or two of the mechanic's varied skills. Technological and organizational change in the shop narrowed and limited his range of traditional skills. For example, the machinist operated a variety of machine tools and used a variety of manual skills at workbench. The specialist, on the other hand, operated only one machine, perhaps a lathe or drill press, and did the bench work associated with that machine. "Machinists, of inferior skill," the census reported noted, "or those who are able to run only a single machine or perhaps do a little bench work, are classed as second class machinists and grouped with machine tenders and machine hands." As the division of labor and machine-tool technology became more sophisticated, the specialist began to lose his combination of mental and manual skills. Taylor noticed this in the machine shop. He reported that the specialist performed "ordinary shop work." His work required "neither especial brains, very close application, nor extra hard work." More and more, the specialist did the monotonous and repetitive work at a single machine. Nevertheless, until the technical revolution in the automobile industry, the specialist was not completely deskilled.[16]

At the time, union members and factory managers voiced considerable concern about the increasing role of specialists in American shops and factories. The International Association of Machinists, for example, railed against the use of specialists and unskilled helpers on new machinery. Reporting on a strike, caused by the assignment of a laborer to an automatic lathe, the *Machinists' Monthly Journal* noted: "The strike is one in support of skilled labor against unskilled labor. . . . A mechanic's skill is to him what the capitalist's money is to the capitalist." In time, the union recognized the necessity for the inclusion of specialists in their organization. Yet, it forbade any skilled machinist to instruct laborers and helpers in the secrets of the trade.[17]

For Taylor, the specialist was closer to the laborer than to the mechanic. Fully acquainted with the latest technical and organizational developments in the machine shop, he had a keen sense of the changes in the wind. "No more should a mechanic be allowed to do the work for which a trained laborer can be used," he wrote, "and . . . almost any job that is repeated over and over again, however great the skill and dexterity it may require . . . should be done by a trained laborer and not by a mechanic." The principal limitation was that there should be enough work to occupy the worker throughout the year. Taylor continued:

A man with only the intelligence of an average laborer can be taught the most difficult and delicate work if it is repeated; and this lower mental caliber renders him more fit than the mechanic to stand the monotony of repetition.

Though narrowly circumscribed, the specialist possessed important recognizable productive skills. Frequently, a specialized job proved an avenue for upward mobility within the working class. Often a young unskilled worker would shift from one specialized job to another within a trade. At the end of this informal apprenticeship, he acquired the skills of a mechanic for that craft.[18]

Thus, at the turn of the century, mechanics, specialists, and laborers were the principal divisions within the working class in American shops and factories. In 1891, the Michigan Bureau of Labor Statistics surveyed the metal-working establishments in the city of Detroit. An analysis of the data confirmed this general occupational pattern. These establishments, including small workshops and large factories, formed the industrial base for the twentieth-century automobile industry. There were machine shops, foundries, carriage and wagon shops, and other establishments. The survey polled 3,920 individual workers and tabulated information on their social and economic condition. A ten percent sample was tabulated by skill and wage levels and by age. An analysis of the sample revealed the following general pattern:[19]

Table 1. *Detroit Workers in Metal Industries, 1891*

Occupation Group	No.	Per- cent	Mean Weekly Income	Mean Age
Foremen	9	2	$19.67	38
Mechanics	153	39	12.58	32
Specialists	117	30	8.18	24
Unskilled Labor	113	29	6.60	27
Total	392	100	9.55	29

SOURCE: "A Canvass of Agricultural Implement and Iron Working Industries in Detroit" in Michigan Bureau of Labor and Industrial Statistics, *Eighth Annual Report* (Lansing, Michigan, 1891), pp. 1–151. These data come from a computer analysis of a one in ten sample of the original data.

In this sample, the mechanics were the largest single group of workers. Although not a majority of the workforce, they clearly influenced the tone and the atmosphere in the shops and factories of the Detroit metal industries. Nevertheless, the specialists and laborers, almost equal in size, also were substantial groups. Foremen constituted a very small group with only two percent. In its modern sense, supervision barely existed. It was either self-imposed as part of the craft traditions or skilled workers directed their informal work groups of specialists and laborers.

Although the sample included 49 different occupations, some occupations dominated their segment of the occupational structure.

For example, iron molders, a traditional craft, and machinists, a relatively new trade, represented about 70 percent of the mechanics. In the case of specialists, machine hands were 29 percent of these less skilled workers. Finally, laborers dominated the unskilled category and made up 65 percent of these workers. In terms of wages, the mechanics earned almost twice as much as laborers, a gap which obviously reflected significant social, economic, and cultural differences. Moreover, with regard to age, mechanics tended to be older; specialists younger. The laborers tended to be older than the specialists. This may have reflected a tendency for laborers to stagnate in their group and for specialists to move into more skilled positions.

Precise occupational data did not survive for the early years of the Ford Motor Company. However, fragmentary evidence suggested the accuracy of the above-noted pattern. For example, even in October 1908, after considerable expansion for Model T production, the Ford Motor Company employed a total of 609 persons. Twelve foremen and 507 workers were employed in "Manufacturing operations." The small number of foremen indicated the more traditional pattern of supervision. The remaining 90 employees were "Persons on the salary role." These included a few managers, engineers, accountants, and salespeople and a large number of clerks and office workers. Another fragmentary and undated document, probably from around 1910, listed on eight pages the names, the occupation or department, and the wage rates of 143 Ford workers. In this instance, the occupation or department and the average wage rates provided a less satisfactory basis for the classification of workers into three categories. Moreover, it was impossible to determine the actual representation of the specialists. They merged into the mechanic category. However, the basic dichotomy between the mechanic and laborer remained, as shown in Table 2.[20]

Due to the data's fragmentary character, only one solid generalization can be made about Ford workers on the eve of the technical transformation of automobile production. Even at this time, traditional work patterns survived in the Ford factory. Laborers still constituted a sizeable proportion of the Ford workforce.

From 1910 to 1914, the new Ford methods of production completely altered the traditional patterns of social relations among mechanics, specialists, and laborers in the Ford shops. Notably, this period saw the rise of the "deskilled" specialist as a significant factor in the Ford workforce. As early as 1914, William A. Logan recog-

Table 2. *Day Wages in the Ford Motor Company, About 1910*

Occupation Group	No.	Per-cent	Range of Day Wages	Mean Wage
Foremen	9	6	$3.00–7.00	$5.01
Mechanics				
High skilled	40	28	1.75–5.20	3.90
Skilled	37	26	2.50–4.00	3.15
Laborers	49	34	1.25–3.00	2.48
Miscellaneous	8	6	2.00–3.00	2.59
Total	143	100		

SOURCE: An eight-page sample of occupations from about 1910 in Box 18, Accession 940, Ford Motor Company Archives, Dearborn, Michigan.

nized "the cold hard fact that the demand for workers with a trade is on the toboggan slide. . . ." "An automobile factory today," he added:

> is nothing more or less than a huge machine with raw materials going in at one end and finished automobiles coming out at the other end. A stream of automobiles passes through the factory, they go from one department to another, from one floor to another and all the time highly efficient specialists, working at top speed, are adding their part of the product to the machine until at last it is a complete machine. The Ford plant is the best example of this system and the Peerless Company . . . have now adopted the same system.

The new Ford production techniques favored the "highly efficient specialist" over the skilled tradesman.[21]

In 1923, Logan again recalled the decline of the carriage and wagon making trade. "The production of carriages, wagons, coaches, and trucks," he remembered, "had been carried on in small shops, with here and there a factory that was considered large." In earlier years, skilled workers dominated the trade. In these small shops, ". . . the work was performed by skilled mechanics, who were masters of their various trades and who did their work from the bottom up, so to speak." The automobile, at first, "an impractical, rich man's toy," had little impact on the methods of production and the skills of the various trades. After the introduction of the Model T Ford, Logan continued, "the automobile had come to stay and revolutionize things in general." With its huge popular demand, the "old-fashioned methods of production" proved inadequate for the manufacture of the new automobiles. Very rapidly, the large factory displaced the small shop; the specialist displaced the mechanic. "Modern machinery," the veteran auto worker concluded, "was installed, new machines were invented, plants were built on a scale hitherto unknown, and a system of acute specialization was introduced to keep pace with demand."[22]

In 1924, Charles Reitell examined and reported on the impact of new industrial methods in the automobile industry. Six years earlier, he had examined the iron and steel industry and concluded that its technology actually raised the skill levels of its workers. Nevertheless, after he studied the automobile industry, he completely reversed his earlier position. The "mechanical achievements" of the automobile industry, he concluded, "proved more a curse than a blessing." The new automobile workers:

are being shaped to meet the demands of these rigid machines. The requirements of dexterity, alertness, watchfulness, rhythmic and monotonous activities, coupled with a lessening of much of the older physical requirements are registering results that require a new type of worker in industry.

In other words, the new industrial technology undermined the traditional structure of occupations in the factory or workshop. In the modern automobile factory, he continued:

... we find skill or long experience at the top and brawn at the bottom both greatly lessened. . . . [This] has meant on the one side a transfer of skill from trained workers into intricate and complex machines; and on the other side the brute force of physical labor into the powerful and gigantic lifting, carrying, and conveying machines.[23]

In fact, the twin pillars of the nineteenth century work force—the skilled mechanics and the muscled laborers—declined in the modern automobile factories. At the same time, the number of machine tenders and of assemblers increased. These two "deskilled" specialized occupations formed the occupational foundation of the automobile industry and represented "the new type of worker in industry."[24]

As the Ford Motor Company's system of mass production neared completion, the structure of occupations began to follow this new pattern. In August 1913, the company conducted a survey of its entire workforce. Its purpose was the systematization of the occupational and wage structure to meet the new conditions of production. The new classification system mirrored the new occupational structure in the Ford factory as shown in Table 3.[25]

Table 3. *Ford Workers, Classified by Occupational Groups, 1913*

Occupation Group	No.	Percent
Mechanics and subforemen	329	2
Skilled operators	3,431	26
Operators	6,749	51
Unskilled Workers (Laborers, helpers, youth)	2,795	21
Total	13,304	100

SOURCE: Oliver J. Abell, "Labor Classified on a Skill-Wages Basis," *Iron Age*, 93 (January 1, 1914), p. 48 and E. A. Rumley, "Ford's Plant to Share Profits," *World's Work*, 27 (April 1914), pp. 665–6.

Compared with the earlier occupational data for Detroit in 1891 and for the Ford shops in 1910, the proportion of skilled workers and laborers underwent a considerable decline. Moreover, the "operators," that is, the specialized workers who performed routine machine and assembly operations, now constituted a clear majority of the Ford workforce.

Finally, in January 1917, the Ford Motor Company made a detailed survey of all occupations in its mechanized plant. The survey listed 71 different occupations, which have been grouped into Reitell's classification scheme for automobile workers. Reitell's three main categories were technical workers, foremen and clerks, and production workers. The last category included machine tenders, assemblers, skilled workers, testers and inspectors, helpers, and common laborers.[26]

Thus, in 1917, the deskilled specialists already completely dominated the occupational structure of the Ford factory. Indeed, these specialists represented more than 55 percent of the total factory population. The overwhelming majority of these specialists were machine hands and assemblers who numbered 17,741 persons. In 1924, Reitell noted that these two groups of workers usually represented from 35 to 55 percent of the entire workforce in the au-

Table 4. *Occupational Classification of Ford Employees, January 1917*

Occupation Group	No.	Percent
Salaried supervisors	198	.4
Foremen	2,523	6.2
Clerks	1,710	4.2
Inspectors	1,533	3.7
Technical workers	5,391	13.2
Skilled trades	1,003	2.4
Specialists	22,652	55.3
Unskilled workers	5,986	14.6
Total	40,996	100.00

SOURCE: "List of Trades and Occupations and Number of Men Employed in Same," January 31, 1917, Box 16, Accession 940, Ford Motor Company Archives, Dearborn, Michigan; Charles Reitell, "Machinery and Its Effect upon the Workers in the Automobile Industry," *Annals AAPSS*, 116 (November 1924), pp. 37–43.

tomobile industry. Moreover, mechanization and the division of labor undetermined the skills of many former mechanics. Their traditional skills, acquired through long years of apprenticeship and work experience, surely lost much of their former meaning and value in the shop.[27]

Both the new industrial technology and the minute subdivision of labor resulted in the rise of the specialist as the predominant figure in the automobile factory. The design of machines and of work routines now contained the skill of many mechanics. Consequently, unlike his nineteenth-century predecessor, the new specialized workman possessed few traditional skills. Skill now could be transferred readily to other machines or other work situations. For the machine operator, the operation of his machine required virtually no thought or judgment. A drill press operator, for example, no longer measured and marked the various holes for a piece of work. He no longer located it on the table of the machine, judged its proper feed and speed, or gauged the proper depth of the holes. Instead, he picked up the piece of work, attached it to its fixture, and threw a switch. Then, a multiple spindled drill automatically made all the necessary holes in the correct location with the proper depth. He removed the piece, placed it for the next worker, and repeated his routine. For the assembler, his work became just as routinized. He performed but a fraction of an entire assembly operation. He no longer assembled a complete part or component. He no longer filed and fitted pieces together. In both instances, the worker readily transferred his skill from one type of operation to another. And, skill now required agility, dexterity, speed, and diligence. The deskilled specialist merely needed the capacity to withstand his inflexible routine with its endless monotony.

Once the predominant occupations in the metal-working industries, machinists and foundry workers saw their traditional crafts destroyed in the Ford shops. Superintendents and foremen claimed that they could make an unskilled immigrant into a "first-class molder of one piece in three days." A man, who had "never seen a core-making bench in his life," could be a core-maker in two days. Arnold reported that "perhaps 5 percent are skilled molders and core-setters." "The remaining 95 percent are simply specialized laborers," he continued, "many of them foreigners who had never seen the inside of the foundry and could not speak one word of English when they began. . . ." Additionally, they preferred to train their own specialized machine operators instead of hiring skilled machinists. "As to machinists, old-time, all-round men," they told Arnold:

> perish the thought! The Ford company has no use for experience, in the working ranks anyway. It desires and prefers machine-tool operators who have nothing to unlearn, who have no theories of correct surface speeds for metal finishing, and who will do what they are told, over and over again, from bell-time to bell-time.

Molders, coremakers, and machinists were all traditional skilled craftsmen. They had long apprenticeships, high levels of skill, and high wages. They were highly skilled mechanics—the aristocrats in American metal shops and factories. Yet, in the Ford factory, industrial technology and work re-organization so diluted and so undermined their craft skills that a man off the street could learn their jobs in a matter of a few days.[28]

To be sure, skilled workers were needed in the Ford plant. But, where and how skill was used changed. For example, the new industry called for large numbers of toolmakers and diemakers. And, the Ford factory had its own apprenticeship school for these crafts. Often Ford workers abandoned the shops in droves to attend these classes whenever possible. In addition, with so many unskilled workers in the shops, foremen and subforemen, the on-line supervisors, had to know how to operate a wide variety of machine-tools. For example, the Ford machine shop employed a number of tool setters on the shop floor. These were skilled mechanics. As H. F. Porter noted:

> Plenty of spare cutting tools are kept on hand and special supervisors patrol the floor, watching for the first sign that a tool is failing to hold the pace or produce the requisite quality. Without waiting for the offending tool to get worse, the supervisor immediately stops the machine and inserts a fresh tool. The operators, with minor exceptions, are relieved of responsibility.

Ford supervisors and foremen considered these tool setters who were skilled machinists indispensable for meeting production quotas. Furthermore, skilled maintenance and repair workers kept the machinery and physical plant in good order. And sometimes, inspectors relied on craft knowledge in order to perform their duties. Nevertheless, the proportion of skilled workers in the mechanized automobile factory was considerably smaller than in the traditional metalworking shops and factories.[29]

The front axle finishing department typified the occupational structure of a single Ford shop and illustrated the social pattern in the mechanized plant. According to Arnold, this department employed about 375 men. In order to oversee its mass of assemblers, the shop had:

> one foreman, who has two assistant foremen, three clerks, and one 'straw boss' for about every 20 workmen, besides tool-setters who are machinists of intelligence, experience, and all-round reliability. The foreman is, of necessity, a competent mechanic and a competent administrator.

To be sure, the administration and supervision of the shop had changed considerably from the late nineteenth-century world of less-formal relationships among the foreman, the skilled mechanics and specialists, and laborers.[30]

For example, the traditional foreman performed a broad range of productive, supervisory, administrative, and clerical functions in his shop. Leon P. Alford reported that the traditional foreman had to:

> look after tools and machines, find materials and supplies for
> his men, instruct them in the manner of doing the work, ar-
> range tasks so that everyone is kept busy, enforce the proper
> pace, write up . . . records, preserve order, make reports con-
> cerning . . . individual jobs, inspect work . . . , lend a hand in re-
> pairs, suggest improvement in equipment, and give opinion on
> which to base promotion and discharges.

In addition, he often hired workers, adjusted wages, and maintained
time cards. Edwin D. Jones noted: "In establishments where the
modern plan of functionalizing and service departments is unknown, each foreman is for his own shop a Jack-of-all-trades, en-
deavouring to deal directly with a great variety of duties."[31]

In the new Ford plant, however, the foreman's duties were more
circumscribed and he had assistant foremen, sub-foremen (straw
bosses), clerks, inspectors, and others to assist him. They all performed low-level administrative and supervisory roles in the new factory. They directed, recorded, or examined the work of others. In
fact, each occupation reflected Taylor's notions of "functional management" and the division of the foreman's job into specific
functional tasks. The principal concern of the Ford foreman was to
get out production. Others tended and adjusted machines, maintained records, and examined the quality of the work.

These new occupations represented an important avenue of
mobility for deskilled craftsmen. In 1891, the foremen represented
two percent of the Detroit sample of workers, clerks and inspectors
did not even make an appearance. However, in 1917, foremen,
clerks, and inspectors constituted 14 percent of the total number of
workers in the Ford factory. This was a huge growth. It surely
created job opportunities for many displaced workers. As the traditional craft patterns of discipline and authority eroded, new ones
had to emerge. With large numbers of unskilled workers in productive operations, foremen saw their jobs redefined as disciplinarians.
Moreover, clerks and inspectors arose to supplement the administrative and supervisory needs of the modern plant.

Unlike his nineteenth-century antecedent, the new Ford foreman
did not supervise groups of workmen for an entire shop or plant,
but only directed the productive operations of his particular department or shop. He insured that his workers reached and main-

tained production standards. The superintendents, factory managers, and engineers determined those standards. In 1912, O. J. Abell reported that "the foreman in each department is purely a production man." His "particular duty" was "to see to it that the men under him turn out so many pieces per day and personally work to correct whatever may prevent it."[32]

In 1914, Arnold listed the types of foremen in the Ford machine shops:

> The machine shop superintendents had under their direction 11 department foremen, 62 job foremen, 84 assistant foremen, and 98 sub-foremen, 255 men in all above the rank of ordinary workmen, and all having the power of discharging workmen at will.

Most likely, the eleven departmental foremen had the broad range of duties, responsibilities, and functions similar to the nineteenth-century foreman. Nevertheless, the remainder had specialized and circumscribed duties and functions.[33]

To the men in the shops, the subforeman was the "straw boss." A notch above the ordinary workman, he was seen as a petty tyrant with an inflated sense of his importance and authority. His task was to drive and to exhort his workers to higher and higher levels of production. Also known as a "working" foreman, he was a predecessor to the later "flying squad" member who filled the gaps on the lines of mass production industries in the 1920s. William Klann, a foreman in charge of motor assembly, recalled:

> We used to have working foremen for every 25 men. If they would go to the toilet the job would stand still and the working foreman would take his place. When we started working faster, we got a working foreman for every fifteenth man. So when a man left the job, the line would never stop. It kept going all the time.

The straw boss became more important as shops and departments attempted to meet production quotas and as factory work became more and more specialized.[34]

Acute specialization facilitated a subsequent influx of large numbers of unskilled immigrant workers. On the shop floor, Arnold observed, the straw boss was important "to the factory manager who wishes to cheapen component production in repetition by the use of specialized laborers. . . ." Especially, as immigrant workers swarmed into the Ford factory, the sub-foreman had to mediate between the supervisors and the workmen. Klann recalled that he had fourteen different nationalities in motor assembly. He added: "We had to have sub-foremen who could speak several languages." As Model T production mushroomed, so too did the demand for specialized labor. Klann remembered the chaotic labor situation: "We took any kind of man the Employment Department gave us and one word every foreman had to learn in English, German, Polish, and Italian was 'hurry up.' " Indeed, as Eastern European immigrants entered the Ford plant, the bilingual straw boss became "indispensable where the immigrant is the principal worker."[35]

In the brief period between 1914 and 1918, the supervision of Ford workers, as evidenced by the increased ratio of foremen to workers, increased at a phenomenal rate. In 1914, one foreman directed an average of 53 workers; in 1917, one foreman supervised an average of 15 workers. These figures did not take into account a probable increase in clerks and inspectors who also served supervisory and administrative functions. To be sure, strict supervision was a key element for successful mass production. Even if workers were not so inclined, the sequential arrangement of synchronized productive processes made the entire system susceptible to interruption or disruption. The careless worker, the aggrieved worker, or the outright recalcitrant worker threatened the smooth operation of the entire system. Close supervision minimized this risk.[36]

In the past, clerks frequently maintained the records and books for the large industrial establishments. In the late nineteenth century, a clerk routinely kept the books or accounts for the small payroll, sales, or shipping department. But, they were few in number. Only a few clerks appeared in the Detroit metal-working shops and factories in 1891. However, in 1917, clerks were essential for the successful operation of the Highland Park plant. Often, they performed the record-keeping functions previously done by foremen. Since tons of raw materials, thousands of parts and components, and hundreds of automobiles passed through the factory each day, records were necessary for the efficient operation of the mechanized factory. The company needed records on the flow of the materials into the factory, on the progress of each part or component, on each piece of machinery, and on each worker and his output. This required a huge staff of clerks to keep and to maintain information.

In 1917, the Ford factory employed more than 1,700 clerks to maintain records for factory managers and superintendents. Aside from a large number of shipping and receiving clerks, many clerks worked in direct connection with productive operations of the plant. Factory clerks, who numbered 272 in 1917, worked closely with department foremen. "Each department," Abell wrote in 1912, "is provided with a clerk who assumes all the duties of keeping time and material records." In the Ford tradition, these factory clerks stood at their desks in their shop or department. They maintained records on production. Usually, they posted this data on a large blackboard for all the workers in the shop to see; then, they recorded it on appropriate forms or ledgers for managers and supervisors. Additionally, toolroom clerks issued and kept track of tools used by specialized workers.[37]

In the Ford factory, the shortage chaser represented a new breed of clerk especially suited to the needs of mass production. Although they only numbered 36, the shortage chasers were a result of the synchronized and integrated factory system. The Ford Motor Company worked on the principle that the storage of parts and components was an unnecessary overhead expense. Nevertheless, a shortage of any materials meant a disastrous and costly interruption of production. Consequently, Arnold noted, the company placed "a maximum sufficiency for 5,000 cars, three days' assembling, with a danger line at components enough for 3,000 cars."[38]

In order to insure an adequate supply of parts and components, the shortage chasers, "brisk and intelligent" young men, went from department to department to search for potential shortages. They ran their circuit of departments and made their reports every two hours. H. L. Arnold displayed an uncommon use of metaphor to describe the young shortage chaser:

> whose face already begins to show the fine lines etched by the stress of concentrated attention, bounds the department by drifting within the sound of breakers, seizes the helm of component production, and pilots the department to smooth water again—sometimes but barely escaping the surf line it is true, but always managing to escape disaster.

Indeed, the new coordinated production techniques demanded a new type of clerk to assure a steady and continuous flow of materials through the plant.[39]

Inspectors were another new category of worker who relieved the foreman from his traditional duties. Again, few inspectors appeared in the Detroit sample of metal workers. But, in 1917, 1,100 inspectors examined and tested the products of the different departments and shops. Machine inspectors examined pieces of work as they progressed through the machine shop. Operation inspectors, stationed at convenient places along assembly lines, accepted or rejected partially completed components. And, floor or final inspectors examined finished parts as they left their section of the shop or their assembly line. Rejected-component, scrap, or "wasters" inspectors checked and examined the work of other inspectors.[40]

Finally, the new occupational structure demanded more powerful forms of managerial control over workers and work processes. These, too, were a significant social consequence of Ford mass production. Of course, a central feature of the advance of industrial capitalism was the evolution of different means to discipline and to control factory workers. Still, skilled workmen traditionally maintained considerable autonomy over decisions about the methods and pace of their work. Their knowledge, skill, experience, and self-imposed discipline insured them a privileged position within their shops. Often, work rhythms fluctuated with the mood of skilled craftsmen and their work groups. However, the mechanized and integrated Ford factory could not function under such an informal and autonomous system of controls. Ford factory managers and engineers became more conscious and more aware about the need for, and the application of, new and different forms of control. These men, who designed and constructed the complex industrial system, also created technical and organizational forms of control over the Ford workforce in their design of work routines, of machines, and of integrated industrial processes.[41]

In 1912, before the realization of line production methods, O. J. Abell recognized three Ford methods for "keeping the human factor up to established rates." These were the large demand for the Ford automobile, the character of Ford foremanship, and the acute specialization of tasks and routines. "No element," Abell wrote, "is more conducive to a continued rate of production than the pressure of rush. . . . In the Ford plant, the spirit of catching up is omnipresent." Furthermore, since the Ford foreman had the assistance of clerks and was "purely a production man," his principal function was to pressure and to drive his workers to greater heights of production. "The particular duty of the foreman," he related, "is to see to it that the men under him turn out so many pieces per day and personally work to correct whatever may prevent it." Finally, Abell continued:

The third essential element is that each employee is alloted one specific operation, and the exceptionally specialized division of labor brings the human element into the condition of performing automatically with machine-like regularity and speed.

This last of the three traditional forms of control was most interesting, particularly given the extent of the division of labor in the Ford factory. Through carefully designed work tasks and routines, Ford managers and foremen readily could spot the inefficient or malingering worker. He did not have the same rhythmic movements as the other members of the shop.[42]

The standard output, or "ratings," of different machines also served as a means for the control over the pace and intensity of production. For managers and foremen, these machine ratings represented a true and scientific standard for the output of machines. With an allowance for time when the machine was not in use, Abell reported, "it is possible to arrive at an accurate expectation concerning the most practicable rate of production." Machine ratings side-stepped the whole question of incentives for the control of output. "It is considered preferable," Abell concluded, "therefore, to accept this rate and bring the human element in step with the rated machine capacity and pay a straight wage for that labor than to accept the variable output under piece-rate or premium inducements." As Fred H. Colvin reported: "Every machine has an alloted daily output, and the work is planned accordingly. Each foreman receives a daily schedule of work to be turned out by his department, and it is up to him to see that it is forthcoming." Since the men were paid day rates, he continued, "the output is largely a matter of foremanship. And it is interesting to note how carefully each workman keeps tab of his output." In other words, the designation of the standard output determined the worker's amount of work, its pace, and its intensity.[43]

In addition, the design of machines also controlled and determined work tasks and routines. In 1914, E. A. Rumley noted that the Ford engineers and toolmakers built "jigs, dies, and special machine tools for 95 percent of all its work." The use of "stop locks and gauges" made it "unnecessary for the workman to caliper or otherwise measure his operations." Rumley concluded:

> A machine that is built to only one piece can easily be made automatically set to the limits of that piece. The task of that workman has been reduced to a simple process of attaching the material and removing it, or moving a lever from one stop to another; thus the skill of the highest grade machinist is automatically obtained. . . . Raw laborers can learn quickly to operate most of the machine tools at a fair rate of speed.

As machines increased in their complexity, routines for the operation of machines became far simpler. Moreover, through their observation of workers with simplified tasks, managers and foremen readily could detect inefficient machine operators and exhort them to improve their output.[44]

While subdivided and simplified machine and assembly operations facilitated the supervision of Ford workers, the sequential organization and complete integration of all work processes had the greatest and most direct impact on the extension of managerial control over the workforce. Simplified tasks and routines arranged in logical sequence, Ralph C. Epstein concluded, "represent the extreme limit to which the extension of the management's control over productive operations can be carried." In addition to the predetermination of "the design, shape, size and quality of the work," he added, "the rate at which each operation must be performed by the workers is rigidly controlled by a power machine, which may even be driven from another building." In this instance, Epstein had the image of the conveyor-driven assembly line in mind. But, the sequential organization of any productive operation controlled the pace and the intensity of the work.[45]

For example, Ford mechanical engineer Oscar Bornholt described the development of sequential machining operations in the Highland Park plant. Using the manufacture of tin cans as an illustration of "continuous" production he noted:

> The first machine sets the pace and the operators of other machines must keep their machines at a similar rate so that the stock will not run short or accumulate. This arrangement therefore helps to increase production. At the Ford plant the machines are arranged very much like the tin-can machines. All

parts of a unit assembly are made on machines that are so laid out that the last operations bring them near together. This applies not only to large pieces, but all parts of a unit which are made in one department under a foreman.

The machines, Bornholt related, "are placed to draw from one machine doing the operation. This gives the effect of the whole operation being done on one machine." The arrangement of individual departments meant that workers had to work at the pace established by the first man or machine.[46]

Others also observed the effect of the continuous flow of work from person to person. One Ford worker reported that on the line, the first "man's speeding up speeds up everything else: the man before him must 'step on it' in order to keep him supplied with materials, and the man after him must increase his pace so that the materials don't pile up." I. T. Martin wrote in the carriage, wagon, and automobile workers' *Journal*:

At the Ford plant the men work in rows throughout the plant, and the march of all the pieces is to a common center, where they are put into place. To each man is entrusted a single operation in the manufacture of the machine, and he is held responsible for a certain amount of work. . . . Each worker must keep pace with the man working below him. Substitutes are kept constantly on hand, at the factory's expense, to meet all emergencies.

As an interconnected social process, the pace and intensity of a single worker affected the pace and intensity of an entire work-group or department.[47]

H. F. Porter detailed a similar phenomenon for the top-making department. It also contained other features to increase production. "Here," he observed:

the operators who are engaged in stitching together the top material are seated at parallel benches. The material starts at the back row and works steadily toward the front. There are five rows in all. By having a little more capacity on the rear row than the one in front of it, and again on the second a slight excess over the third, and so on, the work has a tendency to pile up on succeeding rows. A sporting instinct comes into play, for the operators behind are constantly, with a little handicap, striving to overwhelm those immediately in front; while those in the front are striving as constantly not only to crowd the fellows in front of them but to keep from being crowded by the chaps behind.

In addition to this control through the physical organization of the work process, Ford managers also consciously stirred up competition among workers who performed the same operation. On each row, production boards maintained a record of output. "Here the output of each man," Porter continued, "is posted hourly, and the records of those who equal or better the quota set are written down in colored crayon." Moreover, the company kept a list of "color men" for the selection of supervisors and inspectors. Under this system for the regulation of production, Porter concluded: "There is mighty little chance for the shirker to persist in the Ford plant, even though the entire force is paid on a daywork basis."[48]

H. L. Arnold described an interesting device to control workers for the last procedure on the final assembly line. This final procedure followed the dropping and attaching the Model T body onto its chassis. Then, a worker drove the completed car to a parking area ready for shipment to the dealer. "The early practice," Arnold noted:

> included a run up and down John R street at the discretion of the driver who did not leave the car until he saw fit to do so. The consequence was . . . the street was filled with cars running up and down in no regular sequence and with a considerable waste of time of the drivers. . . .

The Ford solution to this problem involved the "laying down [of] the angle-iron John R street track," which ran under the body chute and went directly to the parking area. The driver had to ride in the track to the parking area. In this instance, Arnold noted the advantage in "keeping work in progress in one well-defined line and thus leaving as little as possible to the whim or choice of the individual workman."[49]

The conveyor, and similar devices, were the mechanisms which provided Ford officials and managers with the greatest amount of control over workers. The Ford foundry best illustrated how technical innovation in the shop evolved into technical control of the workforce. Until 1910, the foundry was a fairly traditional one. Pattern-makers fashioned wooden patterns; coremakers mixed sand and used the pattern to make the mold; and molders poured the metal into the mold to form the casting. Around 1910, the Ford foundry purchased commercial molding machines which made the mold from metal patterns. In 1912, it used mechanized sand-mixing machines which supplied, via chutes, the coremakers and their machines with core-sand. And, in 1913, it had conveyors which carried the mold from the coremakers to the pouring area and finally to shakeout machines which shook the sand from the casting.[50]

These technical changes resulted in organizational changes in the work processes. E. A. Rumley and H. L. Arnold described the impact of the conveyor on work in the foundry. Machine molders placed a mold with their personal brass check on the conveyor. As Rumley related:

> . . . he is expected to place a finished mould upon each platform that bears his number, as it passes him in its continuous rhythm. There is no need for piece work or for a premium system. The man at that particular job is simply expected to finish a mold every time his number comes by, and any failure on his part to keep up the standard quantity becomes evident to every man in the gang and to the foreman as well. The pauses that will give the highest efficiency have been included in the calculations. Piece work, premium systems and other devices to supervise production, with expensive clerks and red tape, are superfluous. The molder's work has been predetermined; he must simply fill his place—be a link in the ever moving chain.

A check-taker removes the brass check near the end of the line and records the number on the molder's record sheet.[51]

Others came to similar conclusions about the influence of the mechanical conveyance of parts and materials. H. F. Porter described assembly operations:

> . . . A major part—an axle or a cylinder block—is placed on a conveyor whose pace is carefully regulated to permit the various subsequent operations to be performed as the piece with its accretions passes by. One may only screw on a nut or two. He may have to more two or three feet while doing this; seldom more. The initial attendant—the man who feeds the chain—

therefore has the regularity of production entirely under his control, and he is especially selected and paid to see that the line is un unbroken procession.

For Harold W. Slauson, the conveyor permitted the mechanical speed-up of the work process:

> Under these conditions of production, is it any wonder that the movements of men become practically automatic and that output is regulated by the speed at which the traveling chains are operated. Speed up the electric motors a notch and—presto! Ford production has increased another hundred cars per day without the necessity of hiring a single workman.

Also, Arnold pointed out the regulatory nature of the chain-driven conveyor for the magneto assembly line. "The chain drive," he observed, "proved to be a vast improvement [over the hand movement of work], hurrying the slow men, holding the fast men back from pushing work to those in advance, and acting as an all-around adjuster and equalizer."[52]

In the late nineteenth and early twentieth centuries, the control and increase of output was a central problem for the management of the machine shop and the assembly room. The proponents of systematic and scientific management, Halsey, Towne, Taylor, Gantt, Gilbreth, and others, wrote extensively on the design of work and on the provision of incentives for greater and greater levels of production. Taylor's classic essay on differential piece rates even had the subtitle, "a partial solution to the labor problem." Now, in the Highland Park plant, Ford managers and engineers discovered their technological "fix" for a long-standing social problem. They controlled and regulated production through the design of machines, the rearrangement of work processes, and the mechanical conveyance of materials past workers.[53]

Finally, as already noted, some occupations were accommodations to the need for new forms of control. Most obviously, Ford officials devised new ways to manage and to supervise masses of deskilled specialists in the recently mechanized plant. The "straw boss" was one such accommodation. The large staff of clerks, who maintained records on the individual workers, was another. At day's end, managers, supervisors, and foremen could go through the records and uncover a worker's or a department's failure to meet production

quotas. Also, checkers and counters insured that a department transferred the proper amount of parts and materials to another section
of the plant. Inspectors also served as a control on the quality of a
workman's output.[54]

For example, "wasters," or rejected components or parts, went to a
scrap inspection department. Here, Arnold reported, the wasters
"undergo individual examination by the twenty scrap inspectors who
place the blame on scrap-making where it belongs." These inspectors
had the authority to contact the head inspector, who in turn could
summon the head of the guilty department. In the end, the waster
"makes plenty of trouble for those whose faults assisted in its production. . . . so that all in fault are very likely to be made fully aware
of vigorous disapproval of scrap production even as a rare performance." H. F. Porter noted that "inspection is to all intents and purposes an integral part in the sequence of productive operations."[55]

Up to this point, the major emphasis has been placed on the
emergence of the Ford industrial technology and its social impact on
the world of work. Within this context, Ford managers, engineers,
and some skilled workers created the conditions which profoundly
altered work routines and social relations in the new Highland Park
factory. In fact, they attempted to establish technical and organizational forms of control over the entire productive process. Nevertheless, they did not operate in a vacuum. They did not have a completely plastic and malleable world to mold and to shape. The
thousands of new Ford workers were not passive objects to Ford
technical and organizational innovation. In different ways and
forms, immigrant industrial novices and American industrial veterans accommodated to, adapted to, or resisted innovation and change
in their factory environment. And, these accommodations, adapta-
tions, and resistances revealed the flexibility, viability, and solidity of
the working class responses to their new conditions of mechanized
work. As Ford mass production became a reality, Ford officials and
managers gradually uncovered a massive labor problem.

4. Ford Labor Problems: Immigrant and Working-Class Traditions

The natural thing to do is work—to recognize that prosperity and happiness can be obtained only through honest effort. Human ills flow largely from attempting to escape this natural course. . . . I take it for granted we must work. All we have comes as the result of a certain insistence that since we must work it is better to work intelligently and forehandedly; that the better we do our work the better off we shall be. All of which I conceive to be merely elemental common sense.[1]—Henry Ford

For as long as one person has worked for another, a labor problem has existed. In the first decades of the twentieth century, manufacturers, factory managers, and social commentators rediscovered "the Labor Problem." In fact, they redefined and reformulated a long-standing and multidimensional American social crisis which paralleled the evolution of industrial society. In the 1880s, the relationship between labor and capital was the social issue of the times. At the turn of the century, the immigrant problem was the principal concern. Increasingly, as large-scale forms of corporate organization, capital intensive industrial technology, and unskilled immigrant workers characterized the American industrial landscape, the labor problem came to constitute a "case of serious maladjustment which has developed in our industrial order." Those who developed the marvelous industrial technology and those who analyzed its social effects discovered "the human element" of production and labeled it the labor problem.[2]

This deep-seated social crisis contained many different aspects which touched all phases of working-class community and industrial life. On the one hand, the labor problem was the problem of the immigrant worker and his relationship to American industrial society. "Fundamentally," Gordon S. Watkins wrote, "the immigration problem is one of preserving American standards and ideals. Civilization is, after all, but a composite of prevailing norms of life and culture, ethical and social standards, and economic practices which people accept as desirable."

In this sense, the problem involved the adjustment and adaptation of immigrant workers to the social and cultural norms of an industrialized America. For Peter Roberts, a YMCA educator, the immigration problem involved "the quality, industrial efficiency, and the relation to the native-born men of the new immigration." According to William Leiserson: "the basis for common thought and action between the native and foreign born lies in the adjustment to the conditions of American economic life." For Jeremiah W. Jenks and W. Jett Lauck, the immigrant problem also related to the standard of the "highest, best civilization in the world." As an industrial problem, it touched on the issues of occupational structure, changes in industrial methods, female and child labor, displacement of American workers, labor organizations, and standard of living.[3]

On the other hand, the labor problem was quite simply the problem of management and labor, or, perhaps, more correctly, the management of labor. In the background, the ominous specter of class conflict moved factory owners and managers to develop new policies for their workers. "Understanding the human element in industry," economist John R. Commons wrote, "is the acid test of the competency of capitalism today. Ignoring this great human problem and fumbling it add fuel to the fires of class conflict, and class conflict and production never go hand in hand."

According to Edgar S. Furniss, the American institutions of "contract, free competition, property rights" failed to function because the "mass of mankind" refused to accept them or worked them in "a spirit of resentment and antagonism." For the employer, he noted, the labor problem was "evident in the disposition of his labor force to shirk and soldier on the job, to render inefficient service, to waste time, material, equipment." Sumner H. Slichter contrasted the remarkable technical and organizational achievements in productive processes with the absence of methods for handling workmen. He commented: "The idea that a definite and well planned labor policy is as necessary as standardized methods of manufacturing, is lacking." Moreover, he added, "a definite plan" is "as necessary in dealing with labor as in controlling manufacturing operations."[4]

According to Watkins, this social problem also meant different things to different classes and groups of people. For trade unionists, it was "the persistence of inadequate wages, excessive hours of labor, and undesirable conditions of employment." For socialist workers, it was "the persistence of the institution of private property and the 'wage slavery' incident thereto." Conservative employers felt that "the labor problem is essentially one of destroying labor unionism. . . ." Liberal ones believed that "the central problem of industrial relations is the establishment of a workable system of joint determination of the labor agreement. . . ." Proponents of the new science of industrial psychology maintained that the social problem "issues from the repressive influence of modern industry." Specifically, they maintained:

> what was once creative work yielding immeasurable joy to the craftsman has degenerated under capitalism into a tedium of repetitive, monotonous operations, exacting discipline, and complete denial of opportunity for originality and self-expression.

Additionally, Watkins noted that the labor problem involved social and economic issues about the community and the factory and touched on the broader question of social justice in modern industrial America.[5]

Fundamentally, the labor problem was the problem of work-discipline for modern industrial society. In recent years, English historians, notably E. P. Thompson and Sidney Pollard, have concluded that the central problem for the development of industrial capitalism was the establishment of work-discipline and work incentives and the adaptation of new workers to the conditions of factory life. For the United States, Herbert Gutman has suggested that successive infusions of preindustrial immigrants, and others from rural areas, into American factories compounded the problem of their adjustment. Moreover, David Montgomery has maintained that even industrial veterans, who were fully acquainted with the regimen of industrial capitalism, presented problems in the area of discipline and incentives to their bosses. And, Daniel T. Rodgers even has claimed that human nature and the regimen of factory life were indeed incompatible.[6]

Against this background, the labor problem, essentially a question of the efficiency and productivity of the workforce, had its roots in the general problem of work discipline. Moreover, it contained two elements associated with the basic character and structure of the American working class. First, preindustrial immigrant workers presented special problems to employers and supervisors in their social and cultural adjustment and adaptation to American industrial life. For the nineteenth century, Alan Dawley and Paul Faler labeled these workers "traditionalists." Their preindustrial social and cultural baggage was not acclimated to the requirements of the urban and industrial world. In a sense, their attitudes and forms of behavior were in Raymond Williams' terms "residual" and "alternative" to the social and cultural norms of industrial society.

Second, many American and Americanized immigrant workers, both skilled and unskilled, were "modernists," either "loyalists," who accepted the principles and promises of industrial capitalism, or "rebels," who rejected them. Loyalist workers did not pose a problem to their employers. Rebel workers, on the other hand, posed a problem since their social and cultural forms were in Williams' sense "emergent" and "oppositional." Not fully accepting the discipline and incentives of modern industrial capitalism, rebel workers individually and collectively resisted the managerial quest for industrial order. Sometimes, this resistance was isolated and only vaguely conscious; other times, it was organized and class-conscious. It included turnover and absenteeism, soldiering, output restriction, militant unionism, and socialism.

To be sure, a blurred boundary line existed between the neutral attitudes and forms of behavior of the foreign-born traditionalists and the aggressive ones of the rebel modernists. For example, turnover or militant unionism often characterized the actions of both groups. And, the shop floor was the perpetual battleground between factory managers and rebel workers in their efforts to win the hearts and minds of immigrants and others who straddled the middle ground of the industrial war. For factory owners and managers, the solution to the labor problem was the "incorporation" of both traditionalists and rebels into more acceptable modes of thought and action which reinforced work-discipline and fostered the continued expansion of industrial capitalism.[7]

As the Highland Park plant moved toward mechanical and organizational perfection, Ford officials, factory managers, and supervisors uncovered their labor problem. Essentially, they contrasted efficient machines with less efficient workers. John R. Lee, the first Ford labor manager, recalled:

> . . . we began to realize something of the relative value of men, mechanism and material, so to speak, and we confess that up to this time we believed that mechanism and material were of

larger importance and that somehow or other the human element or our men were taken care of automatically and needed little or no consideration.

Between 1908 and 1913, Ford officials gradually discovered that workers required just as much attention as machines and the flow of materials.[8]

Around 1912, Ford managers noticed the correlation of worker satisfaction to improved output. Lee related an incident where the standard output of a drop hammer operator fell dramatically. (This was an example of the use of production statistics to check and to control the efficiency of workers.) An investigation of the normally productive operator revealed: "Sickness, indebtedness, and fear and worry of things that related entirely to the home, had crept in and had put a satisfactory human unit entirely out of harmony with the things that were necessary for production." In another instance, shortly after the move to Highland Park, Ford managers noted that worker productivity began to fall in the machine shop. Also, the medical department reported an unusual increase in the number of illnesses and absences. Upon investigation, Ford officials concluded that the concrete floor of the new plant was the source of the problems. They immediately put in wooden flooring and output rose in the machine shop. As a result, they frantically installed wooden floors in all other shops and departments throughout the plant. Ultimately, productivity was the source for the intense concern about the human element in the factory.[9]

And, the Ford Highland Park factory had serious problems with worker productivity as mechanization advanced. By the end of 1913, the new Ford industrial system should have made tremendous strides in worker output. Without specialized machine tools and without the mechanized movement of work and materials through the plant, scientific managers maintained that systematic management with the appropriate incentives would at least double the production of the average worker. Frederick W. Taylor predicated: "The general adoption of scientific management would in the future double the productivity of the average man engaged in industrial work." And, Taylor took the level of industrial technology as a constant.[10]

Theoretically, Ford technical and organizational innovations produced astounding results. Yet, in practice, productivity fell far short of expectations. Under ideal conditions, individual and departmental machine and assembly operations all had remarkable increases in worker productivity. Nevertheless, the overall increase in worker output of the Model T Ford was not quite so dramatic. In 1909, after the first full year of Model T production, an average of 1,548 workmen produced an average of 1,059 automobiles. In 1913, after the installation of the principal assembly lines, an average of 13,667 workers manufactured an average of 15,284 automobiles. (See Table 5.) To be sure, these figures reflected the extremely rapid growth and expansion in both the number of workers and the volume of production. And, the Ford plant certainly should have benefited from the economies of scale. Yet, the productivity of Ford workers increased from an average .70 to 1.12 cars per worker per month. In short, from 1909 to 1913, Ford worker produtivity increased only 60 percent and did not even match Taylor's projected figure of 100 percent.[11]

Table 5. *Worker Productivity for the Model T Ford, 1909–1913*

	Monthly Average			
Year	Cars Manu-factured	No. of Workmen	Produc-tivity	Productivity Index (1909=100)
1909	1,059*	1,548	.70	100
1910	1,704	2,573	.66	94
1911	3,483	3,733	.93	133
1912	6,923	6,492	1.07	152
1913	15,284	13,667	1.12	160

*Monthly average for 11, not 12 months.

SOURCE: "Model T Production Statistics," Accession 922, Ford Motor Company Archives, Dearborn, Michigan. The monthly statistics for "Men on Roll" and "Automobiles Manufactured during Period" were averaged for each year.

Here was a statistical manifestation of the Ford labor problem. While engineers developed mathematical formulations on productivity and output in the abstract under ideal conditions, workers on the shop floor would not or could not match the anticipated goals. A machine or a department might achieve these ratings under carefully structured conditions, but the entire Ford plant did not operate efficiently as an integrated and synchronized industrial system. The "human element" was not a mechanical automaton. Indeed, Ford mass production demanded stricter forms of work-discipline than earlier factories.

The Ford Motor Company's concern with the attitudes and habits of its workers was not entirely new. Well before the evolution of the new industrial technology, it established a company journal, *Ford Times*, for all of its employees. It was one of a dozen or so house organs at the time. Generally, it provided workers and others with information about activities, events, and developments within the company. Moreover, through the use of moral homilies, anecdotes, and short articles, the *Ford Times* repeatedly exhorted Ford workers to work hard and to get ahead.

In one instance, the organ parodied its stereotype of the inefficient and extravagant worker—the "dude employe." The characterization demonstrated what Ford expected from his workers. "The dude employe," the *Ford Times* mockingly asserted:

> stands in his own light. He wears a higher priced hat than his boss; he is immaculately neat; he looks like a fashion plate, but at the same time his tailor bill is not paid; he is owing money left and right. He spends his evenings in cafes, and at odd moments during the day dodges out to look over the racing form and smoke a cigarette. This dude employe sits up late at night. He spends his salary, and more too, in the gay life. He is tired the next morning when he comes down.
>
> The dude employe who wears a high collar is not the one that knuckles down to hard work. Perspiration and high collars do not go well together. The dude employe does not like perspiration, so he sees that he does not exert himself.

Interestingly, Ford officials concerned themselves with questions of dress and life-style and not only ones of behavior at work.[12]

In another instance, the *Ford Times* printed a model New Year's resolution for its workers. Here, the organ emphasized positive virtues. The resolution began: "Of my own free will and accord, I hereby sincerely covenant with myself . . ." It later continued:

> To exhalt the gospel of work, and get action here and now.
> To keep head, heart, and hand so busy that I won't have time to think about my troubles.
> Because—idleness is a disgrace, low aim is criminal and work minus its spiritual quality becomes drudgery.[13]

Also, Norval A. Hawkins, a Ford manager, produced a series of lists which he labeled "Profit Chokers" in the *Ford Times*. Directed toward Ford supervisors, foremen, and workers, these maxims attempted to identify those attitudes and forms of behavior which resulted in inefficiencies in the Ford organization. Some revealed early Ford labor problems and lapses of work-discipline in the shop culture of Ford workers. A number of these maxims aimed at poor work habits: "Waiting for the other fellow." "Chronic strollers and time killers." "Killing time under day-work pay." "Chronic overtimers." "Employes out of tune with their work." "Not focusing your gray matter on the job." "Too little lubrication." "Not keeping important tools properly ground." "Interchangeable parts failing to interchange." Others focused on lapses in shop discipline or infractions of shop rules: "Sulkers, grunters, back-talkers, mumblers, knockers." "Doctoring records to suit the boss." "Keeping the other fellow's time straight." "Workmen guessing their time on the job." "Not watching the 'front-door-ins' and the 'back-door-outs.' " " 'Padded' pay rolls through tardiness and shirking." "Employes not doing what they are told." And, still others indicated an increasing concern for systematic shop management: "Foremen depending on memories." "Foremen using hands instead of eyes." "Not 'tabbing' the productiveness of employes—overlooking loafers." "Not keeping good men to do good work—poor ones cost dollars." "Not developing the ability of employes." "Shop work poorly planned." "Not planning work so that all departments are kept uniformly busy." "Three-dollar men doing $1 work." "Antagonism to improved methods." "Employes working 'their' way instead of the 'Company's.' "[14]

All of these concerns indicated a company groping with labor and personnel problems. But, the labor problem was not yet particularly acute. For the most part, Hawkins' concerns reflected the work habits and shop customs of a more traditional skilled workforce. Gradually, however, as the new industrial technology evolved, the Ford shops took on a very different character and so too did the Ford labor problems.

A massive influx of immigrant workers presented Ford officials and managers with their most formidable labor problem. And, this influx was predominantly former Southern and Eastern European peasants without industrial work-skills and work-habits. In the first decade of the twentieth century, Detroit was a boom town, and automobiles were the basis for the boom. In these years, tens of thousands of workers—immigrants and Americans—flocked to Detroit from the countryside and from other industrial cities. All sought better jobs, more skilled work, and higher pay in Detroit's new automobile plants. And, from 1908 on, the Ford Motor Company expanded at a phenomenal rate and rapidly came to dominate the industry and the city.

In the early years, the small Ford automobile plant employed a workforce which presumably reflected the ethnic and occupational composition of Detroit. Possessing a self-imposed work-discipline and work-habits, skilled mechanics dominated the shops of the small factory and performed the principal production operations. Although the company did not keep records on the national origins of its workforce, skilled American and German workers most likely directed less skilled workers from a mixed ethnic background. Speaking of the early years of the company, many observers repeatedly used the phrase "first-class American mechanics" to describe the Ford labor force. And, Ford himself often used this phrase to describe his skilled workers. Moreover, German workers, who in accordance with company policy rose through the ranks, were the skilled mechanics, foremen, and even managers in the Highland Park factory.

In addition, the ethnic character of Detroit was predominantly American and German. In 1900, Detroit males in "Manufacturing and mechanical pursuits," a category which included laborers, specialists, skilled mechanics, and even some factory managers and owners, numbered 36,598. In terms of birthplace, "native whites" (17,462, or 48.2 percent) and "foreign whites" (18,828, or 51.4 percent) shared an almost equal representation of the factory population. But, most of the American born (12,410, or 71 percent) had foreign-born parents and had a considerable foreign influence on their life-styles, customs, and traditions. In terms of parental social and cultural origins, the Detroit male industrial population included the nations of Germany (13,641, or 37 percent of the total), United States (5,336, or 15 percent), Great Britain (3,697, or 10 percent), Ireland (3,065, or 8 percent), and Poland (2,986, or 8 percent). Other immigrant groups represented smaller proportions of the industrial population. Clearly, English and German social and cultural patterns prevailed in Detroit and in the early Ford plant.[15]

Nevertheless, Detroit's industrial population rapidly increased in size and its ethnic composition dramatically changed with the growth of the automobile industry. According to Lauck and Sydenstricker, the increase in the average number of male wage earners was 129.1 percent for Detroit from 1899 to 1909. (In their data, the next highest increase was 49.9 per cent for Buffalo.) Lois Rankin detailed the origins of Detroit's Southern and Eastern European immigrant communities. For most groups, the 1900s and 1910s saw the principal waves of migration to the city. Some, such as the Italians, Poles, Lithuanians, Syrians, and Hugarians, first arrived in small numbers in the nineteenth century and established relatively large colonies by the early 1900s. Others, such as the Russians, Ukrainians, Rumanians, Bulgarians and Macedonians, Yugoslavs, Finns, and Greeks, did not even begin to arrive until the 1900s. With the exception of some Italians and Greeks who entered petty commercial trades, the overwhelming majority of these "new" immigrants filled unskilled positions in Detroit's automobile industry. Some, notably Finns, Hungarians, Italians, Yugoslavs, Russians, and Ukrainians, came from copper and coal mining districts and other industrial centers. They sought pleasanter and lighter work and conditions in the automobile plants. And, a number of Finns, Greeks, Yugoslavs, Lithuanians, Russians, and Syrians came in a major wave from 1912 to 1914, a period of rapid expansion for the Ford Highland Park plant.[16]

Despite the incredible influx of workers, Detroit shops and factories suffered a perpetual labor shortage. In 1910, the *Detroit Tribune* noted that the automobile companies got "Labor's Cream" and demoralized other industries. It reported that "the insatiable demand of the motor car manufacturers for hands of all classes has paralyzed the labor situation for other industries." Higher wages "tempted" and "lured" common and skilled labor to the automobile shops. For the most part, the main concern was for skilled workers since "in auto making, everything is so specialized and the automobile industry is producing no new skilled mechanics." In 1912, the *Detroit Free Press* reported on the shortage of unskilled foreign labor. It noted: "Detroit is reveling in industrial prosperity such as has fallen to the lot of few other cities." It added: "There is one cloud on the horizon, however, which is proving more or less of a nightmare to some of the larger manufacturers. This is the question of labor, principally of the unskilled variety." The Board of Commerce, the newspaper noted, intended to send "immigration commissioners" to Ellis Island to secure "newly arrived immigrants" and to send them "direct to this city."[17]

At the leading edge of the new industry, Ford technical and organizational innovations were in part a response to the changing social composition of the Detroit labor force. Around 1910, Polish and Italian immigrants, the first Southern and Eastern European immigrant groups to establish themselves in the city, entered the Ford factory in ever greater numbers. "At that time," as the company expanded with its move to Highland Park, William Klann, a German foreman, recalled, "we had all kinds of nationalities working for us. We had Germans, Polish people, Swedes, and some couldn't talk English." At the time, Polish workers became so prominent that Klann felt compelled to learn their language. He continued, "I studied some Polish, too. I learned to talk Polish from these Polish fellows." As the Ford plant mechanized and work became specialized, so too did its social and cultural composition.[18]

By 1914, foreign-born workers, and especially Southern and Eastern Europeans, represented a majority of the 14,000 workers in the Highland Park factory. "Three-quarters of the employees are of foreign birth," O. J. Abell wrote, "a large number of them are non English-speaking and of a grade ordinarily fitted for common labor." And, the new industrial technology provided the means for them to produce high quality work. "In the Ford plant," Abell continued, "they have been trained to a high grade—each for a particular operation." Along similar lines, H. L. Arnold noted: "the Ford Company's unprecedented methods of utilizing unskilled labor in skilled repetition-production are of the highest interest, and should be fully detailed for careful study by all large employers of unskilled labor."[19]

In November 1914, the Ford Motor Company released its first detailed survey on the national origins of its workforce. American-born workers, who numbered 3,771, represented only 29 percent of the workers in the Ford plant. Foreign-born workers came from twenty-two different national groups and numbered 9,109 persons, or 71 percent of the workforce. And, Southern and Eastern Europeans constituted a majority of the Ford workforce. After Americans, the five largest groups were Poles (2,677 or 21 percent), Russians (2,016 or 16 percent), Romanians (750 or 6 percent), Italians and Sicilians (690 or 5 percent), and Austro-Hugarians (657 or 5 percent). At this time, Germans were the seventh largest foreign-born group with 606 workers.[20]

Ultimately, the very heterogeneity of the Ford workforce hindered the efficient operation of the Highland Park factory. In the past, a shop or factory composed of independent and autonomous workgroups could function effectively with different groups having a different ethnic character. Ford mass production, however, required a new degree of cultural conformity. The simplest lapses of communication among workers and among workers and foremen now contained the prospect of the disruption of the synchronized and coordinated flow of materials through the mechanized factory.

Furthermore, aside from being a labor problem to Ford managers, immigrant workers also constituted a considerable social and cultural problem in their urban communities. Employers and skilled craftsmen reviled immigrant workers for their dilution of the "American standard of living." When questioned about the social conditions among workers from his plant, Henry Ford replied that "the most wretched class was composed of foreign workmen, ignorant, and unskilled labor, most of them unable to speak English." In fact, mechanization and large numbers of immigrant workers created a highly stratified occupational structure within the American working class—on the one hand a small fraction of highly skilled American and German tool-makers and machinists, and, on the other hand, a mass of unskilled immigrant specialists. "The effect of immigration upon the occupational distribution of the industrial wage-earners," Isaac Hourwich, a contemporary political economist and statistician noted, "has been the elevation of the English-speaking workmen to the status of an aristocracy of labor, while the immigrants have been employed to perform the rough work of all industries."[21]

And, this social condition of industry spilled over and became a social problem of the industrial city. In the early twentieth century, Lauck and Sydenstricker reported on residential segregation between middle-class and working-class communities and within working-class communities. "Practically every investigation of the environment of wage-earners," they noted:

> has called attention to . . . the general contrast in appearance between those sections occupied by wage-earners' families and the so-called residential sections. In nearly every industrial community whose population is composed almost entirely of wage-earners there is a marked difference between those streets on which unskilled workers live and those on which the better-paid workers have their homes. Since the newer immigration has come so largely into the unskilled occupations, this difference is more plainly evident. Practically all industrial localities now have their 'little Italies' and their 'Hungary hollows.'

The residential segregation, they maintained, was both a cause and a consequence of economic inequality. "It is hardly necessary to enlarge on this often observed condition," they later added:

> beyond pointing out that the influx into industry of southern and eastern European immigrants has greatly intensified it. Their low standards of culture and of living, their isolation from the native-born population because of their inability to speak English and to associate with their American neighbors, and the influence of their own racial and religious institutions, customs and habits in maintaining denominational distinctions, are segregating factors, augmented by an indifference and oftentimes a prejudice on the part of the native-born population. There has grown up in almost every industrial locality . . . a more or less isolated immigrant section with institutions, customs, businesses, and standards of morals and living peculiar to the predominant race or races composing its population. . . .

Indeed, for manufacturers and factory managers, the immigrant problem had its roots in the social and cultural isolation of the immigrant worker.[22]

Peter Roberts, who did educational work among immigrants in the Pennsylvania coal fields, identified the desirable and the undesirable qualities of the Southern and Eastern European immigrant worker. On the positive side, the "new" immigrant worker performed the arduous, dangerous, and dirty tasks in coal mines, iron and steel plants, meat packing plants, slaughterhouses, and tanneries. In these occupations, they were "hard workers, regular, uncomplaining, and submissive." On the negative side, they possessed undesirable traits which affected their work-discipline and productivity in an industrial setting. These included racial hatred and jealousy, too many holidays, the drink habit, an inadequate diet for hard work, thievery, and a tendency to lie. To be sure, these stereotypical images were Roberts' perception of reality and not necessarily reality. Nonetheless, for middle-class factory owners and managers, their perceptions were often their reality.[23]

Next, aside from their immigrant problem, Ford officials and managers confronted the working-class reaction to the new conditions of production. Again, the immigrant problem and the labor problem often converged as foreign-born and native-born workers expressed similar attitudes and acted in similar ways. In both instances, novices and veterans resisted what the new industrial technology had done to their world of work. Sometimes, this resistance was only an individual and semiconscious act; at others, it was collective and class-conscious. In either case, the result of the resistances was a decline in the overall efficiency of the mechanized Ford factory.

First, absenteeism and labor turnover severely disrupted the new Ford methods and techniques of production. Gradually, as the new Ford technology materialized, the rates of absenteeism and turnover reached incredible proportions. In 1913, the "daily absences" in the Highland Park plant amounted to 10 percent of the total workforce. And, in the same year, the rate of labor turnover reached a staggering 370 percent. Both forms of behavior were individual and semiconscious actions against conditions in the Ford plant. For Ford workers, absenteeism often translated into short vacations or respites from the tedium of the assembly lines. Turnover often reflected dissatisfaction with changes in the conditions of work and the character of the workplace. For Ford officials, absenteeism and turnover meant an additional item in the cost of production. It forced them to hire extra men to account for absentees and to bear the cost of breaking in new workers who replaced those who quit.[24]

Frequently, the insecurity and instability of immigrant and American working-class life resulted in the high rates of absenteeism and labor turnover. As already noted, Detroit had an extremely fluid and volatile labor market in this period. O. J. Abell reported that the "rapid growth of the automobile industry brought all classes of labor to Detroit from all parts of the country." "Naturally," he continued, "the men most inclined to shift about were the ones who shifted to Detroit." In addition, Abell added, the seasonality of some automobile factories "contributed its interest to the general unrest." Consequently, "the proportion of floating or transient help has been short of amazing." A leader of the Auto Workers' Union echoed similar sentiments. He noted the difficulty to organize the new automobile workers in the Detroit factories and plants. "Thousands of them," G. Demerest reported to the union, "have been organized into the Carriage, Wagon, and Automobile workers only to be thrown out of work and forced to seek employment elsewhere." Indeed, the seasonal character of the industry augmented traditional patterns of working-class geographic mobility. He continued: "We have a large body of transit [sic] workers connected to our industry. They move from place to place wherever there happens to be a demand for help."[25]

Myron S. Watkins, a first-hand observer of working-class life in Detroit, reported on the almost continuous mobility of automobile workers. He observed that automobile workers "are continually on the alert for 'better pay,' and a difference of five cents per hour in favor of a new job will lead them to 'throw up' an old job without delay." For numerous, and seemingly minor, reasons, Detroit workers readily quit or abandoned one shop or factory for another. He continued:

it may be the opportunity for overtime in the next few weeks, or less bossing, or a larger or shorter noon-hour, or less standing on their feet, or cleaner work, or any of a dozen slight personal reasons that prompt these truly 'independent' laborers to transfer their names to other pay-rolls so frequently.

In numerous instances, the unskilled specialized worker consciously sought small opportunities and small steps upward within the limited boundaries of his world.[26]

Frequently, the unskilled worker abandoned his job in order to broaden his knowledge and experience and eventually to learn a trade. "Many workmen," John W. Love, a journalist reported, "have a series of 'trades' and they vary their lives by changing jobs and changing plants." Frank Marquart first entered the Detroit automobile shops in the 1910s. He detailed this shop tradition. "I know some chaps," he recalled:

that actually learned the toolmaking trade that way. A young man hired out in a factory as a toolmaker. He was placed on a machine, and with the help of the man working on the next machine, picked up a little skill—until the foreman discovered that he was a 'shyster' and fired him. Then he hired out in another plant, picked up a little more skill, and so on until he acquired enough competence to hold a toolroom job. We called it 'stealing a trade.'

Unskilled workers also stole "semiskilled" specialities. "For example," Marquart continued, "a lathe hand always made more money than a drill press hand. Thus a shopmate of mine decided that he was going to quit his drill press job and became a lathe hand. I recall he was fired from three different places before he acquired enough skill to hold down a lathe job in Chalmers. . . ."[27]

Filled with its forms of ironic tragedy, working-class existence endured its minor and sometimes not-so-minor disappointments. Many American and immigrant workers entered Detroit's automobile plants to learn a skilled machinists's trade. And, if they arrived in a newly mechanized plant such as Ford's, they confronted a missed opportunity in its routinized tasks and routines. Nonetheless, resilient and persistent, working-class cultural forms adapted to the setbacks. And, for employers, the result was additional turnover.

In the Ford factory, the new technological and organizational innovations made the industrial process particularly susceptible to the problem of absenteeism. In 1913, a 10 percent rate of absenteeism meant that an average of from 1,300 to 1,400 persons were absent from their place on the Ford production and assembly lines. In order to maintain maximum utilization of machinery and physical plant, the Ford production managers had to take into account the number of absent workers. In order to keep the Highland Park in operation, they either had to find this many replacements each day or to hire a workforce 10 percent above the capacity of the machines and the plant. In either case, large numbers of workers worked inefficiently at unfamiliar machines.[28]

A variety of reasons caused high rates of absenteeism among industrial workers in this period. Many of these reasons related to the unsettled conditions of working-class life and culture. John S. Keir, an early student of the subject, listed lateness, sickness, accidents, high wages, weather, and general dissatisfaction as reasons for absences. Sumner H. Slichter, an early industrial relations expert, reported that the worker simply needed a break from the rigors and the routines of mechanized factory life. Without formal vacations, the voluntary "lay off" was the working-class vacation. According to Keir, " 'sickness' is a term which covers a multitude of sins." He noted an employer who called sickness " 'a lack of gameness,' a giving in to the slightest indispositions." "The two most prevalent diseases," Keir wryly observed, "are alcoholism and stomach trouble." Stomach trouble was the workman's all-purpose excuse for absence. It covered "a multitude of ills, aches, and pains." In this period, industrial workers had their equivalent of "Saint Monday" in the modern malady of "Blue Monday." It was a consequence of general dissatisfaction with work in the factory. " 'Blue Monday,' " Keir added, "has a very real ring from the manufacturer's viewpoint." Mondays, particularly after a Saturday pay-day, accounted for the most absences. Thursday, the day in the middle of the work-week, was next.[29]

For the well-paid skilled worker, the psychological necessity to simply get away from the job or to "lay off" for a few days was an important reason for absences. "The fear of being refused a lay off," wrote Slichter, "causes most men to remain away without requesting a lay off, giving on return the excuse that they were sick." Boyd Fisher, a Detroit business leader, noted: "Strike fever is often vacation fever. Shrewd managers, if they had no more altruistic aim, might well plan vacations to promote industrial equanimity." For the less secure unskilled worker, who constantly searched for higher pay, better jobs, or improved working conditions, sickness provided excuses for their lateness or absence. This was true of the automobile workers in Detroit. "In fact," Watkins wrote, "it is not at all uncommon for employees to use a 'sickness holiday' for tramping about in search of a job."[30]

As in the case with lateness and absenteeism, labor turnover also plagued Ford managers with the disruption of factory operations. With its specialized labor market in a constant state of flux, Detroit's normal rate of turnover was inordinately high. It ranged from 100 to 200 percent per year. Nevertheless, the Ford rate of turnover became unusually high even for Detroit. For example, in 1913 the Packard Motor Car Company had a 200 percent rate of turnover. In the same year, the Ford rate was a phenomenal 370 percent. This meant that Ford managers had to hire more than 52,000 workers to maintain a workforce of about 13,600 persons. In that year, the Ford employment line made the Highland Park factory a stop on the itinerary of Detroit sight-seeing tours. "The long employment line in front of the Ford plant," H. F. Porter noted, "had become one of the sights to whet the curiosity of 'rubber neck' tourists."[31]

Ford officials readily recognized the inefficiency of their high rate of turnover. "Men who are experienced in certain work," the company reasoned, "are naturally more efficient than men inexperienced because of constant shifting." In March 1913, Ford officials conducted a survey of "the number of men leaving the employ of the company." For that month, slightly more than 7,300 workers left the plant. The company discharged 1,276 workers. And, the majority of the Ford workers either formally quit, 870 workers, or were "five-day men," who left without informing the company, 5,156.[32]

The "five-day men," who accounted for 71 percent of the turnover, represented the major problem to the Ford and other Detroit industrial establishments. These workers simply were absent for five days or more and removed from the payroll of the company. Without their formal notification of resignation, the company presumed that these "floaters" quit. A visitor to the Ford factory reported that the fluid Detroit labor market allowed the worker "to quit his job in the morning and find employment in another factory at noon." "Then, too," he continued, "a large number of unmarried men of a roving disposition were among those most attracted to such conditions."[33]

For the employer, labor turnover represented a considerable expense in the operation of the plant. The employment department constantly hired and trained new men. Magnus W. Alexander, the first person to examine the problem, estimated the cost of this process. The "economic loss in the hiring and discharge of employees" included: the clerical work for hiring, the instruction of new workers, the new worker's increased wear, tear, and damage to machinery and tools, his decreased rate of production, and his increased amount of waste and spoilage. He estimated that it cost an average of $35 for each new employee. Boyd Fisher, a leader of the Detroit Executive Club, reported that "Mr. Alexander estimates that it costs $73.50 to break in a new semi-skilled operative and only $8.50 to take on a new laborer, mere percentage figures for turnover mean very little." Even at the $35 figure, with 52,000 workers entering the Ford factory in 1913, the monetary cost of labor turnover to the Ford Motor Company amounted to over $1,820,000.[34]

The reasons for high rates of labor turnover covered a broad range of problems within the factories. In his early analysis of the problem of labor turnover, Boyd Fisher discovered that some reasons rested with the employers and managers and some with the workers. The shop foreman, who possessed complete authority in his shop, accounted for a large number of the discharges. Frequently, he fired workmen because of "religious or national prejudice" or sometimes even whim. At other times he "jobbed" a "good workman" into the streets. Poor planning on the part of factory superintendents and managers resulted in discharges due to the inadequate scheduling of work through the factory. A main reason for workmen voluntarily leaving their jobs, was "the inequalities in the pay system." "Men quit too," reported Fisher, "because foremen or fellow workmen of different races or religions 'gang' them. . . ." He also noted, "Workmen, too, are often ignorant, narrow, highly sensitive to trivial wrongs or fancied oppression by 'capital.' " In this instance, workers quit over issues related to plant conditions, such as lighting, ventilation, toilets and lunchroom or street-car facilities. In many cases, workmen also quit because they were poor and did not have cash. "All the workmen I have known individually," Fisher recalled, "have gone to new jobs 'dead broke.' Often they quit on some pretext, after working a few days, in order to draw pay to keep from going hungry."[35]

And, the acute specialization of labor was another important cause of labor turnover in the automobile industry. With regard to the "comparatively easy . . . shift from shop to shop," Godfrey, who visited the Ford plant, observed that "men are specialized to such a degree that the bulk of the employees are operators and not mechanics in the broadest sense. This makes it much easier to replace them, as well as for them to get jobs in other shops. . . ." In addition, he maintained:

It is perfectly natural that men of the operator class change their jobs more frequently than those in more skilled branches of the trade. This is perhaps due in part to a lesser feeling of responsibility as well as the desire to do something different, after drilling the same-sized hole, in the same place, in the same piece, day after day, for several months. It doesn't require a man with much imagination to get eternally sick of going through the same motions hour after hour and day after day with no prospect of change. The only relief seems to be to either go on a bat or get a new job; and, as the latter is usually cheaper in the end, he usually finds a new job.

Perhaps, John R. Commons eloquently expressed the mood with his comment on turnover among young specialized workers. "They are," he reported, "conducting a continuous, unorganized strike."[36]

Next, soldiering and output restriction directly threatened the authority of factory owners and managers to control workers in their shops and factories. In a sense, these types of working-class behavior were a form of guerilla warfare in the battle over productivity between workers and managers on the shop floor. Also, these activities continued and maintained the independent traditions of the autonomous craftsman to regulate and to control the pace and intensity of factory work. As work became more mechanized and labor more subdivided, skilled and unskilled workers rebelled against their changed conditions of employment in factories. Moreover, with increased attention to greater levels and more efficient means of production, factory owners and managers regarded this labor problem as an insidious threat to the smooth operation of their shops. A fundamental premise of Taylor's system of scientific management was the eradication and elimination of all forms of "loafing" on the job. Taylor first recognized this problem in the 1890s. And, in 1903, he defined it. In "Shop Management," an early classic on labor management, he maintained that "the greatest obstacle" to high output was "the slow pace which they adopt, or the loafing, soldiering, or marking time as it is called."[37]

Taylor distinguished between "natural soldiering" and "systematic soldiering." Natural soldiering came "from the natural instinct and tendency of men to take it easy" and systematic soldiering, later known as output restriction, arose "from more intricate second thought and reasoning caused by their relations with other men." Natural soldiering was the individual act of a single worker, whereas systematic soldiering was the collective act of informal groups of workers within their particular shops or departments. The workman who simply soldiered spent much of his time "improving every opportunity for delay, short of actually sitting down." The workmen who restricted their output secretly conspired against their employer. This systematic soldiering was "almost universal." Under this practice, the workmen had "the deliberate object of keeping their employers ignorant of just how fast the work can be done." The workmen stayed in the factory and collected their wages for an insufficient amount of work.[38]

At the time, most employers believed that only the skilled workers, particularly those associated with the trade union movement, were capable of concerted or systematic output restriction. As a consequence of this belief, the employers charged the American trade union with a conscious conspiracy to impede American industrial progress. Nonetheless, output restriction had deep roots in working-class shop culture. In 1904, Carroll D. Wright, the United States Commission of Labor, reported that some restrictions on output "have been in existence as trade customs or traditions for many years, and when, with modern shop equipment, the employers begin to infringe on the traditions, the union comes in to formulate and preserve them." These customs and traditions frequently lacked formality, but they were important to the social life of the shop. "Even where there are no formal rules," Wright noted, "it has been universally found, both in union and non-union establishments, that the common sentiment of the workmen is strong and severe against those whose output is materially above the average."[39]

In 1931, Stanley B. Mathewson made a comprehensive survey of "the whole messy business of restriction" among unorganized and unskilled workers in a number of mass production industries, including the automobile industry. In this survey, Mathewson:

> saw men hiding finished product under their benches, afraid to turn it in; foremen working at cross purposes with time-study men and showing workers how to make time studies inaccurate; workmen killing time by the hour because the day's 'limit' had been reached; men afraid to let the management learn the improved methods which they discovered themselves; older workers teaching youngsters to keep secret from the management the amount they could comfortably produce in a day.

Mathewson believed that "these workers are practicing restriction under modern management conditions in the same manner and for much the same reasons that their industrial grand-fathers practiced 'ca'canny' and 'soldiering' in this country and Great Britain in years gone by." The working-class customs and traditions of output restriction spanned the nineteenth and twentieth centuries, from the pre-union era to the mass production era. "Restriction," concluded Mathewson, "is a widespread institution, deeply entrenched in the working habits of American laboring people."[40]

In the Ford Motor Company, the development of mass production thwarted, but did not eliminate, the soldiering and the output restriction of the Ford auto workers. Around 1910, after the company moved to Highland Park, William Klann remembered the exhortations of his superior for an increased production quota in the transmission assembly department. "He kept moving it up all the time," he recalled. "It was no easy job since the schedule was up and we had no chance to hide any more parts." Later, in 1913, Klann said:

> . . . we started bunching machines together so you could hardly walk. It was very efficient to do it that way but people never liked it because you weren't carrying stuff; you were just moving from one bench to another and from one machine to the other all the time. . . . The men didn't like it because they had to work

harder. The pieces were there and they didn't have time to walk back and take a rest in between.

Klann's recollection revealed the complicity of foremen and workers in output restriction through informal shop arrangements. In order to maintain the good will of his men, the foreman had to tolerate a considerable degree of worker autonomy.[41]

Furthermore, Henry Ford, a former machinist, knew and recognized the shop customs and traditions of his workers. He frequently railed against the evils of soldiering and output restriction. "More than half the trouble in the world today," Ford proclaimed, "is the 'soldiering' and dilution and inefficiency for which people are paying their good money." In another case, he castigated the shop practice of walking around and looking busy. "The undirected worker," he noted, "spends more time walking about for tools and materials thane he does working; he gets small pay because pedestrianism is not a highly paid line." And, Ford believed that once a worker entered his factory, his obligation was to put in a full day's work. "A day's work," Ford maintained, "means more than being 'on duty' at the shop for the required number of hours. It means giving an equivalent in service for the wage drawn." To be sure, managerial awareness, along with new production techniques, contained and limited the problems of soldiering and output restriction. Nonetheless, automobile workers gave employers what they considered to be "a fair day's work" for their wage.[42]

Myron Watkins reported that high pay attracted automobile workers to the Detroit shops and plants, but "their hearts were not in their work." Soldiering and output restriction expressed their "well-nigh universal dissatisfaction." He described one of "scores of incidents." In one automobile factory, fifteen minutes before quitting time, the entire shop slackened the pace, put away tools, and removed aprons "in preparation for an instantaneous getaway at the first stroke of the gong." "Irish," Watkins' Russian-born shopmate, inspected an almost finished batch of carburetor valves. Instead of completing the batch, he fumbled "over one piece so as not to draw the attention of the foreman to his idleness." Watkins inquired: "Why not finish up the job tonight?" The Russian industrial veteran replied: "Why finish it? It do no good. You never get all those boxes cleared off the floor. As soon as you finish one box, they bring 'nother down. Don't hurry. You never get done anyway."[43]

Frank Marquart related similar incidents from his experiences in

Detroit automobile shops at the time of World War I. In the shop or department, workers had their "unwritten law" for individual productivity at machines. Sometimes, "hungry bastards" violated these working-class norms and faced incredible peer pressure. "They were ostracized," Marquart recalled:

> and no one would talk to them. Every time one of them went for a drink of water or to the washroom, the belts on his machine were cut, the grinding wheel was smashed, his personal tools were damaged, the word 'RAT' was chalked on his machine in block letters. They were treated in the way union building craftsmen treat a scab on the job.

In one instance, two "speed kings" could not tolerate the abuse and quit their jobs. And this was in the technologically advanced and scientifically managed automobile industry. The deskilled immigrant specialist readily adopted the shop rules of workmates who were more familiar with factory life.[44]

Finally, Henry Ford considered any form of unionism a major threat to the efficiency of his mechanized factory. And, at the time, he faced a three-pronged challenge from militant unions. First, the Industrial Workers of the World initiated a militant campaign to organize automobile workers into their "One Big Union." Second, the Carriage, Wagon, and Automobile Workers' Union made its first serious efforts to organize automobile workers into an industrial union. And, finally, the skilled metal trades in the American Federation of Labor attempted to recruit potential members of their trades from the workers in the automobile industry.

Henry Ford's attitude toward organized labor was the classic "open shop" position, i.e., the complete non-recognition of organized labor. After 1902, Detroit was the "open shop" city *par excellence*. At the time, the Detroit Employers' Association waged "a vigorous fight against the various unions in the metal industry" and completely defeated the traditionally strong unions in the metal trades. For the next decade, the skilled workers in the metal trades, such as the machinists and the molders, were without representation in factories and shops connected to the automobile industry. Until about 1912, the Employers' Association's position towards organized labor prevailed, and Detroit had few successful strikes in its automobile shops and factories.[45]

Henry Ford operated in this climate of open hostility between labor and capital. His fundamental objection to labor unions centered on issues connected to production. Labor unions caused strikes, which halted factory operations, or they advocated restricted output, which impeded these operations. "The only true labor leader," wrote Ford, "is the one who leads labor to work and wages, and not the leader who leads labor to strikes, sabotage, and starvation." As with other advocates of the open shop, he often publicly proclaimed that he did not object to labor unions: "I am not opposed to labor organization," he stated. However, he added the usual provision, "I am not opposed to any sort of organization that makes for progress. It is organizing to limit production—whether by employers or by workers—that matters." Like the typical open shop employer, Ford did not care whether or not his workers joined unions, but he would not negotiate with those unions. He said, "We have no antagonism to unions, but we participate in no arrangements with either employee or employer organizations."[46]

Henry Ford, and not labor organizations, knew the best interests of Ford automobile workers. He maintained:

> There is nothing that a union membership could do for our people. Some of them may belong to union, probably the majority do not. We do not know and make no attempt to find out, for it is not a matter of the slightest concern to us.

At best, these statements were insincere statements with a veneer of impartiality and fairness; at worst, they were outright lies.[47]

In the late summer of 1912, an incident at the Keim Mills in Buffalo typified the Ford attitude toward the activities of organized labor. The Keim Mills, which the Ford Motor Company recently purchased, produced and supplied axles, transmissions, and other parts for the Model T Ford. W. A. Walters, who worked at the plant, recalled:

> About a week before Labor Day of 1912, trouble that had been brewing for some time broke out. What we would call a wildcat strike today took place. A number of men ganged up outside in front of the entrance. The factory was closed, that is, open but not working or operating because of a lack of manpower.

Walters said that the plant manager called Ford in Detroit for advice on dealing with the strikers. "Henry Ford said," Walters related,

"'That suits me. If the men don't go to work, get some flat cars and move the presses and machinery to Highland Park, Michigan.' " Rather than negotiate with the patternmakers and molders who called the strike, Ford shipped the machinery of the entire plant to Highland Park. He allowed those workers, who "wanted to work," to follow the machines to the new factory.[48]

In the spring of 1913, the Industrial Workers of the World brought its variety of militant industrial unionism to Detroit. In the wake of its spectacular strikes in Lawrence and Patterson, the IWW initiated an organizational campaign among the unskilled workers in the automobile and associated industries in the Middle West. In February 1913, the campaign began with a massive and spontaneous walkout in the rubber factories in Akron, Ohio. The militant and sometimes violent strike involved from 15,000 to 20,000 American and immigrant workers in the Firestone, Goodyear, Goodrich, and other tire factories. (Firestone supplied the Ford Motor Company with its tires.) When the strike collapsed in March, the IWW organizers moved on to Detroit in an effort to bring unionism to the automobile workers.[49]

In Detroit, the IWW campaign among the automobile workers began at the gates of the Highland Park factory. In late April 1913, the organizers conducted a "free-speech" drive and organized large street meetings in front of the Ford factory. A Ford worker with the organizers stated that "it was the intention of his organization to unionize the men at the Ford plant in an effort to get a higher wage." With Ford workers gathered at the factory windows, a crowd of 3,000 workers attended a rally at the factory gate. When the Ford Motor Company "summarily withdrew the workers' outdoor lunch privileges," the IWW shifted its attention to the workers of other Detroit automobile factories, notably, to the Studebaker plants. In June, some 6,000 workers struck the Studebaker and other plants. Although the strike failed, the arrests of organizers and strikers, the mass demonstrations of strikers, and the police violence against the strikers raised the level of social tensions in Detroit. Moreover, rumor said that the IWW would return in 1914 to organize the workers in the Ford Motor Company.[50]

For a company like the Ford Motor Company, the IWW aroused the greatest fear because it waged a militant rhetorical attack on capitalism and espoused a policy of "sabotage" in American factories and workshops. Although dreaded by employers, some aspects of this policy struck a responsive chord in the factory culture of workers. Sabotage was a word with many meanings. It ranged "all the way from 'passive resistance' at one extreme to violent destruction of property at the other. . . ." In its milder and non-destructive aspects, the IWW concept of sabotage represented an assault against scientific management. As a conscious working-class response to Taylor's efficiency schemes, the IWW proposed a systematic policy of soldiering and output restriction—what they termed "the conscientious withdrawal of efficiency" and "striking on the job." In 1914, the organization directed its speakers "to recommend to the workers the necessity of curtailing production by means of 'slowing down' and sabotage. All rush work should be done in 'wrong manner.' "51

Ralph Chaplin, the Wobbly poet and songwriter, recalled that a "widely circulated jingle" summarized his idea of sabotage:

The hours are long, the pay is small,
So take your time and buck 'em all.

Considered in this sense, sabotage was an equitable and imaginative working-class response to exploitation and had wide appeal among automobile workers. To management, however, sabotage represented a direct and an insidious threat to the high productivity which the employers desired.52

At the same time that the IWW threatened automobile manufacturers, the Carriage, Wagon, and Automobile Workers' Union (CWAWU), a young American Federation of Labor craft union, confronted two important issues—the growth of the automobile industry and the need for industrial unions.

The Detroit local of the CWAWU evolved into a small, but growing, industrial union for automobile workers. In its first decade, the fortunes of this local waxed and waned. Around 1910, "the skeleton framework of an industrial organization was built." For two years, the organization conducted a series of strikes in the smaller shops and achieved minor benefits for its workers. In 1912, the CWAWU "became involved in a strike that spread rapidly until over a thousand men were involved." The strike, which lasted thirteen weeks, involved the painters and the trimmers in the Detroit automobile body shops. One of the struck shops, the American Top and Trim Company, supplied all of its production to the Ford Motor Company. Nonetheless, the spontaneous strike "was beyond the control of the union, which was composed of men who had never been on strike before. . . ." As a result of the strike and its organizational momentum, the Detroit local reported about 1,600 members for the year 1913. In addition, the CWAWU also became involved in the IWW strike in the summer of 1913. Along with the Detroit Federation of Labor, the local AFL city-wide federation, the CWAWU forced the IWW to call a mass meeting and to accept responsibility for the direction of the strike.[53]

Finally, the craft unions in the American Federation of Labor also conducted a major campaign to organize the automobile workers of Detroit. In November 1913 in connection with their jurisdictional dispute with the CWAWU the AFL craft unions asked the AFL Seattle Convention for an affirmation of the autonomy of the various trades in the automobile industry. The convention acceded to their request. As a result of this decision, the Metal Trades Department solicited and received the assistance of the blacksmiths, the machinists, the metal polishers, buffers, and platers, the iron molders, the pattern makers, the sheet metal workers, the carpenters, the painters, and the upholsterers. In January 1914, the representatives and organizers from these organizations reported to Detroit and began their unsuccessful campaign which lasted until June 1914. While they claimed some success in increased membership for some of the unions involved, the drive was an abysmal failure. The Metal Trades Department blamed the failure on the Ford Five Dollar Day and the poor condition of the automobile trade.[54]

By 1913, the Ford Motor Company faced a serious and multidimensional labor crisis. To Ford and his managers, the labor problem involved work-discipline. The immigrant worker was unfamiliar with the values and habits of urban industrial life. And, the American worker was sometimes too familiar with them and was sometimes undisciplined and unruly. John R. Lee, an early Ford labor manager, evaluated the American, immigrant, and second-generation worker:

The American is the past master of bluff, and it takes us a long time to teach him that bluff and appearance count for nothing here. We find the immigrant, substantial, developed physically, which helps him in his work, and his mental powers of thinking are right. . . . he appreciates all that is done for him. It is the children of the immigrant—and his children's children—that cause the most trouble. They try to domineer and resent authority.

In other words, while the immigrant did not have industrial experience, he could be guided in the right direction. The managerial problem was to provide that guidance for the human element and to prevent the assimilation of more class-conscious shop traditions. To this end, the Ford Motor Company instituted a number of labor reforms in 1913 and established the Five Dollar Day in 1914.[55]

5. Toward Modern Labor Management: The Lee Reforms and the Five Dollar Day

The problem of increasing the production per man was one which could not be solved by speeding up machinery and by improving the technical processes. American industry soon found that the proper handling of labor was necessary to realize maximum efficiency. Labor became a production problem which challenged the attention of employers and manufacturers. Businessmen could not ignore it any longer.[1]—Paul H. Douglas, Political Economist, 1919

... but the human element enters into the consideration, and this is, in reality, the one *variable* that must be dealt with. But to hold this variable within as restricted limits as possible, and in fact, to reduce it to a *constant*, the Ford plan, dealing with the men and their compensation, was evolved.[2]—Harold Whiting Slauson, Industrial Journalist, 1914

The Ford labor problems had a chaotic and amorphous character. Nevertheless, Ford factory managers and engineers, who rationalized work process and the entire Highland Park plant, struggled to resolve these human problems in the same manner as they did with their technical problems in the Ford shops. In their eyes, the human element was neither more intractable nor more insurmountable than the mechanical element of production. As with the design of machines, work processes, and the entire industrial system, the methods and procedures for the management of labor required reexamination, reorganization, and rationalization in order to suit the needs of mass production. At this time, the modern "science" of management was in its infancy and Ford labor policies were quite conventional. And these labor policies matched Sumner H. Slichter's contemporary observation on "the traditional management of labor." It "had two principal characteristics: crudity and the reliance on drive methods as a means of increasing output." Both unsophisticated policies and the use of foremen for handling workers were important features of the early Ford managerial tradition.[3]

95

However, in the first decade of the twentieth century, two other managerial traditions coexisted with these conventional methods and countered the cruder aspects of these customary practices. And, both traditions attempted to extend management's control over the industrial workforce. First, scientific management, as already noted, had an important influence on the technical evolution of Ford mass production. Moreover, it focused on certain areas of the labor question with its emphasis on the coordination of workers and industrial processes. It proposed a more systematic and scientific adjustment of the labor problem. Second, industrial betterment attempted to extend management's reach beyond the purely technical realm of working-class life to the broader social and cultural ones of values and forms of behavior. Deeply paternalistic, the industrial betterment movement sought to improve the social and moral condition of labor in order to alleviate worker dissatisfaction with modern forms of factory production. Although they sometimes overlapped and interconnected, the scientific management tradition formed the basis for modern personnel management, and industrial betterment grew into welfare capitalism. Both were the foundation for modern labor management in the Ford factory and in other modern industrial establishments.[4]

In the Ford factory, the two more progressive traditions coalesced and partially transformed the cruder and more authoritarian one. In 1913, John R. Lee, the first modern Ford labor manager, rationalized Ford labor policies in the same way that others rationalized industrial processes. And, in early 1914, Ford officials established the famous Five Dollar Day—a unique and thoroughly paternalistic profit-sharing plan for Ford workers. At the same time, they created the Ford Sociological Department, which attempted to manipulate and to mold working-class social and cultural forms to suit the requirements of mechanized production. In fact, the Lee reforms and the Five Dollar Day extended the frontiers of managerial control from the shop and factory into the homes and communities of Ford workers. Furthermore, the Ford Sociological Department tossed a wide-ranging and tightly-knit web of social controls over the Ford workforce in order to create, to develop, and to instill positive industrial values and disciplined work habits in the Ford labor force.

While principally concerned with the technical processes of production, scientific management also addressed the more general problems of labor. In 1903, Taylor expressed his views on the economic and moral well-being of workers. He believed that the worker must be adequately paid, but not overpaid. He felt that too much money led to the worker's moral decline. "If overpaid," he noted, "many will work irregularly and tend to become more or less shiftless, extravagant and dissipated. It does not do for most men to get rich too fast." Nonetheless, he concluded that, "most men become more instead of less thrifty when they receive the proper increase for an extra hard day's work. . . . They live rather better, begin to save money, become more sober, and work more steadily." Hard work with appropriate pay was the path to spiritual and material contentment and to productive and efficient workers.[5]

Moreover, Taylor proposed the formation of an employment bureau as a part of the planning department for the well-managed factory. The "competent man," who operated this office, should "inquire into the experience and especial fitness and the character of applicants and keep constantly revised lists of men suitable for the various positions in the shop." Furthermore, this employment clerk should maintain an "individual record" for each worker

> showing his punctuality, absence without excuse, violation of shop rules, spoiled work or damage to machines or tools, as well as his skill at various kinds of work, average earnings, and other good qualities.

In fact, Taylor's employment bureau represented a step towards the modern centralized personnel office.[6]

The industrial betterment movement originated with the late nineteenth-century proponents of the social gospel and constituted the basis for American welfare capitalism in the Progressive Era. Opposed to the crude self-interest of social Darwinism, the adherents to the social gospel articulated and proposed a Christian humanism in their effort to provide a conscience and a soul for industrial capitalism. Figures such as Josiah Strong and William H. Tolman called for the moral, social, and material uplift of workers. But, it was paternalism of the worst variety. Indeed, Tolman concluded his pioneering work, *Social Engineering*, with Carroll D. Wright's conception of the social role of the employer:

> The rich and powerful employer . . . holds in his influence something more than the means of subsistence for those he employs; he holds their moral well-being in his keeping, in so far as it is in his power to hold their morals. He is something more

than a producer; he is an instrument of God for the upbuilding of the race.

In an age of international imperialism, the American industrial elite had its internal domestic imperial policy. It took the form of the "successful man's burden" to direct and to guide the spiritual and moral well-being of "heathen" American workers.[7]

However, the proponents of the social gospel wanted more than manufacturers and industrialists with a social conscience. They also wanted to adapt and to adjust workers to the new urban and industrial civilization. Acutely aware of problems brought about by the advance of industrial capitalism, Strong summarized its impact:

> . . . The substitution of mechanical for muscular power by the introduction of machinery, the rise in the standard of living brought about by the increase in wealth, intelligence and culture, and discontent arising from the yet unsolved problem of the equitable distribution of that wealth, the creation and growth of the modern city and its social conditions, the organization of industry which divides labor and centralizes profit,—all have combined to create new and strange conditions which tend to make this a period of transition and of social adjustment.

For Strong, the transition to a new industrial order demanded that man and society be remade to face the changed conditions. "For lack of such readaptation," Strong concluded, "we have bitter strife between capital and labor, strikes and lockouts, discontent and riot, anarchy, murder, and suicide." In order to ease the transition and to ameliorate worker disaffection, industrial betterment evolved into welfare capitalism which provided housing and educational programs, religious and recreational facilities, profit-sharing and stock ownership plans, medical facilities, pensions, and other welfare programs for workers.[8]

In the Highland Park plant, the more forward-looking managerial traditions of scientific management and industrial betterment coalesced and became a new strategy for the control of workers. This new strategy overcame the more primitive and conventional forms of labor management. For example, even in the early years, scientific management expressed itself in the drive for technological and organizational efficiency in the Ford factory. And, at the same time, industrial betterment manifested itself in the extensive range of welfare activities and programs for Ford workers. H. F. Porter returned from the Ford plant "impressed with the excellence of the working conditions, the emphasis on good light, ventilation and sanitation, the provisions for safety and the cheerful, busy atmosphere of the place." In addition, the *Ford Times*, one of the few house organs of the period, attempted to foster an attitude of harmony and cooperation between company and workers throughout the factory. In 1910, the company organized the 55-member Ford Motor Band. And, by 1920, the company listed many activities which had an industrial betterment character, notably many schools including an English school, apprentice school, trade school, and service school, and a 20-acre Ford athletic park with facilities for football, baseball, and tennis, a children's playground, a rest park, and a bandstand.[9]

Additionally, sometime betfore 1913, the Ford Motor Company established a medical department to provide for the medical needs of Ford workers. Most likely, the Medical Department was the result of the new Michigan Workmen's Compensation law in 1912. In July 1912, the Detroit *Free Press* noted the concern of Detroit manufacturers over the implementation of the "employer's liability act" in September. Many decided to construct hospitals and first-aid departments to prevent claims of compensation from their workers. In early 1914, a government investigator reported that the Ford Motor Company gave physical examinations to all prospective employees. "The prime purpose," he concluded, "as told me by one of the doctors is to discover cases of hernia in order to forestall future claims against the company for compensation."[10]

In addition to recreational, educational, and medical programs, the early Ford labor practices also included bonuses for the automobile workers. In December 1905, each worker received a Christmas bonus of $1,000. In 1908, as the company expanded for the production of the Model T Ford, it began to provide a year-end bonus on a "seniority basis." A worker with one year's service received 5 percent of his annual wages; with two year's service 7½ percent. As Ford production increased in scale and as work became more coordinated and specialized, the Ford Motor Company recognized the necessity for a stable and experienced workforce that understood the prevailing practices of the Ford shops. In the years 1909 and 1910, the company extended the bonus to workers with three year's service. These workers received 10 percent of their annual wages.[11]

In 1911, the company added an "efficiency" bonus to "a select list of employees." It ended the one- and two-year service bonus and kept the three-year service bonus. In 1913, the efficiency bonus went to "foremen, superintendents, and other salaried men." About 200 persons received an average of $1,000 at the end of the year. The efficiency bonus went into effect shortly after the company moved its major productive operations to the Highland Park factory. And, it reflected a greater awareness of, and concern for, the general problems of turnover, efficiency and productivity.[12]

Nevertheless, despite the best efforts of scientific managers and the limited generosity of welfare programs, Ford workers remained extremely dissatisfied and expressed their discontent through their industrially inefficient behavior. In 1913, the Ford Motor Company set out to solve its problems of general worker dissatisfaction and low rates of worker productivity. In order to deal with the crisis caused by this problem, the company turned to John R. Lee. In 1911, when the company purchased the John R. Kiem Mills in Buffalo, Lee was the general manager of the plant. At the time of the machinists' strike in September 1912, Lee helped move and set up the Kiem machinery in the Highland Park factory. After this, he directed the employment office and oversaw the personnel matters of the large factory. The employment office simply processed and maintained the records of the men hired by the departmental and shop foremen. Gradually, Lee developed his talents for handling men and brought order to the chaotic labor practices in the hiring and in the discharging of the workmen.[13]

Sometime around the summer of 1913, the Ford Motor Company directed Lee to examine the causes of Ford worker dissatisfaction and to find possible solutions to the Ford labor problems. At the time, the central concern was labor turnover, because it was the most visible manifestation of factory problems. Lee conducted an investigation and issued a report on the problems to company officials. It concluded that the "chief causes of dissatisfaction and unrest among employees" were:

1. Too long hours. A man whose day is too long and whose work is exhausting will naturally be looking for another job.
2. Low wages. A man who feels that he is being underpaid will always be looking for a change in occupation.
3. Bad housing conditions, wrong home influences, domestic trouble, etc.
4. Unsanitary and other undesirable shop conditions.

5. Last and perhaps the most important cause of dissatisfaction is the unintelligent handling of the men on the part of the foremen and superintendents.

This list generally reflected the factory manager's perceptions of labor's problems and indirectly touched on worker dissatisfaction with their new conditions of production. For Lee, poor housing and home conditions were important sources of worker inefficiencies. Most important, however, was the crude ineffective handling of men. For workers, long hours, low wages, undesirable shop conditions and arbitrary and capricious foremen mirrored their concerns about their new work tasks and routines in the mechanized plant.[14]

Ironically, Ford workers were predominantly Southern and Eastern European immigrants who supposedly endured such intolerable working conditions. The contemporary conventional wisdom of managers maintained that these workers tolerated unbearably long hours, miserably low wages, and the worst shop conditions. But, the Highland Park plant was a new breed of factory with an entirely different pace and intensity of work even for unskilled workers. Like the peasants of the old world, Ford immigrant workers voted and voiced their opinions with their feet and abandoned the Highland Park factory in droves.

Next, Lee tried to discover solutions to these problems. In an interview with Rose Wilder Lane, Ford related that the company studied "relief plans, German methods of shop management and welfare work." The Detroit *Tribune* reported that Ford "sent John R. Lee on a trip to most of the large manufacturing plants in the country to study the wage scale system." However, Lee did not uncover a program which suited the needs of the Highland Park labor force. The newspaper report continued: "it was found that conditions were generally the same all over the country. After Mr. Lee's return an entirely original system had to be worked out." And, after Lee instituted his reforms, the company reported that it was "necessary to go a little further than where other firms left off and that if it hoped for success it must be necessary to consider the human element."[15]

As a result of Lee's comprehensive investigation of existing labor management programs, the Ford Motor Company instituted a broad and extensive new labor program on October 12, 1913. It went into effect as of October 1, 1913. First, the new program increased the wages of Ford workers by 15 percent. Second, it instituted a new "skill-wages classification system," which rationalized Ford wage policies. And, third, it created an Employees' Savings and Loan Association, which alleviated the financial insecurities of working-class life. The two latter policy changes moved Ford labor management into the direction of a centralized employment department. And, relatedly, with these changes, the role of the foreman declined in the management of the labor force. The Employment Office, which simply processed job applications, became the Employment Department, which handled all phases of Ford labor relations.[16]

The skill-wages classification system rationalized the occupational and the wage structure for workers in the company. This system sought to insure "each employee that he is being paid all to which his productive ability and period of service entitles him, both in dollars and cents and in comparison with other men." Since mass production changed the traditional job structure of the Ford workforce, the company required a new method and new standards for the organization and the categorization of its workforce. The traditional categories of mechanic, laborer, and specialist proved inadequate for the classification of the large numbers of "routinized" specialists in the Highland Park factory. In the development of the new classification system, Lee and his staff analyzed the content of each job in the factory, reorganized these jobs into groups with similar levels of skill, and established a graded hierarchy of jobs from the least to most skilled. Instead of following the customary wage scales of the workers, their foremen, or unions, Lee created a range of wage rates which followed the pattern of the new job hierarchy (see Table 6).[17]

Most important, the new classification system provided a ladder for social mobility within the factory. It gave the worker an automatic wage increase as soon as he reached a specific standard of efficiency. Also, if the worker increased his skill, he moved on to the next grade of skill. Prior to the new plan, the worker who failed to get a raise in pay usually "knocked" or "kicked" about the company or his foreman. Now, the worker could blame only himself when he failed to maximize his earnings. This ingenious system internalized within the worker the self-discipline required for industrial efficiency in the mechanized plant. If craft traditions no longer produced the self-disciplined worker, Lee and other managers created a hierarchical structure for this purpose.[18]

Prior to the implementation of the new wage system, the company had neither a rational policy nor clear guidelines for the payment of Ford workers. A company-wide wage policy, a fundamental element in modern labor management, simply did not exist. Before the re-

Table 6. *The Ford Skill-Wages Classification System, October 1913*

Skill Rate	Hourly Wage Rate	Number of Workers	Grade
A–1	.51	2	Mechanic and subforeman
A–2	.48	45	
A–3	.43	273	
B–Service	.43	51	Skilled operator
B–1	.48	606	
B–2	.34	1,457	
B–3	.30	1,317	
C–Service	.38	19	Operator
C–1	.34	348	
C–2	.30	2,071	
C–3	.26	4,311	
D–1	.34	31	Helper
D–2	.30	137	
D–3	.26	416	
E	.26	2,003	Laborer
Special	.23	208	Women and Messengers

SOURCE: Oliver J. Abell, "Labor Classified on a Skill-Wages Basis," *Iron Age*, 93 (January 1, 1914), p. 48 and E. A. Rumley, "Mr. Ford's Plan to Share Profits," *World's Work*, 27 (April 1914), pp. 665–6.

forms, Lee recalled sixty-nine different wage rates throughout the Ford shops. "We, like other employers," he related:

> had gone on for years, hiring men at the back door for as little as we could get them, putting them into the shop and making them work at the same job for as long as they would stick, and not giving them an advance until we had to.

E. A. Rumley, who visited the Highland Park plant, reported that "it was left to the foreman to recommend an advance of a cent or two as he thought the earning power of a particular man increased." This often resulted in inequities and abuses and added to the general insecurities of workers in the shops. "Some men," Rumley continued:

> advanced rapidly because of their efficiency; others, because they knew how to handle their foremen and were self-assertive in their demands. Other men of a retiring nature in the same department hesitated to ask for higher pay and went on working at a lower rate when they really merited an increase.

Frequently, workers, who performed similar or even identical jobs or who possessed the same level of skill or efficiency, received completely different rates of pay. Indeed, the irrationality of Ford labor policy contrasted sharply with the incredible rationality of the Ford technical system.[19]

According to O. J. Abell, the mid-Western correspondent for *Iron Age*, among the consequences of the new wage system were the end of discrimination against individual workers, the reduction of the number of different wage rates, the use of a worker's skill as a basis for classification, the recognition of service with the company, and the creation of "a well regulated" system of wage increased by "fixed amounts." The new system, Lee concluded, was "a broad plan for the stratification of workers in the plan along clearly defined lines and on the basis of definite standards." (See Table 6.)[20]

The new classification system established six ranked groups or grades of workers—mechanics and subforemen, skilled operators, operators, helpers, laborers, and "special" workers, i.e., women and children. It designated the first five groups with letters from "A" for mechanics and subforemen through "E" for laborers. Within each group, the system further classified each worker according to his level of skill—"1" meant a first-class workman, "2" a man with average ability, and "3" a beginner. The Ford work standards department determined these levels of skill on the basis of the machine ratings or the productivity of these different groups of workers. With the addition of two service rates for operators and skilled operators, the new system established a ladder with sixteen different levels of skill and experience and with eight different wage rages. "The plan," observed Abell, "contemplates the advance of employees from one grade of skill to a higher grade and also from one class of work to a more highly paid class."[21]

For example, if the company hired a man as a machine operator, he entered his shop at the skill-wage rate of C−3. On the basis of the standard of productivity for his particular machine, the company expected him to advance to the rate of C−2 within six weeks. This meant an automatic raise from 26 to 30 cents per hour. In time, the company expected him to become a first-class operator and receive 34 cents per hour. If the worker was especially proficient, i.e. productive, or capable of operating other machines, he became a skilled operator and moved to the "B" skill-wage rates. If not, after two years, he received his "service" rate. This rate afforded "a recognition of faithfulness of those operators who have acquired a proficiency in their particular work, but lack the ability to advance to higher grades of usefulness."[22]

Under this new labor program, the Employment Department replaced the foreman as the final authority on labor questions and assumed a larger and more prominent role in the management of Ford workers. It became the "clearing house" for the transfer or the discharge of Ford workers. "No longer," Rumley reported, "is any man discharged on the word of the foreman alone." Under Lee's direction, the new department maintained records on the progress and the efficiency of each worker in the Ford shops. It gradually acquired and centralized the functions of the traditional foreman.[23]

As director of the new Employment Department, Lee headed a special committee which investigated each foreman's recommendation for the discharge of a worker. H. F. Porter described this new "court of appeal":

Now if a man fails to get along with his foreman he comes before this court, is carefully questioned, plainly talked to if at fault, and sent back to work in another department. Often it is a case of a 'square peg in a round hole,' and the man is shifted around until the work that he can do best is found.

Denied his authority to hire and to fire workers, the foreman now had to assist and to work with his men in the shop in order to achieve prescribed levels of productivity. "It is impressed upon the foreman," Abell noted, "that their departments and their own showing are handicapped by the presence of men who cannot make the expected progress." Foremen now had "the incentive to help the employee as much as possible." If a worker did not or could not function in a particular shop, the foreman retained the power to "discharge from their departments, but not from the factory."[24]

An important principle of the new system was the investigation of the Ford workers. A few months later, through the examination of the individual worker's pay record, the Employment Department, Lee noted,

put a check upon each individual case, so that he would not have to wait for an increment in recognition of his ability and worth through any one agency, but was automatically looked up in case his advancement did not come within an average time set for such development.

For the beginner, the department examined the new worker's pay envelope for three consecutive weeks. If the worker did not receive a raise, the Employment Department took up his case with his foreman. "Six weeks after a man is hired," Rumley stated:

> if his pay does not increase from the beginner's pay to the second stage of a fair workman, his name automatically came to the attention of the superintendent who investigates the case. "Why has this man's wage not advanced?" is asked of the foreman. If no very definite reason can be given, or if the answer is, "He is not worth more," the answer is "Why do you keep him? What are you doing to do to place him where he can be profitable both to the company and to himself?"

In fact, the Employment Department's "court of appeal," and not the superintendent, investigated the worker.[25]

Generally when the company transferred a man for the benefit of the company and to the man himself, the principal motivation was the high cost of labor turnover. According to Lee, the company believed that "it is a great deal cheaper for us to take him from one department to another than to discharge him." In the instance of the worker, who "overrates his ability" and who "falls considerably behind the rate or class of work," he "is given the option of work he can do, at lower wages, or of being discharged." Ultimately, the worker who did not meet the company standards of efficiency faced discharge.[26]

Although the new labor program contained some progressive features, the basic standard of the entire system rested on the productive efficiency of the Ford worker. The purpose of the system, said Lee, was "to grade the men in our employ according to their efficiency and to see that every man gets a square deal and receives the wage he is entitled to as soon as he reaches our different standards of proficiency progressively arranged." The inefficient workman always faced the threat, and sometimes the fact, of discharge. If the inefficient worker was "in the employ of the company for any length of time," Lee noted, "he is let out, the company figuring that he is holding back the output of that department, if he does not increase his earning ability." Abell reported that the company discharged a workman "on the basis of efficiency alone." "A man is discharged," he said, "only when it seems impossible to work him efficiently in any department of the shop. . . ." In early January 1914, Henry Ford stated: "No man will be discharged if we can help it, except for un-faithfulness or inefficiency." An unfaithful worker was not "honestly trying to render good service" to the Ford Motor Company.[27]

The establishment of an Employees' Savings and Loan Association was the second major change in the company's labor policy. It made "possible for every employee to secure funds without inconvenience and at a nominal charge." Whereas the skill-wages classification eliminated certain abuses against the worker in the factory, the Savings and Loan Association provided for the general economic security of immigrant and other workers. For the most part, the association focused on the problems of the economic insecurities of immigrant life. Immigrant workers were the principal beneficiaries of the new Ford institution. "An observation of the type of men generally making up the borrowing line," recalled Abell, "seems to point clearly to the fact that these men are largely of the improvident and undependable type normally comprising the shifting class of labor." In the terminology of the early twentieth century, the phrases "the improvident and undependable type" and "the shifting class of labor" were very definite and precise references to immigrant workers. Another observer connected the function of the Ford Savings and Loan Association to the economic abuses of the immigrant boss. H. L. Arnold reported that membership in the association made the borrower "his own loan shark." He no longer went "to an outside Shylock for assistance."[28]

The Ford Motor Company created the Savings and Loan Association for two specific reasons: first, "the encouragement of the saving habit among the employees," and, second, the provision of "small temporary loans" to Ford workers "with little expense and no loss of time." The membership in the association was voluntary, but any Ford worker could take out a loan. The company appointed a committee to insure the proper financial administration of the association. And, it bore the operational expenses of the institution. The association required its members to deposit one dollar each pay day. Moreover, the depositor underwent the actual ritual of presenting his dollar to a representative of the association. "The $1 is not taken out of the pay envelope by the paymaster, but is required to be deposited by the member with the individual in his department authorized to receive it." The company believed that this interpersonal ritual developed the "saving habit." Additionally, the association distributed earnings on the deposits each quarter. These earnings came from the loan fees, the bank interest, and the investment of the funds.[29]

The Savings and Loan Association had a special window near the paymaster's office to process the loans to Ford workers. According to Abell, "most of the borrowers are not members of the association." Presumably, the American workers took advantage of the savings feature and the immigrant workers took advantage of the loan feature of the association. The worker borrowed on his future pay at the rate of ten cents per $5.00 up to $20.00. "Loans may not be applied for oftener than once between pay days and cannot exceed $20.00, except by special arrangement with the administration committee." On the next pay day, the paymaster deducted the amount of the loan and the loan fee.[30]

As in the case of the skill-wages classification system, an investigation of the Ford worker was an important feature of the new Savings and Loan Association. "After the employee has made three loans," Abell noted, "he is questioned closely to discover whether borrowing has a basis in real need or not, and the investigations thus far have shown a preponderance of deserving cases." Indeed, when the company questioned the worker on the necessity of his loans, it began an intrusion not only into the economic affairs of the worker, but also into his personal and domestic life. In fact, Abell felt that the loan program catered to "the undesirable element in the shop." Nonetheless, if the loan program assisted in the "uplift" of the bad element, it was a good program. Moreover, "if it results in creating the habit of steady employment and continuous service, it may also develop other traits that naturally associate with steadiness in any direction."[31]

The Ford Five Dollar Day, the most famous labor-management reform in the annals of American business, supplemented and extended the Lee reforms for the more efficient administration of the Ford factory. Whereas the October reforms emphasized the more scientific management of labor, the Five Dollar Day added an extra dimension to the industrial betterment and welfare activities of the company. It was a unique profit-sharing plan with a powerful monetary incentive to mold and to shape Ford workers in order to nurture more disciplined work habits for mechanized factory work. Ford officials created the Sociological Department to administer the plan. The Five Dollar Day became a formidable instrument for the social control of Ford workers. All Ford workers received their wages, but only those who met Ford standards received their profits. Based upon the premise that a sound home environment produced and efficient worker, the Sociological Department reached into homes and communities to resolve problems with traditionalist and rebellious workers. In the short run, money proved a strong incentive for the alteration of habits and behavior.

A cloud of uncertainty covered the actual origins of the Five Dollar Day. Different company officials presented different accounts of who originally had the idea and what happened at specific meetings. The decision to pay Ford workers the Five Dollar Day seems to have occurred by chance in the form of a dare or challenge to Henry Ford. In the first days of January 1914, the Ford Motor Company's board of directors convened a series of meetings to discuss plans and policies for the forthcoming year. At one of the meetings, they discussed wages. In the course of the discussion, a few of the directors, amazed at Ford's liberal wage proposals, literally dared him to keep raising the projected figure until it reached $5.00. At the time, this daily income was an exhorbitant amount for an unskilled factory worker. However, Ford insisted that the anticipated profits justified the high daily income. At a subsequent meeting, the directors continued to develop the new plan. They decided that approximately half of the company's anticipated profits, a sum of $10,000,000, would go toward the Five Dollar Day and that the new program would take effect on January 12. They selected John R. Lee to implement the plan and to work out its details.[32]

On January 5, the company publicly announced the new plan to share profits and to establish the minimum income of five dollars per day. The public announcement proclaimed:

> The Ford Motor Company, the greatest and most successful in the world, will on January 12, inaugurate the greatest revolution in the matter of rewards for its workers ever known to the industrial world.

The company announced the reduction of the hours of work from nine to eight and the raise in pay from $2.50 to $5.00 per day. In order to utilize the full productive capacity of the Highland Park plant, the company also shifted from two nine-hour to three eight-hour shifts. The company presently employed 15,000 workers and intended to hire an additional 4,000. "All but 10 percent of the employees," the announcement stated, "will *at once* share in the profits." (Italics mine). The company intended to exclude young workers under the age of twenty-two.[33]

Moreover, the new plan also established more general principles and qualifications of the older Ford workers. Henry Ford, the company president, spoke on the idealistic and benevolent practices and objectives of the new plan. "No worker," he proclaimed in the announcement, "will be discharged if we can help it, except for unfaithfulness or inefficiency." "We believe," he added, "in making 20,000 men prosperous and contented. . . ." James Couzens, the practical vice president, noted: "Thrift and good service and sobriety will be encouraged and rewarded." From its inception, the new Ford Profit-sharing Plan amalgamated the basic premises of scientific management and industrial betterment.[34]

Contrary to Allan Nevins' statement that the Ford program was not a profit-sharing plan, but "simply the establishment of a high minimum wage out of profits," the Five Dollar Day was undeniably a profit-sharing plan. The profit-sharing feature was the essential element to induce Ford workers to change their ways. An early memorandum on the plan for company managers noted: "Impress upon your employees that . . . the increase they are receiving from it is *their part and parcel of a division of profits* obtaining for the current fiscal year and [is] in no wise to be construed as anything else." [Italics mine]. Moreover, as the memorandum emphasized, the Profit-sharing Plan was temporary and experimental. In August 1914, a federal government reported stated: "The plan was adopted for one year as an experiment and may be continued or discontinued at the end of the year, depending on the profits of the company or on other considerations." From the beginning, the Ford Motor Company hoped to establish a profit-sharing plan which included the two important considerations of industrial efficiency and industrial betterment. The specific details of the plan evolved in the course of the first year of its existence.[35]

A fundamental premise of the new profit-sharing plan was that workers brought into the factory their poor attitudes, their bad habits, and their economic worries and insecurities. All of these affected the efficiency and the performance of the workers of the assembly lines. In essence, the company connected a worker's living conditions and his attitudes and values to his industrial efficiency. For example, Henry Ford and other factory managers regarded thrift as a positive virtue. "Thrift," a company pamphlet reported, "is an index of character. It indicates self-control, self-respect and some plan and purpose in life looking toward the future." Simply because a worker saved his money, he possessed a number of other positive personal virtues. The company presumed that he worked steadily and diligently and that he was responsible and efficient. A personal virtue from a man's domestic life supported a range of virtues which affected his factory life.[36]

Within this context, the worker's income was the mechanism to increase his overall efficiency in the Ford factory. The Ford Motor Company controlled the income of its workers by making a crucial distinction between wages and profits. It explicitly defined its Five Dollar Day as a profit-sharing plan, and not as an increase in wages. The company supplemented the worker's existing wage rate, determined by the "skill-wages classification" plan, with an additional profit-sharing rate. "As is well known," John Fitch stated, "the five dollar wage is made up of two elements: the daily rate, which is the wage proper, and the difference between that and five dollars, which is termed profits." (Under this plan, the skilled worker with a higher daily rate received a smaller proportion of his daily income as profits.) In the case of an unskilled worker, for example, his normal wage rate was $2.34 per day and his profit rate was $2.66. Samuel M. Levin, who wrote on the unique Ford plan in the 1920s, described the effect of the distinction between wages and profits: "It offered separate stipends to the men in this double capacity, so that a man in the lower ranks of labor might receive $2.34 per day for working (this was the minimum) and $2.66 for living as the company wanted him to live." In its literature for its workers, the company clearly distinguished between wages, "which the Company will pay him for his services and labor" and profits "over and above the sum earned and paid as wages." In accordance with Ford policy, wages were the "earned" result of "services and labor." Profits were the conditional gift of the Ford Motor Company.[37]

The company repeatedly emphasized the distinction between wages and profits to its workers and employees who participated in the Ford Profit-sharing Plan. Each worker had the amount of his wages and the amount of his profits recorded separately on his pay envelope. Shortly after the plan went into effect, the home office reprimanded a branch manager for his loose use of the two terms: "we would emphasize the fact that the increases we are granting according to the schedule are all based upon *profit sharing*. You continually refer to the increase in wages and in this you have not caught the very essence of the plan."[38]

The essence of the Ford Five Dollar Day and Profit-sharing Plan was the use of profits to alter and to control the lives and the behavior of the Ford workers. Ford profits added the necessary flexibility for rewarding and disciplining its workforce. "It is the Ford theory," noted John A. Fitch, "that a man is entitled to his wages, if he is kept on the payroll at all, but that he is entitled to profits only in the case of his adhering very strictly to the rules laid down." To secure "these exceptional earnings," O. J. Abell related, the company "requires conformity with its general plan for the betterment of its employees." The worker who did not conform was not fired or laid off in the traditional sense. The company retained the worker and attempted to change him. "After having become a profit sharer, an employee may be discharged, or he may be *laid off as a profit sharer,* although retained as an employee." When the company laid off a worker as a "profit sharer," it did not incur the expense of finding a replacement and training him.[39]

The worker without profits was in a personally and psychologically difficult situation. Compared to his fellow shopmates, he did the same work and received half their daily income. He had few choices. He could avoid his awkward situation and quit to seek work elsewhere. He could remain obstinate and ignore the rules and requirements. Or, pressured by family and friends not to be foolish, he could mend his ways, conform, and live and work according to the company standards.

The Ford Profit-sharing Plan possessed a special feature for the obstinate worker who continued to ignore the company rules and standards. While the non-conforming worker earned only his wages, the company withheld his profits and noted the amount withheld on his pay envelope. As the withheld profits accrued, the company enticed the worker to meet its requirements by offering him a proportion of the accrued profits in a single lump sum. In order to hasten the worker's change in life and habits, the proportion of returned profits decreased as time passed. The company believed that the worker had to change within six months:

It was expected, however, that he would make good within a period of six months. If he requalified at the end of thirty days he got back his share of the profits; if at the end of 60 days—75 percent; 90 days—60 percent; four months—40 percent; five months—25 percent. If there was no improvement at the end of six months, it was deemed that *the employee had duly qualified himself for discharge.*

Under this system for the proportional repossession of his withheld profits, an unskilled worker, who received $2.44 in wages and $2.66 in profits, received his accrued profits according to the schedule in Table 7.

Table 7. *Total Wages, Profits Withheld, and Profits Returned for an Unskilled Worker*

Month	Wages	Profits Withheld	Profits Returned
1st	$ 60.69	$ 69.12	$ 69.12
2nd	121.69	136.24	103.68
3rd	182.37	207.36	124.42
4th	243.16	276.48	110.59
5th	303.96	345.60	86.40
6th	364.74	414.32	0

Of course, the amount of profits returned varied with the worker's basic wage rate as determined by the "skill-wages" pay schedule.[40]

Since the company recorded the amount of withheld profits on the worker's pay envelope, each pay day the worker had a reminder of the folly of his obstinacy. For an unskilled worker who earned about fourteen dollars per week, the prospect of receiving a sum as large as one or two month's pay proved an enormous incentive to alter his living conditions, his behavior, his attitudes, or anything else the company desired. And, if he chose not to change, the worker ultimately faced the traditional form of factory discipline—dismissal. He then faced tramping the streets of Detroit in search of work with lower pay and a less rigid and more satisfactory factory environment.

In 1920, I. Paul Taylor, a Ford critic and a commissioner of Highland Park, captured the essence of the Ford Profit-sharing Plan. On the issue of wages and profits, he noted: "I believe that it is illegal to withhold a man's wages if he has earned them, but when you call part of them 'profits' or a 'bonus' you get away with the reduction a lot easier." Moreover, Taylor connected the Ford Profit-sharing Plan to the new Ford industrial system:

A man is late to work once or twice—and with the conveyor system, that throws a monkey wrench in the machinery—and he is threatened at once with a loss of the 'profits.' There are all kinds of things that you can do under this system—from compelling men to tell how much they spend for groceries, furniture and recreation to coming to work regularly.

Given the deep-seated economic insecurity of the worker in the early twentieth century, the worker forgot his dignity and pride and permitted these intrusions. He traded pride and privacy for the economic security of a job with high pay.[41]

Ford officials were acutely aware of the uniqueness of their profit-sharing plan. Given the opposition of trade unions and workers to patenalistic welfare programs, they made every effort to separate their plan from conventional forms of industrial betterment or welfare capitalism. To visitors, who were "interested in welfare work," the company noted: "We haven't a thing to show them, because ours is not that kind of welfare, ours is a man-to-man, character, building proposition." In a pamphlet for workers, the company suggested that industrial betterment plans, which purchased "gymnasiums, lunch rooms, swimming pools, etc.," spent money "FOR the men." This contrasted with the Ford program. "Mr. Ford's idea is to give his employees the profits in money in their pay envelopes. This is spending money THROUGH the men." In the eyes of Ford officials, the uniqueness of their plan rested on the principle that the company directly gave its workers their profits every two weeks in their pay envelopes.[42]

But, they believed that if the company provided the workers biweekly profits, it also had to guide them in the expenditure of their higher income. For this reason, Lee established the Sociological Department. Possibly, the name came from a similar welfare institution with Rockefeller's Colorado Fuel and Iron Company. In this era, sociology had matured and gained acceptance as an academic discipline for the study, analysis, and management of the affairs of men. Yet, in time, Ford workers even disapproved of the name Sociological Department because its intrusive activities developed unfavorable connotations. In late 1915, when S. S. Marquis took over the department, he changed its name to the Educational Department. This new name emphasized teaching and instruction rather than examination and investigation.

From the very beginning, the company and newspapers referred to a "sociological department" as a new institution to handle and to manage the new Five Dollar Day. Nevertheless, a formal institution did not emerge until April 1914. At this time, the company proposed to make "the investigation a permanent institution." The investigation determined a workman's eligibility for Ford profits. And, when it became permanent, so too did the Sociological Department. However, the first company memorandum about welfare work among Ford employees first appeared with "Sociological" at his head in November 1914.[43]

The Ford Medical Department was an antecedent to the Sociological Department. Shortly after the announcement of the new Profit-Sharing Plan, Henry Ford told *New York Times* reporter: "We have had a sociological department connected with our first-aid department for some time." In this instance, Ford referred to the Medical Department and the work that it did in the area of health and its effect on lateness, absenteeism, and efficiency. In this interview, Ford also said that "doctors are in a better position to exercise a sort of watchfulness over the men than lawyers and superintendents, and our method is to have them to straighten out men who show evidences of not keeping up to their standard." Thus, well before the establishment of the Ford Profit-sharing Plan, the Medical Department exercised two important functions of the new Sociological Department—watching the men and straightening them out.[44]

The public announcement of the Five Dollar Day contained several references to the specific conditions and requirements which made a Ford worker eligible to share the company's profits. At the time, Henry Ford implied that a worker needed to be faithful and efficient. And, James Couzens specifically listed thrift, good service, and sobriety. For the young worker, the company listed sobriety, thrift, steadiness, and industriousness. Official statements and literature repeatedly listed similar attributes for the "worthy" or "deserving" worker.

In 1914, a pamphlet, which explained profit-sharing to Ford workers, noted: "A worker is only put on the list of profit-sharers after he has been carefully looked up, and the company is satisfied he will not debauch the additional money he receives." Moreover, the "duty" of the Sociological Department's investigator was "to correct the morals and the manner of living" of those workers who failed to receive his share of the profits. In 1916, another pamphlet stated that the Sociological Department "teaches employees in the manner of thrift, sobriety and better living generally." Another pamphlet encouraged workers to live "under conditions that make for cleanliness, good manhood and good citizenship." From the start, Henry Ford noted that he wanted "a very definite incentive to better living, and . . . the very best incentive was a money premium on proper living." John R. Lee said that a worker received profits "according to his worth and what his skill and ability merit for him." The home office advised a branch manager: "The very essence of this plan of profit-sharing is to know beyond a shadow of doubt, that the money is paid to those deserving and to no others, and the manager will be held accountable in this respect."[45]

The Ford Sociological Department investigated every Ford employee who made less than $200 per month to determine whether or not that employee was eligible to share in the profits. The company investigated everyone except high level managers and supervisors. It investigated salesmen, foremen, clerks, and factory workers. The investigation became the main object of sociological educational work in the Ford factory. For the investigation, Ford told reporters: "We require and learn the nationality, the religion, the bank savings, whether the man owns or is buying property, how he amuses himself, the district he selects to live in—this and much else are tabulated."[46]

A general letter from the home office to the branch offices in January 1914 indicated precisely how much else:

> In our investigations here we use the following questions: Are you married? If married, how many dependent upon you? If single, how many dependent upon you and to what extent? Relationship of dependents? Residence of dependents? Married men: do you live with your wives? Have you ever had any domestic troubles? Are your habits good or bad? Have you a bank account? What is the name of the bank and the number of the book? Last employment? Reasons for leaving? Would your home conditions be bettered were your income increased? Would you be willing to follow some systematic plan of saving suggested by the company?

Some of these questions probed deeply into the personal and domestic lives of Ford workers. Until the rules and procedures become more formalized, the company intended that such questions guide the Sociological Department's investigators. Shortly thereafter, a special form, the "Record of Investigation," collected and tabulated information on Ford workers.[47]

Initially, three categories of workers were eligible for participation in the Ford Profit-sharing Plan. These included married men of any age, single men over twenty-two, and single men under twenty-two with dependents. After some public controversy, women with dependents were later included in the plan. Throughout 1914 and 1915, the Sociological Department developed and refined its conditions and standards for worker participation in the Ford welfare plan. By early 1916, the Sociological Department had a set of "Sociological Department Instructions," which served as the basis for investigations and which detailed methods for the determination of eligibility for profits.[48]

For example, the "Instructions" provided a general summary of Ford standards: "The requirements by which the Company regards a man as eligible to receive profits vary according to age, marriage, habits, dependents, etc." In general, all Ford workers had to exhibit or to demonstrate thrift, good habits, and good home conditions. However, the specific requirements were loose or stringent according to the age, marital status, or family size of the worker. For married men, the company demanded:

Living with and properly supporting his wife and family.
Legal marriage assurance of Investigator's affirmative opinion,
    preferably the former.
Home conditions good.
Habits good.
Thrifty.

For single men without dependents:

Twenty-two years of age. (Verified up to 26 years).
Home conditions good.
Habits good.
Proved signs of thrift.

For single men with "proved total dependents" the requirements "are the same as above, with the exception that he need not be twenty-two years of age." For women, the company required an "immediate blood relation totally dependent upon her" and:

Home conditions good.
Habits good.
Thrifty.

While the "Instructions" detailed specific standards and requirements, they allowed the investigator considerable flexibility on his interpretation of them. For instance, the married worker with a large
family did not have to have as large a bank account or as nice a
home as the married, but childless, worker.[49]

In addition to its standards for personal and domestic life, the
Ford Motor Company expected increased efficiency and greater
productivity as a condition for the Five Dollar Day. With the announcement of the plan, Henry Ford stated that the increase in pay
was "neither charity nor wages. It is simply profit-sharing."
Moreover, he added, "In a way it is efficiency engineering, too. We
expect to get better work more efficient work, as a result." In reference to the lowly sweeper who also received the Five Dollar Day,
James Couzens stated, "We think it will increase his efficiency, as indeed it will that of all our employes. Workers who are worrying
about how to make ends meet inevitably are unfitted for that concentration which insures high efficiency."[50]

A pamphlet for Ford workers stressed the necessity for greater efficiency in the factory. The company, it argued, generously provided
its workers with a greater income and expected something in return
from the workers. "The Ford Motor Company," it reminded workers, "does not believe in giving without a fair return. So to acquire
the right to participate in the profits a man must be willing to pay in
increased efficiency." It also reiterated the connection between a
worker's home life and his performance in the plant: "Especially he
must do everything in his power to improve his standard of living
and to make his environment more wholesome, both for himself and
for those dependent upon him." "Of course," the pamphlet later
added,

> the workers are bound to appreciate the fair treatment of Henry
> Ford, and there is bound to be an increased spirit of loyalty and
> efficiency all the way from the sweeper to the department man-
> ager.[51]

Also, in January 1914, the home office sent a letter to the branch
managers and explained the initial rules and procedures for the new
sociological work. The letter advised the managers on the matter of
efficiency:

> You should get greater efficiency out of your men now and if
> you have used a reasonable amount of care in selecting them

and hiring them in the past, they should respond now with greater alacrity to your demands. Do not keep anyone who has proven inefficient and has been given a fair trial in more than one capacity.

The high income of the Five Dollar Day provided the "carrot" to induce Ford workers to match the efficiency of mechanized factory production. And, when goodwill failed, the company resorted to the "stick" and discharged the worker who did not produce.[52]

At first, the Ford Profit-sharing Plan offered the Five Dollar Day to all those workers who met these various requirements for eligibility. In its announcement of the plan, the company said that all but ten percent of the workers would receive the Five Dollar Day "at once." However, as the Sociological Department defined its standards, it excluded workers from the Profit-Sharing Plan. The Sociological Department did not finish its investigation of each worker until April 1914. At that time, Lee told the investigators that "the 40 percent who are not (getting their profits), are striving their very best to qualify." Aside from the ten percent who were ineligible because of age or sex, forty percent of the Ford workers did not meet the company standards and did not receive the share of the profits. On the other hand, each eligible worker, who met the requirements, received his share of profits retroactively to January 12, 1914.[53]

Although the general requirements—marital status, age, dependency, home conditions, habits, and thrift—remained constant throughout the existence of the Profit-sharing Plan, the specific requirements changed in response to altered conditions in the Detroit labor market. At first, a residency requirement did not exist. But, as thousands of workers flocked to Detroit to earn "the big money" at Ford, the company insisted that job applicants reside in Detroit for six months prior to application. Also, as Detroit's industrial economy expanded and as the labor shortages appeared, the company lowered the minimum age for eligibility, increased the wage rate in proportion to profits, eliminated unnecessary investigations, and even established a Six Dollar Day.[54]

All in all, the Lee reforms and the Five Dollar Day provided short-term solutions to the Ford labor problems. H. L. Arnold felt that the Ford innovations solved the problem of labor turnover. "The high mark of the Ford employment department," he related, "was 526 men hired. This number immediately fell off after the discharge appeal was inaugurated, and has now dropped to what appears to be a legitimate normal." H. F. Porter listed the advantages of the Ford Employment Department:

> The direct saving to the company through the greatly lessened employment expense was large, but the indirect saving through greater efficiency of a reasonably permanent and contented working force, although more difficult to measure, was much larger. A decided decrease in the number tardy or absent was another result which had its financial compensations.[55]

Interestingly, Ford officials frequently pointed to the Five Dollar Day, and not the new industrial technology, when they spoke of increased efficiency or productivity. Shortly after the announcement of the Profit-sharing Plan, a reporter asked Ford what he expected "to result from this distribution?" Ford replied, "For one thing, we shall get increased efficiency. . . . The men will get half the profits. Is it not in their interest to increase their output and thus increase their share of profits?" A year later, in 1915, Ford told the Industrial Relations Commission:

> The increased efficiency of the men under the plan has been from 15 to 20 percent with reference to the work produced, which is further emphasized when you consider that the improvement was made in an eight-hour day versus the comparison in a nine-hour day.

John R. Lee told an interviewer that the Five Dollar Day "has resulted in increased efficiency and has paid from that standpoint as well as from the humanitarian point of view." S. S. Marquis echoed his predecessor: "Ford's most valuable contribution thus far has been the discovery of some very profitable philanthropy."[56]

And, finally, a reporter asked Ford why he established his Profit-sharing Plan. Ford replied that he "concluded that machinery was playing such a part in production that if men could be induced to speed up machinery, there would be more profit in the high wage than at the low wage." But, money alone was not enough to induce workers to speed up machinery. It was simply a key to open the door to the source of the labor problems. It allowed Ford sociological investigators to enter the homes of Ford workers and to gather information on their values and styles of life. And, with this information, the investigators used the monetary incentive to change what they considered inefficient aspects of working-class life and culture. The Ford investigators and their investigations aimed at the formation of the new worker for the new industrial technology.[57]

6. The Ford Sociological Investigations

... They went out to the home and they had a regular form that they filled out. They picked on your life history.

They went to my home. My wife told them everything. There was nothing to keep from them. Of course, there was a lot of criticism of that. It was kind of a funny idea, in a free state. . . .[1]—William Pioch, a Ford Worker.

The Five Dollar Day and Profit-sharing Plan represented an ambitious program to transform the attitudes and behavior of Ford workers. The Sociological Department was the institution for social and cultural change. The investigator, later called the advisor, was the agent. Indeed, the principal objective of the Ford welfare program was to remake social and cultural values for men to fit the regimen of the mechanized plant. In E. P. Thompson's insightful phrase, the entire program sought to restructure working habits and to create "new disciplines, new incentives, and a new human nature upon which these incentives could bite effectively."[2]

A fundamental premise of the Ford program was a particular middle-class vision on the role of the family and the home in the formation of social and cultural values. And, although this was a paternalistic vision, it marked a progressive shift from the older idea of individual and moral causes of poverty to the more modern idea of social and environmental ones. To be sure, the Ford plan relied on traditions of individual self-help and moral uplift, but it did mark a transition to newer social attitudes on the causes of working-class poverty. In the eyes of Ford, his officials, and his factory managers, a workman's efficiency in the factory and his home and family environment were thoroughly intertwined. H. F. Porter reported that Ford managers believed that "what a man *is* on the outside is reflected to a greater or lesser extent in his demeanor and the quality of his workmanship. . . ." John R. Lee often stressed the important influence of domestic life on factory production. In 1914, he told a group of Ford sociological investigators that "Mr. Ford believes, and

123

so do I, that if we keep pounding away at the root and the heart of the family in the home, that we are going to make better men for future generations, than if we simply pounded away at the fellows at their work here [in the factory]."[3]

S. S. Marquis, who later directed the Sociological Department, voiced very similar sentiments of the relationship between the home and the factory. "The environment of a man," he told an audience of educators, "must be right if you expect him to come clean and strong out of it." He later added: "When the efficiency of a good workman begins to decline, we have come, as the result of past experiences, to look into the home for some kind of domestic trouble. . . . Family quarrels have an almost immediate effect on the output of lathes and drill presses." In another speech, he strengthened this connection between a worker's family life and his work in the shop. "You have all heard," the former minister stated:

> that the family is the foundation of the church and the state. We found that it is the foundation of right industrial conditions as well. Nothing tends to lower a man's efficiency more than wrong family relations.[4]

On the basis of these premises, the Ford Motor Company established its Sociological Department in order to insure the formation of the right environment and to make efficient workers. With the announcement of the Five Dollar Day, the company immediately initiated a series of investigations to determine whether or not each Ford worker possessed the proper home environment. In February 1914, John A. Fitch described the excitement in Detroit's working-class communities. "Fifty investigators," he reported, "are dashing about Detroit in Ford automobiles, accompanied by interpreters and armed with long lists of employes." One investigator stops his automobile at the house of "some lucky bolt-screwer." This "advance guard of the new pay envelope" enters the house and conducts his character investigation:

> 'Does Joe Polianski live here,' he asks.
> 'Yes, he lives here all right.'
> 'What sort of man is Joe—pretty good fellow?'
> '*Sure* he's a *fine* man.'
> 'What does he do evenings?'
> 'Always home evenings, goes to bed early.'

'Does he drink?'

"No! No! He not drink.'

'What does he do with his money—does he save any?'

'Sure, he save. Some of it he sends to the old country to help old folks, some of it in the bank.'

'Well, now, if Joe should get more wages what do you think he would do with it?'

'Save it and buy a house, I guess.'

'All right,' says the investigator snapping his book together. 'Tell Joe to bring his bank book with him when he comes to work next week.'

So it goes. Wife, landlady, neighbor, and friend all speak a good word for Joe. But the investigator makes up his mind as to Joe's character by noting the manner in which he lives, and the kind of people his friends seem to be. Furthermore this outside investigation serves as a check on information already secured in the shop. Every man has been canvased and asked to tell his age, whether married or single, and whether he has money in the bank. If anyone is found to have misrepresented, he will not be kept on the company payrolls. If he is careless in his habits or unthrifty, he will not share in the profits, but will only get his old hourly rate for his day's work. But he will not get that for long if he does not show that he deserves the $5 minimum.

At this time, the investigations were "superficial." However, Fitch concluded: "When the time is not so limited, and, when the whole community is no longer in a state of tense excitement over the very situation that has made the investigation necessary, a better technique and standards may be anticipated."[5]

As Fitch's account suggested, Ford workers had to meet very strict social and moral requirements. In order to receive the Five Dollar Day, the company noted, a young worker "must show himself sober, steady, industrious and must satisfy the superintendent and staff that his money will not be wasted in riotous living." In the first weeks of the plan, the company reported that not all workers would receive the high income. "A worker," it added, "is only put on the list of profit-sharers after he has been carefully looked up, and the company is satisfied that he will not debauch the additional money he receives." These attitudes reflected a profound distrust of the capacities and abilities of Ford workers.[6]

Upon completion of the first round of investigations, Ford officials made the investigation a permanent feature of the profit-sharing plan. In 1915, Henry Ford explained the purpose of the Sociological Department to the Industrial Relations Commission. Its main objectives were to:

> ... explain opportunity, teach American ways and customs, English language, duties of citizenship. . . . counsel and help unsophisticated employees to obtain and maintain comfortable, congenial and sanitary living conditions, and . . . exercise the necessary vigilance to prevent, as far as possible, human frailty from falling into habits or practices detrimental to substantial progress in life. The whole effort of this corps is to point men to life and to make them discontented with mere living.

Essentially, the Ford program sought to remake and to restructure working-class culture on sound middle-class, industrial values.[7]

The Ford investigator had a central role in this paternalistic transformation of working-class values and ways of life. In the course of the Ford investigation, the company urged both investigators and workers to develop a close personal relationship. On the one hand, an instruction sheet to guide investigators advised: "Please throw into the investigation of each case a deep, personal interest and state as briefly and concisely as you can all of the facts and features for making a well rounded judgment." On the other hand, a booklet issued to workers stated:

> Employees are urged to consult often with the Company's investigator assigned to the locality in which they live, and to ask his advice on matters relative to their welfare and that of their family. Be honest and truthful with the investigators and see if they cannot be of assistance in straightening out difficulties.

As Samuel M. Levin concluded: "The Company was not only to be an employer of laborers, but also a sort of first friend, a foster father, a critic of their outside affairs, their conduct, and ways of life."[8]

The Ford sociological investigators were living examples of the qualities and virtues which the Ford plan sought to encourage in the labor force. For the most part, they were American white-collar or supervisory employees recruited from within the Ford factory. Initially, the very name Sociological Department brought applications from college-trained sociologists, "who wished to become connected with our work, and how obviously would have difficulty in it because they would have so much to unlearn. . . ." Also, the title investigator resulted in "numerous applications from members of private detective agencies, etc., men who thought that their experience would qualify them for our work." Nonetheless, in the first days of the plan, the company noted that the investigators were "Auditors, Foremen, Assistant Superintendents, the keenest, best men we have, whose characteristics for carefulness and thoroughness have been proven in faithful service." And, Lee also emphasized recruitment from within the Ford enterprise. "The whole work," he reported, "was put into effect and supervised by employees of the company—no outside talent or assistance was asked. We worked the whole scheme with Ford men."[9]

At first, the Medical Department formed the core of the staff for the sociological department. Prior to the Sociological Department, medical investigators examined such problems as health, safety, absenteeism, turnover, and efficiency. And, some of these areas became the domain of the new Sociological Department. In late January 1914, O. J. Abell estimated nearly 100 investigators. "These investigators," he reported, "are for the most part physicians who have been associated with the medical staff; others of the investigators are among the oldest and most trusted employees of the company." Later in the year, there were 200 investigators. But, gradually, the number leveled off to a permanent staff of about fifty investigators. In addition, clerks, stenographers, and translators assisted and supported them. The company supplied an automobile for making the rounds to workers' homes. In 1915, it cost about $9,000 per month, or about $108,000 per year, to operate the Sociological Department. And, in that year, the company distributed about $7.9 million in profits to approximately 19,000 workers in the Highland Park plant.[10]

For the first investigations, the company intentionally selected a large number of investigators. It relied on a process of natural selection to filter out those men with the best traits for the job. One pamphlet noted:

At the outset a corps of about 200 men (and this force was purposely large at the beginning, so that the best qualified for the work might ultimately be selected), picked for their peculiar fitness as judges of human nature—men who had made a success in the running of their departments—was organized and put to work gathering facts and figures with reference to every employee of the Company.

For sociological investigators, the desired traits were "originality, personality, tact, diplomacy and clear and correct interpretation of the Ford Profit-sharing Plan." In time, the Sociological Department underwent its own division of labor and occupational specialization. In 1916, Lee stated that "we have divided the whole number so that the especially gifted in cases of domestic infelicity might tackle jobs of that type; those who have evidenced unusual skill in handling men with criminal records are detailed to such cases, and so on."[11]

In 1917, a Sociological Department report provided a detailed examination of its wide range of activities. At the time, it had fifty-two investigators on "regular work" and fourteen on "special work." Earlier, C. T. Shower distinguished between outside men and inside men. He noted:

> The outside men, formerly called investigators but now termed advisors, investigate the housing condition of the employee, whether or not he practices thrift, whether he is on a solid wholesome basis of living, whether he needs medical attention, also whether or not he is in debt. This investigation is made within 30 days after the man is hired, after which a recommendation is made to the proper inside department.

The man who worked with the inside department, Shower continued, "takes care of one phase of work: real estate matters, garnishments, legal matters, etc." The investigators on regular work visited the worker in their homes; those on special work attended them in the factory.[12]

The Ford Motor Company compiled detailed information on the work and the activities of its sociological staff. The efficiency-conscious company expressed concern about the outside investigators's unsupervised travels around the city. The Sociological Department report noted:

> Work of each advisor outside is closely checked up by the daily count of regular and special investigations turned in, quality of work, number of absentee reports, and the method of handling

them, in such a way that it is impossible for an outside man to 'loaf' much on the job and get away with it.

According to the report, the fifty-two outside investigators visited in seventy-seven districts throughout the city and its suburbs. Each district contained an average of 523 Ford workers. Each investigator had an average caseload of 727 workers. And, each day the investigator made 5.35 "regular investigations," five "absentee calls," and a total of fifteen "outside calls." Moreover, the report noted that the outside investigator also examined and questioned workers in the Ford plant. "This necessitates," it noted, "advisors being in at the time the shifts are out, and they average five men each day."[13]

The inside department consisted of a staff of fourteen investigators under the direction of G. M. Rounds. These "special" investigators performed a combination of Ford sociological, traditional welfare, and modern personnel work in thirteen different areas. The special investigators worked on those cases that best suited their particular talents. The sociological work included the investigation of office, low level supervisory (i.e., general foremen and foremen), and female employees. These groups of employees required the special attention and the tact of a particularly talented investigator. And, another investigator looked after the special needs of immigrant workers who shipped money to their relatives in the old countries.

Special work also included those activities and services directed towards the physical and mental well-being of Ford workers and their families. This included aid for sick employees, special assistance for charity cases, medical care for the crippled children of Ford workers, help for epileptic and insane employees, and assistance for "deficient" children. Also, Ford investigators performed duties similar to the modern welfare worker or probation officer. They handled problems with "anti-social cases," criminal cases and suspects, and Ford workers "brought up before city police, courts and jails." And, in the area of personnel work, different investigators looked after factory sanitation, the quality of food service in the plant, and the excuses of absentees and workers who lost their badges. Finally, an investigator provided legal advice and appraisals for Ford workers who purchased property or a home.[14]

The Ford Sociological Department investigated every Ford employee who earned less than $200 per month. This meant that it investigated salesmen, clerks, foremen, and factory workers. That is, it examined everyone except high level managers and supervisors. For each investigated employee, the company maintained a "Record of Investigation." And, the company insisted that the Ford worker provide all relevant documentation for the sociological investigation. In order to obtain information for the workman's record, the investigator "consulted every available source of information—churches, fraternal organizations, the government, family bibles, passports— everything that would give the truth about the men was scrutinized." Moreover, the company held the worker responsible and accountable for the outside witnesses to his character. "In cases where it is impossible to find someone who knows the habits and home life of the employe," the home office instructed Ford branches, "we withhold the increase [in profits] otherwise to be granted him under the plan, placing the burden of proof upon him." And, the company ordered investigators: "Get all the information you can to corroborate the employes' statements."[15]

The "Record of Investigation" examined three distinct aspects of the lives of Ford workers. First, it recorded a wide range of social and biographical information on each worker. Second, it gathered information on the economic and financial condition of the worker and his family. And, third, it explored the worker's morality, his habits, and his life-style.[16]

The social and biographical information included some information which any employer might need to know, but it also included information which probed deeply into the personal lives of Ford workers. The record listed the worker's date of initial employment along with whether or not he had left the company and had been rehired. It also recorded the date of the first sociological investigation, and all subsequent investigations, of the worker at home or in the factory. The detailed data also included—the workman's address, age, date of birth (with the notation that young workers had verified their age with a birth certificate), religion, whether or not the worker spoke English, nationality, marital status (appropriately verified), how long the worker had been in Detroit and in the United States, whether or not the worker was naturalized, and the number of dependents. For each dependent, the company required the worker to provide the same, the relationship, the address, and the extent of dependency.

The economic and financial information on Ford workers grew from the company's effort to determine whether or not the worker utilized his profits wisely. "Every worker," the company ruled, "must account for his share of the Profits." In other words, the worker "must show the Company how he is handling the money given him over and above his skilled rate." To this end, the company wanted to know whether or not the workman owned or was purchasing property or a home, whether or not he had a savings account in a bank, and whether or not he was in debt. Furthermore, it required information on the location and value of the property, the name of the bank, the account number, the balance in the account, the holder of the debt, the reason for the debt, and the balance due. The company also wanted to know whether or not the worker carried insurance, the kind of insurance, the amount, and the size of the premiums. Again, the investigator demanded supporting documentation— deeds, bank books, receipts, bills, etc.—to confirm the worker's statements. In subsequent investigations, the investigator carefully reexamined the worker's financial condition to determine whether or not the worker used his profits to his best advantage.[17]

The Sociological Department expressed especial concern about the thrift of Ford workers. The Ford notion of thrift demonstrated how an economic virtue became a moral and cultural one. The company believed that a thrifty worker was a reliable and efficient worker. The single man received the special attention of the investigator with regard to thrift. The company presumed that these young workers did not possess the stability and responsibility of married workers. As a consequence, the single worker not only had to be thrifty like all other workers, he also had to demonstrate "proved signs of thrift." As early as January 1914, the company carefully defined its notion of "proven thrift:"

> By this we mean that the employe shall not be addicted to the excessive use of liquor, nor gamble, nor engage in any malicious practice derogatory to good physical manhood or moral character; shall conserve his resources and make the most of his opportunities that are afforded him in his work.

Within this context, thrift assumed a broad social and cultural dimension. Thrift did not simply mean saving money in the bank or investing it wisely. It meant the elimination of those activities which tired or wore down body and soul. Alcohol resulted in hangovers and lateness or absenteeism; gambling—in worries about debts; women—in late hours. John R. Lee once said that the company did not want a worker to share in profits if he was "wasting away his substance." In the Ford enterprise, thrift meant that the worker should not squander those mental and physical resources that were necessary for efficient production.[18]

Finally, as a condition for the five dollar income, the company also scrutinized the Ford worker's morality and habits. In this area, the Ford Motor Company clearly and concretely attempted to reform and to remake men in the Ford image. In its instructions to investigators, the company noted that habits were "one of the most vital points" of the Ford investigation. "To grant a share of profits," it reasoned, "to a confirmed drunkard, gambler, or to one addicted to any other evil habit, would be largely instrumental in promoting his degradation, and quickening his downfall." The sociological instructions noted that the "drink habit" was the principal problem. The company encouraged the investigator to give "good advice and encouragement" until the worker overcame his habit and regained "his will power and self-respect." However, if this failed, the company advised, "it is then well to see that he take the 'Cure.' " In the end, the instructions concluded:

> One attempt is not always sufficient to bring about the desired results; but, as one of the principles of the Ford Plan is to elevate mankind, every conceivable effort should be made to reform an unfortunate of this type and instill him with new ambition, which will enable him to have higher and better ideals.

In this area of morality and habits, the published "Records of Investigation" revealed more about the Ford ideals and values for Ford workers.[19]

The Ford Motor Company permitted the publication of typical cases to illustrate the nature of its industrial welfare program. One case, a Catholic Armenian worker who was a skilled machine operator, represented the ideal worker. His record indicated that he had lived in Detroit for three years and in the United States for five years. He supported a mother and two sisters who lived in Turkey. The investigator judged his habits as "Good." His recreations included "Theatres" and "home reading." The investigator also evaluated his home conditions as good. The Armenian machine operator boarded in a room which cost two dollars per week. It was an apartment: "Five rooms and bath, occupied by two men and one woman. Nicely furnished, clean and neat." From the time the worker first received his share of the profits, the investigator noted:

His bank savings, since May 11th, 1914, have been increased $725.00 (v). April 7, 1915, sent to Old Country $50.00 (v) through American Board of Commissioners for Foreign Missions. This man was granted a share of profits on 5−25−14 and up to the present time has saved $740.00 (v), an excellent showing. He is very saving and worthy to continue a share of the profits.

A model worker, even by the rigorous Ford standards, the Armenian sent the company a photograph of himself and a letter, which expressed his appreciation for the Ford Profit-sharing Plan.[20]

In another instance, a German Catholic worker who came from a German area of Poland, lived under conditions which typified the new Southern and Eastern European immigrants. He had a large family, a wife and four children. When first investigated in January 1914, his habits were poor—"Drinks and smokes." He lived in a two-story frame house that was in "poor condition." The neighborhood was also unacceptable: "Very bad. This is an alley with one and two storey houses in poor condition on one side only—Foreign." The investigator detailed his impressions of the Ford worker's standard of living:

This man lives in a dirty unsanitary hut and has a room full of boarders, who sleep 3 and 4 to a room. Some of the boarders go through the room where the man and wife sleep to reach their own room. Wife looks haggard from overwork. She and the children are as dirty as their surroundings.

Living under such conditions, the investigator did not approve the worker for a share in the profits. Instead, he "advised" the worker not to have boarders, to move to a better neighborhood, and generally to improve his living conditions.

By May, provided with the incentive to more than double his pay, the worker began to follow his investigator's advice. He purchased a "lot in the suburbs and has built a 3-room shack on it; occupied by his family only." Eventually, the workman planned to build a house on the lot. He also enrolled in the Ford English School, a new institution for teaching the immigrant worker the English language and American values and customs. "The furniture," the investigator observed, "is not excellent, but it is enough for their immediate needs. The family, as well as the home, show cleanliness." Indeed, the man and his family demonstrated "a great improvement since the last investigation." However, the workman had to wait until August before he received the investigator's approval for profits.

A subsequent investigation in December revealed the continued improvement in the living conditions of the family. By this time, they had built their new home. The family also purchased new furniture. In August 1915, the investigator praised the remarkable progress of the worker and his family:

> Our employee is making wonderful progress with his share of the profits. His home is comfortably furnished; the family is neat and clean. He can now speak English, and has taken out 1st naturalization papers. They are a happy and contented family.

In this case, the incentive of the Five Dollar Day provided the stimulus for the immigrant worker to alter his habits and his lifestyle to meet Ford's American standards.[21]

In a third example, a young American worker illustrated the company's fear that an increased income would result in a self-indulgent and profligate existence. In fact, the company believed that Ford wages alone were adequate for a comfortable life for single workers. Therefore, youthful workers had to show a better accounting of their share of Ford profits than older or married workers. The company reminded its investigators that a single man without dependents "must account for all of his profits outside of his general living expenses," which included "rent, board, clothing, etc." It also instructed them to know "the extent of their indulgences that makes for good or bad manhood."[22]

In January 1914, upon the completion of his investigation of the twenty-three year old skilled worker, the investigator noted that the young American was an exemplary employee. He had a high school education. He carried a life insurance policy. He boarded in a good home in an "American residential" neighborhood. Because the workman lived with a "respectable family" and because he "started a savings account," the investigator granted the worker his profits as the result of his initial investigation.

However, a follow-up investigation in July revealed that the young worker did not use his share of profits in the acceptable manner. The investigator reported:

> The profits have been a detriment to this young man. After getting a share of the profits he started having a good time. He not only spent all of the profits he received, but the money he had in the bank as well. He has absolutely nothing to show for the wages and the share of the profits he has received since the last investigation.

Consequently, the investigator took away the profits and advised the young worker to mend his ways.

Once again, the monetary incentive, backed by the ultimate threat of dismissal, convinced a Ford worker to change his habits and lifestyle. By December 1914, the young worker "realized his mistake." He began a new savings account and "now stays in nearly every evening." The investigator reapproved the worker for a share of Ford profits. By August 1915, the investigator noted changes in the young worker—his neighbors spoke well of him, he planned to marry and to build a home, and he enrolled in a YMCA technical course. While the increased income initially caused the young worker to fall to evil ways, the Sociological Department's vigilance and guidance assisted his return to "right" living.[23]

Finally, the case of a young American machine operator typified the company's more charitable motivations. Normally, the company excluded workers under the age of twenty-two from its profit-sharing plan. However, this young American worker had a mother, a brother, and a sister, who all were totally dependent on his income. These dependents made him eligible to receive Ford profits. In January 1914, the investigator wrote:

> This boy lost his father by death about 6 months ago, and the mother has had a rather hard struggle to make both ends meet. The father did not carry life insurance, and they are still in debt for the funeral expenses. This son is very good to his mother. He turns his pay envelope over to her each pay day. A very worthy case. Mother has no other means of support.

Under these circumstances, the investigator immediately granted the family a share of the profits. As time went on, the living conditions of the family steadily improved. They moved to a new apartment.

They bought new furniture. They eventually purchased a little cottage "in a neighborhood not very thickly settled." In October 1915, the investigator concluded: "This family is getting along very nicely. They are very thrifty. The share of the profits has been put to good use, and they are very happy and contented."[24]

Aside from the Records of Investigation, a number of Ford "Human Interest Stories" also detailed the procedures and concerns of the Ford social investigators. Around 1915, the Ford Sociological Department collected these stories as examples of Ford welfare work, most likely for public relations purposes and as examples for other investigators. Ford officials seem to have instructed the investigators to search their files and memories to discover the cases that best illustrated the uplifting character of Ford sociological activities. And, while these cases were hardly typical ones, they did demonstrate how the program should work and how the investigators should perform their duties. For the public and for other Ford investigators, the human interest stories provided models of the social uplift and the moral salvation of Ford workers. Most of the stories followed a standard and ritualistic pattern. First, the Ford sociological investigator uncovered a problem with a Ford employee, his family, or his home life. Once discovered, the Sociological Department moved to alleviate and to correct the problem. And, finally, the worker and his family recognized their problem, changed their attitudes or forms of behavior, and dutifully expressed their gratitude to Henry Ford, the Ford Motor Company, or the investigator for their new and improved life. Four human interest stories served as examples of Ford sociological work for the correction of the drink habit, marital separation, and a malingering worker.[25]

In the first instance, Ford investigator William E. Hakes wrote about "a good, faithful workman," who unfortunately "was addicted to drink." According to Hakes, the worker's home reflected his poor moral condition. At his visit, he discovered:

> what they called a 'home' in absolute poverty; the wife in bed with erysipelis on her face, and a little deranged, as her conversation showed. Her son, about seven years of age, a bright, flexen-haired little fellow, had recently had the misfortune to have his eye put out by falling on a sharp stick. The other child, a bright little girl about five and one-half years of age, was playing on the floor, and none too clean. The rooms were furnished in the most scanty manner: one iron bed for the whole family,

and an old rickety table, and bench and boxes used for chairs. No rug or carpet on the floor. And this was the home of an American workman.

The middle-class investigator confronted a harsh reality of some aspects of American working-class life. Hakes talked with the worker's wife and then "went after the husband." He did not detail his conversation with the worker, but he secured "promise to do better." And, on this basis, Hakes conditionally approved the worker for profits. Whatever the investigator said, it had its proper effect. After he received his first large pay envelope, the Ford workman was "radiant." "He came up to me," the investigator related, "and shook my hand, and thanked me for what I had done for him." At the time of Hakes' report, the worker and his family moved to a comfortably furnished cottage, paid their doctor bills, and wore decent clothes. Also, Hakes added: "He has gotten away from his associates of the drink habit." And, the Ford worker "did not think there were words to express the gratitude he has to offer the Ford Motor Company for his help."[26]

The second story involved an American worker who fell from grace because of his affection for women and drink. On the surface, things looked well at the initial sociological investigation. "When the investigator made his first call on this couple," Charles R. Chamberlain noted, "he found what was apparently a very happy couple." Some minor problems existed. For example, although married only one year, the young couple splurged and purchased expensive furniture on the installment plan. Nevertheless, "with economy and thrift, they could reasonably look forward to becoming clear of debt." Moreover, shortly after the initial visit, the young couple had "a fine baby boy" and appeared "very proud and happy." It was not until the third investigation that the Ford investigator uncovered serious domestic troubles.

After "a rigid investigation," the Ford sociological worker discovered that as the wife convalesced from the birth, the husband began his downfall. He started "spending his evenings away from home, generally under the influence of liquor." Money for food, medical bills, and furniture all went for drink and good times. Throughout, the young wife covered for her husband and told the investigator "a great many untruths." She "feared he would lose his position, become discouraged and go further on the downward path, if the real condition of affairs became known." Just prior to the third investigation, the worker drew his pay and abandoned his wife and infant child. The furniture was repossessed. An endless line of bill collectors called for payment of the debts which the worker incurred.

The Ford investigator brought the case to the attention of the Ford legal department which agreed that "the woman was worthy of help." The company offered her a profit-sharing job with the same pay as her husband. For the moment, however, the company recommended a three-month rest for the worried and nursing mother. It planned to pay her ten dollars each week from the Ford charity fund. In addition, the investigator arranged that the furniture be held until the final few payments could be made.

Shortly thereafter, the prodigal worker returned to his wife. According to Chamberlain, he was "very travel-stained and repentant." "He had been traveling all over the state on freight cars which had not helped the appearance of his clothes any, and with a week's growth of beard he was not a pleasant sight." The young wife was not quite prepared to "forgive him," but was "ready and willing to give him another chance to make good." The Ford investigator developed a plan of salvation for the fallen workman. First, the Catholic worker had to sign "a pledge to keep away from women and liquor" in the presence of his two parish priests. Then, the investigator took a copy of the pledge to P. E. Martin, the plant superintendent, and requested that the man be given a second chance in the Ford factory. Martin agreed since "to let him go at this time might mean his ruin while helping him would in all probabilities make him once more the good husband he had been before the slip." Finally, the company allocated the worker's pay to his wife "until time had proven that he could use it judiciously and for the best interest of his family."[27]

Another domestic relations case involved "an employee whose wife had left him." Prior to his employment with the Ford Motor Company, the wife sold their furniture, sent the children to friends in the country, and hired out as a domestic in the city. According to Ford investigator C. M. Groat: "She instituted divorce proceedings and he filed a cross bill." Apparently, the man was unemployed and economic insecurity exacerbated domestic tensions. Meanwhile, he got a job at Ford. At the initial investigation, the Ford sociological worker unraveled the worker's domestic troubles and brought together husband, wife, and children. "The family," Groat reported, "was reunited and with the money that this man had been able to save through the profit-sharing plan, they were able to rent and comfortably furnish a modern flat, and clothe themselves and children." Groat further related that in the last six months he had handled about forty "domestic relations cases." Moreover, "with one exception, the families have been reunited and are living happily together." Groat then related his personal philosophy for these cases. In most instances:

> ... all that is needed is for someone to point out to both husband and wife their duty to each other and to their children, and many a family blesses the day when a Ford sociological representative entered their home and gave them the needed encouragement.[28]

Finally, C. R. Chamberlain reported the "strangest" case that came to his attention in the past year. This worker apparently could not face going to work in the Ford plant each day. From November 1914 through March 1915:

> ... he had only worked altogether for about six weeks. He would work for a week or two and then lay off for a few weeks. Part of the time he was sick, but a greater part of the time was simply because he could not work up enough ambition to come out to work.

Each morning, his wife packed a lunch and he told her that he was off to work. Instead, "he would go to one of the saloons in the neighborhood of Clark Park and generally spend the entire day there, or until the saloon keepers got tired of seeing him around and threw him out." His family lived on charity and relied on friends and neighbors for food and clothing. Chamberlain did his best to get the man to come to work. He "called every day and often twice a day to induce [the worker] to brace up and come back to work. On each visit his answer would invariably be that he would be at the factory the following morning, but he always failed to keep his promise."

As the family situation deteriorated, Chamberlain devised a drastic plan of attack. Since the family had no food, the rent was overdue, and the children needed clothes for school, he went to the legal department for advice. He and the lawyer instructed the wife "to swear out a warrant for her husband on a charge of non-support." The warrant was served and the worker went to jail for four days. At the trial, the judge paroled the worker: "over to Parole Officer Dickenson for a period of one year. The provisions of his parole were that [he] must keep out of saloons and work steadily every day. Both . . . were to report every Friday evening to Mr. Dickenson." Additionally, Chamberlain spoke with the plant superintendent; the worker "was put to work with the understanding that his pay be turned over to his wife." After the man worked steadily for two months, the wife:

> was beginning to feel very much pleased at the way things had turned out. She was paying up her debts as fast as possible and hoped soon to be clear, when they intended to move into a better neighborhood away from the husband's evil companions.

Once again, Ford sociological work with its powerful financial incentive had its intended effect.[29]

The Ford attitude toward women workers mirrored its attitude towards home and family. In 1914, the Highland Park factory employed from 250 to 300 female workers. They worked in the magneto, top-making, and upholstering departments. Ford officials believed that their nimble fingers were well-suited for winding wire and for sewing. When first announced, the Five Dollar Day excluded women from the Ford Profit-sharing Plan. Indeed, the company believed that women "are not considered such economic factors as men." The reason for this, James Couzens stated, "is because they are not, as a rule, the heads of families." Moreover, he continued, "women are likely to throw up their positions at any time, without notice for any reason that may happen to influence them." (Given the high rates of labor turnover for the entire plant, women did not seem more unreliable than male workers.) Nevertheless, the "few" reliable women, Couzens added, "not infrequently make sudden announcement of their marriage and leave." Consequently, the company considered all women, regardless of their family status, as youths: that is, as single men under twenty-two without dependents and, therefore, ineligible for Ford profits. As the result of criticism from women's rights advocates, the company eventually allowed some women, who were the heads of households, to participate in its welfare plan.[30]

On the other hand, Ford sociological policies still reinforced traditional family relationships. As earlier examples illustrated, Ford sociological investigators devised ingenious and comprehensive schemes to reunit the families of Ford workers. The Ford sociological "instructions" noted that "domestic trouble" required "considerable tact and diplomacy." And, they suggested a strategy for investigators:

> Where the result of the interviews shows that both husband and wife are at fault, each should be shown wherein they have been in the wrong and convinced of their duty to go to the other and acknowledge it, at the same time accept the acknowledgement of the other in good spirit. Each should be advised of the kindly feeling the other has in the matter. When this has been accomplished, and they have been called together, there is little doubt of a satisfactory result.

And, the "instructions" concluded that "the object of the Ford Motor Company is to *protect and to build up happy homes* and in no way assist in tearing them down." Additionally, the wives of Ford workers were not permitted to have their own jobs. In a general discussion of policy, the company emphasized that "if a man wants to remain a profit sharer, his wife should stay at home and assume the obligations she undertook when married."[31]

The Ford investigators were not perfect. And, they sometimes made serious mistakes in their zealous efforts to obtain information on the Ford workforce. John R. Lee related an incident which caused considerable trouble for his department. In this case, a young man in the "student course" was transferred from department to department a number of times. Obviously, this called for further investigation. So, two investigators went to his home. "They were impressed," Lee noted, "by the fine neighborhood, and wondered how a man earning his 29 cents here could live in such a building; so they asked the same questions, trying to get information on this man, the same as our other employees." But, the young man was the son of Seaborn Livingstone, "president of the Dime Savings Bank—of prominence all over the Great Lakes—whom the great Livingstone Channel is named after . . . member of all prominent organizations, The Detroit Club, etc." Soon after the investigation, the father called Ford officials. And, within minutes of each other, Ford, Couzens, the vice president, and Klingensmith, the treasurer, all spoke with Lee about the investigation. "I then decided," Lee continued, "to pull his sheet from the records, and kill the whole thing right there, but in some way it slipped by, and the other day Mr. Hakes got hold of the sheet, and of course, went down to the Livingstone home again." Another complaint went straight to company officers. Couzens called Hakes into his office. And, he "explained the matter satisfactorily. It developed that he had not asked hardly any questions, but the talking was all from the members of the household." Lee related this incident to other investigators in order to illustrate the need for tact and caution. The investigation of upper and middle-class families brought swift and effective protest. He wanted to show them "just how these things are hurled back at us, and I wish, from this time on, if any doubt arises in your mind, you will go back after you have thought the matter over."[32]

And, other problems plagued Ford sociological investigators. Initially, Ford workers and the general public expressed their dissatisfaction and hostility towards the Ford welfare program. After the first series of investigations in April 1914, Lee conducted a number of meetings with different groups of investigators. He wanted to avoid the troubles and difficulties encountered in the first investigations and to establish new procedures and policies for future investigations. In the early investigations, the Ford investigators faced "a great many difficulties and a great many handicaps." Most important, "the first work engendered a lot of apathy and ill-feeling on the part of outsiders towards the Ford Motor Company. . . ." In particular, he urged the investigators to "guard against" and to use the "utmost care" in "the delving into strictly personal things—things that are strictly private, that do not concern our work in the least." He reported that a Sacramento newspaper wanted to visit the Highland Park plant and to discover exactly what the investigators did. Lee said that the paper sought:

> to find out that we were not going into the home, regulating the size of the home—how the home should be, what schools the boys should attend, the progeny they should have, etc. That we were not working on eugenics, nor hygienics, nor any thing of that nature.

He also related that a Ford worker wrote the company and complained about unnecessary questions—"if he had any children—if he had done anything to prevent children." He then warned the investigators about the potential newspaper headlines: " 'Ford Trying to Regulate the Size of Families,' 'Ford Delving into the Secret Affairs of the Home,' etc."[33]

Obviously, Ford investigators were indiscreet in their interviews with Ford workers and their families. And, Lee urged them to use more tact, caution, and diplomacy. "Unless we work like Trojans now," he advised, "we are going to have some notoriety that we do not want." In the future, "you will have to use all the skill and ingenuity you can muster to get the desired results." The previous investigations, he continued, uncovered "faults," now the task was "to find the good things in the men, and to keep adding to these just as much as possible." Since the Sociological Department now possessed records on the workforce, it was no longer necessary "to ask the same questions as to age, religion, number of children, their names, ages, etc. . . ." In the next investigations, he concluded:

> all we want this time is to learn the progress of the lack of progress. We want to know whether this plan has benefited or degraded, and if we possibly can, get an idea of the degree of progress that the man has made.

Indeed, the Ford sociological program generated suspicions and resentment among workers and the public. This forced Ford officials to reevaluate and to change their methods and procedures.[34]

And, the more cautious strategy appeared to have some success in the company's relations with its workers and with outsiders. In 1915, William M. Purves, an investigator, reported on "The Investigators' Standing with Employees and Others." Of course, he recognized that in the past, "private affairs were needlessly pried into, confidences violated and ungentlemanly acts perpetrated in the employes' houses." Nonetheless, he cited a gradual change of opinion, because the workers and others realized the purpose of the investigation and that the company was "altogether back of [i.e., behind] the investigator." In Purves' view, workers now understood that "the object of the investigation is to help, and not to cause trouble for, the employe" and should understand that "the investigator is the personal representative of the Company, and consequently their best friend." Whereas earlier it was difficult to obtain information, now workers volunteered it and actually sought out "the investigator to ask advice regarding their private affairs."

Furthermore, the Sociological Department developed its rationalization for those who objected to the home investigation. With the dissenter, Purves continued, "it can now be taken as a sure thing that he has something to hide and has been doing something underhanded which he is afraid will be found out." S. S. Marquis, who later directed the Ford program, echoed this theme in his speeches on Ford educational activities. "Often," Purves added:

> after this type of man has been reasoned with and the kinks in his habits or morals straightened out, and a new page in his history started, he has confessed he is happier than for years and is deeply gratified to the Ford Motor Company and its investigators for starting him on the right path.

Still, Purves' comments had a self-serving and overly positive tone on the success of the Sociological Department. Most likely, Ford workers took their profits and kept their mouths shut. In 1916, when Marquis directed the program, he changed the name to Educational Department, because workers still expressed their opposition and hostility to Ford welfare work.[35]

The Ford Motor Company also classified and graded the social, cultural, and moral standards of Ford workers in the same manner as it classified and graded their skill and efficiency. Upon completion of the first investigations in April 1914, the home office reported:

> . . . we are now dividing our whole force into three groups.
> *First:* Those who have qualified and are now receiving a share of the profits.
> *Second:* Those who have qualified by a very small margin and whom we believe will need a tremendous amount of help and supervision in order to continue sharing in the profits.
> *Third:* Those who have not qualified and whom we are working upon with every agency possible that we may bring them into a realization of the fact, that by living up to the standards we have set, will enable us to give them a share in the profits.

Additionally, Ford officials selected investigators with "the personal characteristics that will appeal for best results to each of these three classes." In order to contain and to reform the human element, Ford officials and managers felt the need for an acute sense of order and structure for all aspects of its factory workforce.[36]

The second and third groups received the most attention of sociological investigators. In the second group, the Ford officials worried most about married workers who were in debt. They wanted to know "that in liquidating their obligations . . . , they do not come out with a clean slate into an atmosphere of extravagance or selfish-ness or any bent or trait that would be detrimental to good man-hood." They also expressed concern about those who did "particu-larly good work in the shop" but turned out "anything but thrifty" in their "outside life." The third group primarily consisted of immi-grant workers. These were "the men who do not speak English or who live in dirty squalid conditions, who are improvident, and who, unfortunately for the most part, have not squared away for a number of reasons." If approached properly, they responded "readily." Some workers in this group presented special problems to Ford investigators. These were immigrant boarding-house operators, "who are turning over their houses to boarders for the sake of a meager return and who are wearing their families and wives out." Ford officials believed that the boarders, especially single men, violated the sanctity of the family unit. Nonetheless, many im-migrant entrepreneurs did quite well in the provision of room and board for their compatriots. Some became "disgruntled and an-tagonistic" and did not realize "the fundamental things this plan stands for or are unwilling to do so." Ultimately, Ford officials "eliminat[ed] such from our employ. . . ."[37]

By November 1917, the Sociological Department carried the prin-ciples of organization and rationalization of the labor force to their most extreme limit. At this time, the sociological investigators grouped Ford workers into four classes: Honor Roll, Class A, Class B, and Class C. The Honor Roll workers were "in the employ of the company a sufficient length of time—say at least one year—to make it clear that they are of the sober, thrifty, properly housed and prop-erly living class of whom further investigation is unnecessary, and who may safely be left alone." The Class A workers had "satisfac-tory" investigations, but were not employed "quite long enough" to be "permanently established in habits of thrift, industry, sobriety, etc." The Class B workers were "men who have been recently em-ployed and who have not been long enough with the Company to determine whether they will develop into a problem or be of the kind who will ultimately be placed upon the Honor Roll. . . ." The Class C workers were "the problem class." These workers received the full attention of Ford investigators. "In Class C," a company let-ter stated, "you will place all men who for any reason—such as drink, lack of thrift, domestic trouble, indebtedness, etc.—present them-selves to you as a problem requiring special attention."[38]

The Honor Roll contained model Ford employees. It, too, had different requirements for married and single men. Married men:

> Should be thirty years of age, living with and taking good care of their families; of excellent habits and positively no domestic troubles; home conditions beyond reproach; unquestionably thrifty and with at least one year in the Company's service.

Single men:

> Should be thirty-five years of age; habits unquestionable; home conditions beyond reproach; an excellent showing of thrift, even beyond that of married men; and with three or more years constant service with the Company.

The Sociological Department "Instructions" also indicated "Secondary Honor Roll Men." These workers qualified "in every respect the same as the first Honor Roll man except possibly for lack of thrift." Since their home conditions were "beyond reproach," these workers could "be called into the factory at regular intervals and a strict accounting of thrift taken."[39]

The Honor Roll was "the secret issue of sociological work." Presumably, it formed a potential pool of Ford workers for promotion to more interesting and more prestigious jobs in the factory—subforemen, inspectors, foremen, and toolroom workers. In 1917, a company document listed approximately 1,000 "Star" employees. Most of these workers had English or German names and were subforemen or foremen. About 80 either quit and left the Ford plant or were demoted to production jobs. Notations near these names indicated that they were "off the Star Roll." They also gave the reason for the quit or demotion. These notations illustrated the strict standards for Ford "Star" workers. Some could not handle the men under them or did not desire to be foremen. Others had poor habits—"Polish wedding, Drunk," "Too irregular," "borrowing money from his men," "stealing tools," "occasionally sober," "selling real estate," "crap game while on duty," "domestic trouble," and so forth. Many of the workers who left refused to accept disciplinary transfers within the Ford plant.[40]

All of these examples and episodes illustrated the most salient feature of the Ford welfare program—its deep-seated middle-class arrogance and paternalism towards Ford workers. Undeniably, some investigators approached their jobs with a reforming or uplifting spirit and with true altruistic sensibilities towards the men in the Ford shops. Some rose from the shops themselves as part of the American quest for upward social mobility. And, the sociological investigators did alleviate some of the most deleterious aspects of American and immigrant working-class poverty. However, they approached Ford workers from a distance delineated by the boundaries of class. Also, they carried a conviction of the moral superiority of middle-class social and cultural values. The investigators emphasized middle-class patterns and standards of life—the nuclear family, a pastoral home or cottage for that family, cleanliness in personal and domestic life, thrift, sobriety, traditional morality, family-centered recreation and entertainment, and most of all hard work. And, Ford workers had little room for self-initiative and self-expression. In the Progressive Era, Ford workers and their families suffered the humiliations and indignities of our modern welfare clients. The Ford investigators were fathers who rewarded and punished the behavior of their wayward working-class children. But, nowhere was Ford paternalism more evident than in its treatment of immigrant workers.

7. Assembly-Line Americanization

The apperception mass [sic] of the immigrant, expressed in the attitudes and values he brings with him from his old life, is the material from which he must build his Americanism. It is also the material we must work with, if we would aid this process. Our tools may be in part American customs and institutions, but the substance we seek to mold into new forms is the product of other centuries in other lands. . . . A wise policy of assimilation, like a wise educational policy, does not seek to destroy the attitudes and memories that are there, but to build on them.[1]—Robert E. Park and Herbert A. Miller, 1921

Americanization was the social and cultural assimilation of immigrants into the mainstream of American life. And, it was also a unique, and distinctly American, method for the resolution of a key industrial problem—the problem of work-discipline and of the adaptation of new workers to the factory environment. Americanization usually has not been the concern of labor or industrial historians. Historians of Americanization generally have emphasized the differences between American and immigrant cultures.

Edward G. Hartmann, the movement's principal historian, examined the early Americanization campaign from this perspective. According to his investigation, American middle-class and business elites, "the intelligentsia, the educators and social workers, the industrialists, and . . . business and civic groups," were the leaders and organizers of this "educative movement." He concluded that:

the Americanization effort stressed the desirability of the rapid assimilation of the millions of immigrants who had come to America during the pre-war decades, through the attendance of the newcomers at special classes, lectures, and mass meetings, where they might be instructed in the language, the ideals, and on the life which had come to be accepted as the American way of life.

149

In this form, the Americanization campaign was voluntary, benevolent, and educational. Nevertheless, when the programs emanated from within factory gates, they had their darker side. The issue was not simply different national or ethnic cultures, but also preindustrial and industrial cultures, and even class cultures. Americanization was an important movement for the adjustment of immigrant workers to a new industrial environment and to American urban and industrial society, not just to American society in the abstract.[2]

In recent years, Thompson, Pollard, Gutman, Montgomery, and others have suggested the importance of culture as a concept for the examination of the history of the working-class and industrialization. Their work suggested that the adaptation of a new industrial workforce involved a complex matrix of interrelationships between industrialization, social class, and culture. The new industrial worker needed a new culture, i.e., a new set of attitudes, values, and habits, for his survival and for his very existence in the factory and in industrial society. In the United States, the Americanization movement attempted to provide the necessary industrial culture for immigrant workers in American factories. Imposed from above, it was a middle-class industrial ethos for immigrant workers. And, while the Ford Americanization program was unique in some of its elements, it typified some of the experiences of many other American manufacturers and industrialists of the period.[3]

The profound paternalism of the Ford Profit-sharing Plan captured the Progressive Era's contradictory attitude toward the unskilled immigrant worker. On the one hand, it attempted to assist the worker and to elevate him to a better standard of life. On the other hand, it sought to manipulate or to coerce the worker to match a preconceived ideal of that better life. John R. Commons, the progressive labor historian, noted the double edged character of the Ford program. The Ford plan, he reported, "is just old fashioned industrial autocracy tempered by faith in human nature." A benevolent end—the uplift of the unskilled and unschooled immigrant worker—justified a manipulative and coercive means.[4]

From the very beginning, the Ford Profit-sharing Plan attempted to fit the immigrant worker into its preconceived mold of the ideal American. An early memorandum clarified the objectives of the Ford plan to a branch manager. "It is our aim and object," the home office noted, "to make better men and better American citizens and to bring about a larger degree of comforts, habits, and a higher plane of living among our employees. . . ." Henry Ford expressed his concern about non-American workers to an interviewer: "These men of many nations must be taught American ways, the English language, and the right way to live." He then elaborated on the "right" life for the foreign-born worker. Married men "should not sacrifice family rights, pleasure, and comfort by filling their homes with roomers and boarders." Single men should live "comfortably and under conditions that make for good manhood and good citizenship." A company report on progress among immigrant workers noted that the Ford ideal was to create "a comfortable and cozy domesticity."[5]

In its literature for workers, the Ford Motor Company repeatedly advised them where and how to live. A pamphlet pointed toward "right" living conditions:

> Employes should live in clean, well conducted homes, in rooms that are well lighted and ventilated. Avoid congested parts of the city. The company will not approve, as profit sharers, men who herd themselves into overcrowded boarding houses which are menaces to their health. . . .
>
> Do not occupy a room in which one other person sleeps, as the company is anxious to have its employes live comfortably, and under conditions that make for cleanliness, good manhood, and good citizenship.

Ford and his managers deeply believed that tenement life in the immigrant neighborhoods of the city polluted body and soul. They also considered physical and moral cleanliness important attributes for work in modern industrial society. A clean home reduced the chances for illness and absenteeism. A clean mind provided the sound foundation for the construction of good work habits.[6]

The Ford Sociological Department even extended its interest and attention to the children of immigrant workers. It prescribed a strong dose of Victorian morality for them in order to promote and develop good bodies and souls. "Choose a home," a pamphlet advised:

> where ample room, good wholesome surroundings, will enable the children to get the greatest benefit possible from play, under conditions that will tend to clean helpful ideas, rather than those likely to be formed in the streets and alleys of the city.

Particularly in adolescence, young men and women "should be guarded well, and not allowed to contract habits and vices injurious to their welfare and health."[7]

S. S. Marquis, who headed the Ford Sociological Department, recalled Ford's own reason for this concern about the morality of children. "By underpaying men," Ford told the Episcopalian minister:

we are bringing up a generation of children undernourished and underdeveloped morally as well as physically; we are breeding a generation of workingmen weak in body and mind, and for that reason bound to prove inefficient when they come to take their places in industry.

The good worker was both physically fit to perform his tasks in the factory and morally fit to perform these tasks diligently.[8]

Often, Ford's paternalistic advice on the care of the home and family contained overt manifestations of middle-class arrogance towards the new immigrant workers. In one instance, a Ford pamphlet advised:

Employees should use plenty of soap and water in the home, and upon their children, bathing frequently. Nothing makes for right living and health so much as cleanliness. Notice that the most advanced people are the cleanest.

Again, the advice cut in two directions. On the one hand, health and cleanliness were important for immigrant workers. On the other hand, the assumption was that lower classes were generally unclean. Indeed, these sentiments typified upper and middle-class American attitudes towards Southern and Eastern European immigrants.[9]

Boris Emmett examined the Ford Profit-sharing Plan for the U.S. Bureau of Labor Statistics. He discovered a class and ethnic bias in the administration of the Ford program. Although the rules and standards of the plan were "strictly applied," he reported that the "rigidity of application" depended on "the specific character of the group of employees concerned." Overall, the Sociological Department and its investigators tended to favor the life-style and the culture of American workers and office employees. "The company," Emmett wrote, "pays very little attention to the manner of life, etc., of their office employees." It believed that "the employees of the commercial and clerical occupations, who mostly are native Americans with some education, need not be told how to live decently and respectably." Consequently, the Ford welfare program concerned "chiefly the manual and mechanical workers, many of whom are of foreign birth and unable to speak the English language."[10]

Additionally, the instructions to the Ford investigators indicated that even American factory workers received preferential treatment. For example, as part of the sociological investigation, the worker who lived with a woman had to furnish proof of marriage. Yet, "especially in American homes," the company left "the question to the discretion of the investigator." If the worker lived in an exemplary American home environment, he need not embarrass the worker with this question. He simply assumed marriage. "If it is the opinion of the investigator," the instructions noted, "that the surroundings and the atmosphere of the home are such as to be above reflecting suspicion on the marriage relation, it is not necessary to obtain documentary proof.[11]

Furthermore, two Ford "Human Interest" stories illustrated how Southern and Eastern European immigrant workers met their good fortune in the form of the Five Dollar Day. One story involved a Russian immigrant and his family; the other a Turkish workman.[12]

F. W. Andrews, a Ford investigator, wrote his story on Joe, a former peasant, his wife, and their six children. Three years earlier, they left Russia for the United States. "Life was an uphill struggle for Joe since landing in America," Andrews reported. Nevertheless, he had a positive trait—his willingness to work hard. "He was a willing worker and not particular about the kind of employment he secured." In the recent past, he dug sewers and worked as an agricultural laborer. When work ran out, he moved to Detroit with his family. "And here," Andrews noted, "for five long months he tramped with the 'Army of the Unemployed'—always handicapped by his meager knowledge of the English language, and was unable to find anything to do." Consequently, his wife bore the "burden of supporting the family." She "worked at the washtub or with the scrubbing brush when such work could be found."

Fortunately, the tale continued, Joe applied for and received a job at the Ford factory. After the company hired him, Andrews went to Joe's home to determine his eligibility for the Ford Five Dollar Day. The scene could have been from a Dickens novel. He discovered "an old, tumbled down, one and a half story frame house." The family's apartment, Andrews related, "was one half of the attic consisting of three rooms, which were so low that a person of medium height could not stand erect—a filthy, foul-smelling hole." It had virtually no furniture, only "two dirty beds. . . . a ragged filthy rug, a rickety table, and two bottomless chairs (the five children standing up at the table to eat)." The family led a precarious hand-to-mouth existence and ate only when the wife earned enough to purchase food for the evening meal. They owed money to the landlord, the grocer, and the butcher. The oldest daughter went to a charity hospital a few days earlier. The wife and the other five children "were half clad, pale, and hungry looking."

This scene of poverty and misery set the Sociological Department's paternalistic programs into motion. Through special arrangements, the pay office issued Joe's wages each day instead of every two weeks. The company provided him with an immediate loan from its charity fund for "the family's immediate start toward right living." However, the investigator, and not Joe, took the fifty-dollar loan and paid the bills and rented a cottage. He also purchased inexpensive furniture and kitchen utensils, provisions, and cheap clothes for the wife and children. (Andrews reported that he bought "a liberal amount of soap" and gave the family "instructions to use freely.")

After Andrews arranged for this initial assistance for Joe and his family, a remarkable ritual followed. The Ford investigator:

> . . . had their dirty, old, junk furniture loaded on a dray and under the cover of night moved them to their new home. This load of rubbish was heaped in a pile in the back yard, and a torch was applied and it went up in smoke.
>
> There upon the ashes of what had been their earthly possessions, this Russian peasant and his wife, with tears streaming down their faces, expressed their gratitude to Henry Ford, the FORD MOTOR COMPANY, and all those who had been instrumental in bringing about this marvelous change in their lives.

In this ritual of fire, an old life went up in smoke as Joe and his family expressed their gratitude and loyalty to Henry Ford.

In time, the children were well dressed and clean. They attended public school. The wife wore "a smile that 'won't come off.'" Joe soon repaid his loan and expected "to soon have a saving for the inevitable 'rainy day.'"[13]

Another investigator, M. G. Torossian, reported on the case of Mustafa, a young Turkish worker. He also was a former peasant. In

his homeland, Mustafa "was the sole help of his father in the field."
Nevertheless, he had positive virtues and the potential for right living even in an industrial job. "Young Mustafa," Torossian related,
"unlike his race, who mostly wander in the mountains and make
money quickly robbing others, had a natural intuition for an honest
living." He learned about "this land of wealth and happiness" from
friends, left his young wife and child with his parents, and went to
Canada. Again, through friends, he learned about work with the
Ford Motor Company. He came to Detroit and obtained work in the
Ford factory before the announcement of the Five Dollar Day.

As in the case of so many other Southern and Eastern European
workers, Mustafa lived in an immigrant boarding house. Torossian
noted that he lived "with his countrymen in the downtown slums in a
squalid house. . . ." However, even in this atmosphere, Mustafa
demonstrated his abilities and his potential to change and to live in
accordance with American standards. The Ford investigator pointed
out that "he used to wash his hands and feet five times a day, as part
of their religion before praying." But even in his native religion, the
Turkish worker learned and accepted American socil and cultural
norms. In America, he only prayed three times a day. "This," said
Torossian, "was modified from five times a day washing on account
of time being too valuable."

With the announcement of the Five Dollar Day, Mustafa's "almost
unimaginable dream came true." At first, he did not receive the "big
money," because he did not speak English and did not comprehend
"his trouble." Among other things, the investigator "advised [him] to
move to a better locality." The Turkish worker even demonstrated
his initiative and "voluntarily took out his first naturalization papers." In the end, he too received the Ford Five Dollar Day.

With the prospect of doubling his income, Mustafa readily abandoned his traditional customs and values for American ones. Torossian concluded:

> . . . Today he has put aside his national red fez and praying, no
> baggy trousers anymore. He dresses like an American gen-
> tleman, attends the Ford English school and has banked in the
> past year over $1,000.00. Now he is anxious to send for his
> young wife and child to bring her and to live happily through
> the grace of Mr. Henry Ford.

Moreover, the Turkish worker also dutifully expressed his gratitude for Ford's paternalism. Torossian related Mustafa's words: "Let my only son be sacrificed for my boss (Mr. Ford) as a sign of my appreciation of what he has done for me. May Allah send my boss Kismet."[14]

Against these uplifting cases, a single and revealing incident demonstrated the nature of the company's concern for the ways in which immigrant traditions affected industrial efficiency. In January 1914, a few days after its impressive gesture—the announcement of the Five Dollar Day—the Ford Motor Company dismissed "between eight and nine hundred Greeks and Russians, who remained away from work on a holiday celebration." The holiday happened to be Christmas. Using the Julian calendar, the Greek and Russian Orthodox Christian workers celebrated Christmas thirteen days later than the rest of the Ford workforce. As justification for this large-scale dismissal, which amounted to about six percent of the Ford workforce, a Ford official stated that "if these men are to make their home in America they should observe American holidays." The absence of this many workers disrupted production in the mechanized Highland Park plant. "It causes too much confusion in the plant," the official concluded, ". . . when nearly a thousand men fail to appear for work."[15]

The Ford English School extended the Ford Americanization program into the classroom. Its exclusive concern was the Americanization of the immigrant worker and his adaptation to the Ford factory and to urban and industrial society. In the English School, as adult immigrant workmen struggled to learn and to comprehend the strange sounds of a new language, they also received the rudiments of American culture. In particular, they learned those habits of life which resulted in good habits of work. In 1916, S. S. Marquis defended the objectives of the Ford educational program before an audience of American educators. The Ford English School, he noted, "was established especially for the immigrants in our employ." It was one part of a total program to adapt men to the new factory system. "The Ford School," he reported, "provides five compulsory courses. There is a course in industry and efficiency, a course in thrift and economy, a course in domestic relations, one in community relations, and one in industrial relations." Later, using the Ford factory as a metaphor for the entire educational program, he added:

This is the human product we seek to turn out, and as we adapt the machinery in the shop to turning out the kind of automobile

we have in mind, so we have constructed out educational system
with a view to producing the human product in mind.

The Ford managers and engineers devised a system wherein men
were the raw materials which were molded, hammered, and shaped
into products which had the proper attitudes and habits for work in
the factory.[16]

In April 1914, the Ford Motor Company called upon Peter
Roberts, a Young Men's Christian Association educator, to develop a
program of English language instruction for immigrant workers in
the Highland Park factory. In 1909, as the result of his activities
among immigrant coal miners in Pennsylvania, Roberts published a
preparatory course of English language instruction, *English for Coming Americans*. This course provided a complete package of materials
to teach the basic elements of the English language. The core of the
program centered around a domestic, a commercial, and an industrial series of lessons. Each series applied the English language to a
different aspects of the immigrant worker's life. This Roberts package formed the basis of language instruction in the Ford English
School.[17]

The domestic series provided specific English lessons for the immigrant workers in his role as the head of an "American" family
unit. This series, Roberts explained, identified "the experiences
common to all peoples reared in the customs of western civilization."
The ten lessons included such topics as "Getting Up in the Morning," "Table Utensils," "The Man Washing," and "Welcoming a Visitor."[18]

The commercial series supplied the immigrant worker with the
vocabulary to serve in his role as consumer. In particular, it attempted to break the economic power of immigrant bosses, who sold
goods and services, who served as employment, travel, and shipping
agents, and who functioned as bankers in the immigrant neighborhoods. Moreover, the lessons emphasized and encouraged the virtues of thrift and property ownership, which created stable and reliable citizens. "These lessons," Roberts noted, "describe the acts
which foreigners in a strange land daily perform. When they are
mastered the pupils will be able to transact their business outside the
narrow circle of places controlled by men conversant with their language." The lessons intended to make the immigrant worker a consumer of American goods and services from American merchants.
In this series, the subject matter included "Buying and Using

Stamps," "Pay Day," "Going to the Bank," "Buying a Lot," "Building a House."[19]

Finally, the industrial series provided flexible lessons to meet the immigrant worker's needs as a producer in the factory. The aim of this series was "to meet the need of thousands who have common experience in industrial life." Here, the lessons included "Beginning the Day's Work," "Shining Shoes," "A Man Looking for Work," and "Finishing the Day's Work."[20]

The lessons in each series had characteristically prosaic titles. And, indeed, the lessons provided helpful and useful information for the immigrant worker. Nevertheless, each lesson contained specific social and cultural norms for life in urban and industrial America. Ford workers learned the value of time in their personal and working lives. They learned the importance of cleanliness and health. They learned self-discpline through regular habits of saving and work. They learned to invest in and to purchase property and to become responsible citizens. These positive virtues—timeliness, cleanliness, thrift, self-discipline, regularity, and citizenship—represented the Ford, and generally the American middle-class, ideal for remaking former European peasants into reliable and efficient factory workers. The English language was an important means for the adaptation of immigrant workers to the regimen and the discipline of the mechanized factory.

As part of its instructional program, the Ford English School also taught immigrant workers not to offend their social betters in their manner and their behavior. For this reason, table manners and etiquette were important parts of the curriculum. "Last, but not least," S. S. Marquis reported, "must be mentioned our professor of table manners who with great dramatic art teaches the use of napkins, knife and fork and spoon." The Ford instructor taught the immigrant worker "the art of eating a meal in a manner that will not interfere with the appetite of the other fellow." In addition, Marquis continued, "We also have a professor of etiquette, such as is required for the ordinary station in life." Moreover, Ford English instructors expected their students to dress properly for the classes. "A by-product of the classes," a report noted, "was a rise in the 'standard of living' by making men conscious of their personal appearance." Instead of going directly from work to school, the instructors required that "class members first go home, wash, and change clothes."[21]

In 1919, Clinton C. DeWitt, the director of the Ford English School, defended the Ford system of industrial Americanization with its practical teachers from the shop floor before an unfriendly audience of American educators. He argued that "a real live American born man, who is a leader among the fellows of his department" would make "in a short time out of Europe's downtrodden and outcasts, good Americans." He also catalogued the advantages of the industrial teacher:

> . . . both teacher and student have so many things in common. He works for the same employer, he works the same hours, he has the same pay day, he has the same environment, he has the same legal holidays, he refers to the same head office, the same pay office, the same superintendent's office, the same safety department, the same Americanization school. The main doorway, the different buildings, and all the printed signs are thoroughly common to teacher and student.

From DeWitt's perspective, the factory hierarchy facilitated instruction. The foreman, the natural leader in his shop, instructed his subordinates in the English language, American values and customs, and Ford shop practices.[22]

In 1915, Oliver J. Abell, an industrial journalist, praised Ford's "benevolent paternalism" in industry. He maintained that the "greater must care for the less." Furthermore, he continued, "we provide schools for the child. Instruction and discipline are compulsory, and it is well. But we forget that measured in the great scale of knowledge, there are always children and grownups, pupils and teachers, and age is nothing." Here, Abell captured the essence of Ford paternalism and of the relationship between dominant and subordinate groups in American society. Superiors considered their inferiors—Blacks, servants, women, and even workers—as no more than children. Indeed, the Ford immigrant worker was no more than a child to be socialized, in this case, Americanized, to the reigning social and cultural norms of American society.[23]

S. S. Marquis, the liberal clergyman, explained how the company coerced workers into attending their English lessons. "Attendance," he reported:

> is virtually compulsory. If a man declines to go, the advantages of the training are carefully explained to him. If he still hesitates, he is laid off and given uninterrupted meditation and reconsideration. When it comes to promotion, naturally prefer-

ence is given to the men who have cooperated with us in our work. This, also, has its effect.

In the early twentieth century, Ford officials duplicated the disciplinary patterns which early industrialists utilized in eighteenth-century England. The carrot and the stick rewarded or punished the worker as though he were an errant child.[24]

Gregory Mason, a strong advocate of Americanization programs, questioned "the grotesquely exaggerated patriotism in the Ford plant." In the course of the English lessons, "the pupils are told to 'walk to an American blackboard, take a piece of American chalk, and explain how the American workman walks to his American home and sits down with his American family to their good American dinner.' " "The first thing we teach them to say," Marquis related, "is 'I am a good American,' and then we try to get them to live up to that statement." "It is a very common thing," DeWitt noted, "to have a fellow born in Austria yell to a teacher passing by, 'We are all good Americans!' " In this period, Ford and other employers began to give good citizenship and Americanism their own definition. A Ford pamphlet noted:

> Automatically, upon graduation, the English School alumni become members of the American Club. At weekly meetings they practice speaking, reading, debating, and discuss points of history, civil government, and national problems of current interest.

By the end of the First World War, Americanism countered those social and economic philosophies which threatened managerial prerogatives of production, namely Bolshevism, socialism, and even trade unionism.[25]

The mass ritual of graduation was the most spectacular aspect of Americanization in the Ford factory. Ford English School graduates underwent a symbolic ritual which marked the transformation from immigrant to American. DeWitt described the ceremony as:

> a pageant in the form of a melting pot, where all the men descend from a boat scene representing the vessel on which they came over; down the gangway . . . into a pot 15 feet in diameter and 7½ feet high, which represents the Ford English School. Six teachers, three on either side, stir the pot with ten foot ladles

representing nine months of teaching in the school. Into the pot 52 nationalities with their foreign clothes and baggage go and out of the pot after vigorous stirring by the teachers comes one nationality, viz, American.

Marquis enriched this image and emphasized the conformity of the one nationality: "Presently the pot began to boil over and out came the men dressed in their best American clothes and waving American flags."[26]

Following this pageant, teachers and community leaders gave speeches which praised the virtues of American citizenship. When the graduation ceremony ended, all went on "a trip to some park, where American games are played by teachers and students for the rest of the day." In the evening, the company rewarded its volunteer teachers for their time and their efforts. It held "an entertainment and banquet for the volunteer instructors and their wives. The expense, of course, being paid by the company." At this celebration, DeWitt reported, "the teachers meet with Mr. Ford and other high officials of the company, and a great spirit of one for all and all for one predominates the entire evening."[27]

Americanization in the Ford factory was important for a variety of reasons. First, the Ford programs touched the lives of tens of thousands of Ford workers in its effort to influence those institutions which shaped immigrant working-class culture, particularly the family, the home, the neighborhood, and the factory. From 1915 to 1916, the company reported that some 16,000 workers graduated from the Ford English School. Moreover, Ford statistics indicated that while 35.5 percent of the workforce did not speak English in 1914, only 11.7 percent did not speak the language in 1917.[28]

Second, the Ford Americanization program indirectly captured the American imagination in the prewar years. The Ford program served as the model for a city-wide Americanization campaign in Detroit. And, in 1915, Detroit in turn became the model for the National Americanization Day Committee and its national campaign for the assimilation of immigrants into American society.[29]

Finally, Ford was neither alone nor entirely unique in its attempt to adapt immigrant workers to factory and industrial life. In fact, American industrial leaders and managers developed a new strategy for the management of an immigrant workforce in this period. Whereas the traditional managerial practice divided ethnic groups and played their national and cultural rivalries against one another, the new one emphasized conformity with American social, cultural, and industrial values. During the First World War, as manufacturers and others became increasingly apprehensive about aliens in their midst, they viewed Americanization as a means to remake immigrant workers into their image of the efficient and productive worker. In 1919, George F. Quimby, the keynote speaker for the National Conference on Americanization in Industries, emphasized that the proceedings should be "based on the fundamental principles of American life—a sound social order." In 1920, Peter Roberts gave American citizenship a broad social and economic definition. "Good citizenship," he noted, "means each one in his sphere keeping busy, doing honest work, and contributing to the sum total of wealth for the support of the nation." In the postwar labor upsurge, industrial leaders considered Americanization as a cure for the social ills of society.[30]

In many ways, Ford officials and factory managers considered the Five Dollar Day and the Sociological Department a success. And, they used statistical evidence to measure that success. Most significantly, it reduced the incredibly high rate of labor turnover. In 1913, the rate was a phenomenal 370 percent. It fell to about 54 percent in 1914 and dropped to a low of about 16 percent in 1915. During the First World War, it gradually rose to about 42 percent in 1917 and to about 51 percent in 1918. And, the latter figures included men who left to enter the armed forces. Additionally, the rate of absenteeism also decreased to more manageable proportions. In October 1913, this rate was about 10 percent; in October 1914, it was 2.5 percent.[31]

Furthermore, the productivity of Ford workers increased as a result of the monetary incentive and welfare work. "From the statistics at hand," a Ford pamphlet related:

we found an almost immediate increase in production. For instance, in the Motor Department, we found that with relatively the same number of men there was an output of 7200 parts in eight hours as against that of 6125 in nine hours.

It reported similar increases in the rates of production of radiators, fenders, and gasoline tanks. "These increases," it noted, "were produced with practically no additional increase in equipment." Ford seemed to find a secret to industrial success in shorter hours and increased production. "Increased production," the pamphlet concluded, "is the result of increased energy, and efficiency, and good will, plus improved methods and machinery."[32]

In January 1915, O. J. Abell assessed the first year of the "unorthodox and unprecedented plan of sharing profits" and summarized its positive influence on Ford profits and production. A comparison of the financial statements for September 1913 and September 1914 revealed "the remarkable increases in cash and every other 'assets' item." And, he added, "over one-half of the assets of the company exist in the form of cash or the most liquid securities." These assets increased from just over $35 million to over $61.6 million. At the same time, the record of production indicated a substantial increase despite changes and obstacles within the Highland Park factory. "In the past year," Abell reported:

> the Ford Company has added to its own factory operations all of the machine work formerly conducted by Dodge Brothers, the work of a large plant in itself; it has assumed the manufacture of several additional parts of its car, formerly purchased; it has shortened the hours of labor from 9 to 8; it has increased the daily production of cars fully 15 percent, and at the same time the number of employees is less by nearly 2,000.

Furthermore, Abell believed that "an additional thousand employees could be dispensed with tomorrow without affecting the production by as much as a single car."[33]

Also, Ford officials and investigators collected and tabulated "sociological" data on Ford workers from 1914 to 1917. After the Five Dollar Day, more and more American workers entered the Ford shops to obtain high wages. While approximately 75 percent of Ford workers were foreign born in 1914, only 58 percent were in 1916 and 60 percent were in 1917. Ford statistics also demonstrated an increase in the average size of bank accounts of workers from $75.20 in 1914 to $223.29 in 1917. The same period saw increases in the average amount of life insurance, the average value of homes owned or on contract, and the average amount of monthly rent or board. And, a higher percentage of Ford workers had bank accounts, owned or were purchasing homes, and had life insurance. This financial information, Ford officials believed, showed the increased prosperity of the Ford workforce. Furthermore, more immigrant workers spoke English and were naturalized. And, Ford workers improved their home conditions, neighborhoods, and habits. The proportions of workers classified as "good" in these areas ranged from about 80 to 90 percent in 1917. Finally, the number of married workers increased from about 59 percent in 1914 to about 70 percent in 1917. In the eyes of Ford officials, these social and economic statistics indicated a more stable, more reliable, and more responsible workforce.[34]

In addition, many outside commentators considered the Ford welfare program a successful effort to reform and to remake the Ford workforce. On the Five Dollar Day, Harold Whiting Slausen noted the relationship between high wages and degraded work:

> But as much as the monotony of each man's work might be expected to lead to discontent, the prospect of wages double those that could be obtained in any other factory for the same work serves as a deterrent and positions in the Ford factory are eagerly sought for. This has resulted in the elimination of what had previously been one of the serious problems of the organization—the instability of the personnel of the workmen.

On sociological work, H. F. Porter believed that Ford investigators had to pry into "[m]en's private affairs." And, he provided the justification: "Men, the slaves of all manner of bad habits, the victims of new-world vices and old-world standards of living, had to be made to see the worthwhile side of manly attributes and decent, clean home conditions." In his opinion, the Ford welfare program was "practicable and effective social welfare work." Also, Ida M. Tarbell, the Progressive social critic, visited the Highland Park factory with the intention to expose the abuses of the Ford system. After her visit, she told the Detroit Executive Club: "I don't care what you call it—philanthropy, paternalism, autocracy—the results which are being obtained are worth all you can set against them, and the errors in the plan will provoke their own remedies."[35]

Some still voiced criticism about the Ford labor policies. For example, an investigator visited the Ford plant for the Commission on Industrial Relations. He reported, "To the student of industrial democracy the Ford works offer very little. Everything is being done from above. The role of the employe is merely so to mold his conduct and personal habits." In order to counter such opposition, Ford officials marshaled positive testimonials from middle-class community leaders. "The doctors, lawyers, and businessmen of the city," a Ford investigator related, "are willing to cooperate with the investigators at all times." Moreover, he added, they "are heartily in sympathy with the work being done here." And, local governmental, religious, and educational leaders praised the social uplift of Ford workers and their families. For instance, a Polish priest remarked: "The investigation . . . has resulted most favorably in this parish. Probably the most noticeable feature is the decrease in heavy drinking, which is characteristic among our people. Sobriety is now the rule rather than the exception." And, many other community leaders expressed similar sentiments on Ford sociological work.[36]

Nonetheless, Ford workers grumbled and griped, and knocked and kicked about Ford sociological investigations. Some changes in Ford welfare policies reflected this working-class antipathy and dissatisfaction with the welfare program. In 1914, Lee cautioned investigators about probing too deeply into the personal lives of Ford workers. In 1916, Marquis chose the name Educational Department to avoid the unfavorable connotations of the older name. And, at the same time, "investigators" became "advisors." In 1917, he expressed a "desire to eliminate as far as possible all unnecessary investigations." From this point on, his department no longer investigated workers with more than a year's service with the company. And, William Klann provided the views of his workers:

The Sociological Department helped a lot of cases and a lot of cases it didn't help. Some of the fellows felt that they didn't want that done and they wouldn't have the fellows come to the house., They asked them whether they were married or not, and if they weren't they would have a minister marry them. And, they didn't like those things. . . . They felt they were interfering in their private lives.

William Logan, the Auto Workers' Union leader, focused directly on the question of Ford paternalism. "The workers," he said, "are not little children who need some fatherly minds to guide them, to tell them how much they may earn and what they shall do with it." Indeed, the Ford sociological investigations certainly generated a general and pervasive uneasiness among Ford workers.[37]

In 1915, the Detroit *Journal* reported on many letters received from "disgruntled job seekers." These letters mirrored some disaffection with Ford policies and programs. One worker criticized Ford discipline and employment policies:

. . . do the inspectors and investigators really pick out the most needy or do they select those who will slave in the foundry eight hours a day and be yelled at and cursed at by their boss and say nothing for fear of losing their positions? This last I know to be a fact, for a certain man in my neighborhood with a family of seven children to look after was dogged so he just had to quit and let his family suffer hardships until he found something else to do.

Another provided a catalogue of grievances about the regimen of the Ford shops:

If you forget to ring up your clock card in the morning and evening you lose a day's wages even if you have a time card to show. Four or five minutes late, two hours docked. No helpers for mechanics. Multitudes of unwritten laws. No redress for wrongs. No safety first, although there is a mere pretense. A man who has never been a mechanic until he enrolled with Ford's factory will receive bigger wages than an expert. In fact, Ford's factory is a grouch hole and no place for a sane man.

And, still another worker complained that only the hardy and healthy could tolerate Ford assembly lines. "Ford's system" he noted, "is such that a man who dissipates on booze or dope may be detected by his lack of efficiency."[38]

Of course, members of the Automobile Workers' Union also criticized the Ford sociological program and conditions in the shops. One auto worker complained about the six-month probationary period required for profit-sharers. During this period, the workers received their wages and not their profits. He noted that in some shops with periods of "rush work," this period was "the secret part [of the Ford plan] where the automobile worker gets the worst of it." New workers had "to make good to qualify for the $5.00 day." And, frequently, "a percentage of the men are usually compelled to quit, being physically unable to stand the pace, or all of the work is cleaned up and the men are laid off and Mr. Ford has the entire amount done at 30c per hour." W. E. Schneeberg, another au-tomobile worker, praised the high income, but called for more humane working conditions. "Although the Ford workers are the highest paid in the automobile industry," he wrote, "they will see that such deadly monotony is not the best thing for their health. . . ."

He concluded: "This big pay goes all right, but the conditions must be more human to be ideal." And, William A. Logan believed: "There is a limit to human endurance. Any man or set of men who are keyed up to the last notch will eventually break down, it matters not whether they get $1 or $10 per day for their work." Generally, an unsettled and ominous mood characterized worker reactions to, and dissatisfaction with, the sociological investigations, the Five Dollar Day, and the shop conditions.[39]

More unsettled and ominous was the financial and economic status of the entire Ford Profit-sharing Plan. It was an expensive program and costs grew as the Ford workforce expanded. Also, a tightening Detroit labor market forced officials to increase the basic wage rate. This decreased the profit rate as a proportion of the Five Dollar Day. In 1914, Ford officials set aside $10 million for its welfare program. Earlier, the employment office estimated that the reduction of turnover alone would save $5 million due to reduced costs for hiring and training new workers. In fact, in 1914, the company paid out about $5.8 million in profits to workers in the Highland Park plant and about $8.4 million to all employees in all Ford establishments. And, in 1917, it paid out almost $20.7 million to Highland Park workers and nearly $26.3 million to all Ford employees. Added to the administrative costs of the Sociological Department, this represented a considerable financial expenditure and presented a possible area for reduced costs as the automobile industry became more competitive at the end of the decade.[40]

At the same time, the Detroit labor market wreaked havoc on Ford wage policies. In 1914, approximately one-half of the unskilled worker's income was wages and one-half was profits. This provided an enormous inducement for workers to change their attitudes and habits, or, at least, to give the appearance of change. In 1916, the wage policy changed in order to meet a severe shortage of workers and to remain competitive with other automobile and metal industries in Detroit. "In order that men shall receive during the first six months of their services, approximately the same amount as their efforts would net them in the labor market," the company decided "to pay newcomers at the rate of 43c per hour, or $3.44 for an eight hour day." This meant that an unskilled worker's daily share of the profits was $1.44 instead of the earlier $2.66. In 1917, Ford officials lowered the minimum age for profit-sharers from twenty-one to eighteen and eliminated unnecessary investigations. In 1918, it raised the minimum wage rate to 50c per hour, or $4.00 for an eight hour day. At this time, a worker's profits amounted to only 20 percent of his income. Finally, in 1919, officials established the Six Dollar Day in their effort to retain a meaningful incentive for the welfare program. However, it did not go far enough. Wartime inflation so brutally undermined the value of the Ford worker's dollar that, at the time, the Ford plan needed a Ten Dollar Day to maintain the same inducement as in 1914.[41]

So, as the United States entered the World War in 1917, the Ford profit-sharing program was on unsettled ground. To be sure, it produced some positive benefits and accomplishments. Most notably, the rates of absenteeism and turnover fell dramatically and the labor force was much more stable than in 1913. And, productivity also rose to more satisfactory levels. Furthermore, Ford workers demonstrated a marked improvement towards a middle-class standard of living. Nonetheless, problems loomed on the horizon. Ford paternalism apparently altered the actions and behavior of Ford workers, but it did not capture their thoughts and feelings about the welfare program. It treated them as individuals and perhaps solved the outward manifestations of some individual problems such as absenteeism and turnover. But, paternalism did not respond to other personal and social needs for dignity or self-respect. For example, what did the Ford worker and his wife think or feel when a middle-class investigator questioned their conjugal relationship, or what were the inner thoughts and feelings of the immigrant worker forced to abandon his personal history and to participate in a humiliating public ritual of Americanization? Nor did paternalism satisfy the needs for individual or collective self-initiative and self-expression. How fast did a worker or groups of workers produce when the foreman did not look in their direction? How many machines broke down because of a conscious mistake? And, what did the worker really think about trade unions and socialists? For Ford officials, the war-time experience revealed that national identity and consciousness remained an important aspect of the immigrant worker's world. And, it also indicated pro-union and even radical sentiments existed in the Ford workforce. In the end, the World War demonstrated the carefully architected Ford program of social control did not win completely the hearts and minds of Ford workers.

8. The End of Ford Paternalism: World War, Labor Militancy, and Political Repression

I don't care what you say but I say that it is a damn dirty trick to squeal on a man and I think that he is the meanest thief that works at night.... This government is so damned rotten that a man can't say a word anymore![1]—A Ford worker

The First World War had a profound impact on American political, social, and intellectual life. It marked the end of American innocence. It brought a new toughness to American social and industrial relations. The Great War was a watershed for American social and political history. The prewar period was the Progressive Era. Its attitude towards the plight of labor and the poor was idealistic, reform-minded, and sympathetic. In contrast, the postwar years were the "Lean Years." The tone of the period was hard-nosed, pragmatic, and tough. And, the Ford labor programs mirrored their times. In the course of the war, the Ford labor policies underwent a transition from a variant of welfare capitalism, which captured the mood of the Progressive Era, to a version of the American Plan, which typified the more recalcitrant employer attitudes of the twenties.[2]

For workers, the war meant a deterioration of working and living conditions as goods and materials went to European battlefields. While American industries geared up for war production, the new technologies and new forms of work organization, which had their origins in factories such as Ford's in the prewar decade, became more and more common features of the American industrial landscape. With increased war production, American workers saw their jobs change, skills diluted, and pace of work intensified. At the same time, real wages declined with war-induced inflation as European battlefields commanded a larger share of American agricultural and industrial resources. This inflation eroded the modest and marginal standards of living of skilled American, and less-skilled immigrant, workers. Consequently, native-born and foreign-born workers became increasingly militant in order to defend or to recapture their earlier working conditions and standards of living.[3]

Additionally, the European war had a significant impact on the attitudes of immigrant workers towards the United States and their homelands. As immigrant workers took sides on the World War, their national identities and feelings of national pride vigorously reemerged. German and Austro-Hungarian workers sometimes sympathized with kin and homeland and thus with America's enemies. So too did Irish workers who often sided with Great Britain's archrival in the international arena. Also, Southern and Eastern European workers tied their national and cultural aspirations to different dominant powers in the region. The war also bred revolution. And, with the Russian Revolution in 1917, many immigrant workers, and some American workers too, tied their hopes and dreams to the creation of a new social and economic order. For employers, this chaotic situation called for renewed and more intense efforts to bring immigrant and other workers within the confines of the dominant social, cultural, and political norms.[4]

Finally, the World War tremendously expanded the power and authority of the national government. As new federal agencies emerged to organize and to rationalize the American war effort, the federal government asserted its right and obligation to defend national and public interests. For example, the War Labor Board became the public arbiter of the contentious relations between labor and capital. In order to insure working-class support of the war, it often recognized organized labor's demands for higher wages, shorter hours, improved working conditions, and most important collective negotiations with their representatives. But, the rapid extension of federal power also had its negative side for labor in the appeals for increased war production, patriotic unity, and moderation in their demands. A repressive conformity characterized Americanization campaigns, periodic subscription drives for Liberty Loans, rigid enforcement of conscription laws, and general repression of the Industrial Workers of the World, the Socialist Party, and other critics of the American war effort.[5]

In 1914, the Ford high-income and welfare policies contained or reduced many of the earlier labor problems. Yet, in 1917, some problems reemerged or remained unsolved. For example, labor turnover increased, although not to the inordinately high levels of 1913. It rose from a low of 16 percent in 1915 to 24 percent in 1916,

42 percent in 1917, and 51 percent in 1918. But, military quits accounted for 7 or 8 percentage points in the 1917 and 1918 figures. Also, throughout the war, low worker productivity plagued Ford foremen, supervisors, and factory managers. Of course, the Highland Park plant produced helmets, ambulances, trucks, and aircraft engines for the war effort. These different products required different manufacturing techniques. Naturally, this reduced worker productivity. Also, soldiering and output restriction continued to trouble Ford managers. Moreover, the wartime social and industrial conditions produced fragmented immigrant loyalties and increased worker discontent. Under these conditions, working-class militancy and radicalism grew among the deskilled and unskilled Ford workers. The skilled American or German craftsmen favored a return to former shop methods and conditions. The unskilled Southern and Eastern European specialists recognized that the operation of a specialized machine no longer opened the door to a skilled trade. The result was a militant upsurge for industrial unionism in the automobile industry.[6]

In 1914, Ford labor policies temporarily thwarted the organizational campaigns of the Industrial Workers of the World, the American Federation of Labor's Metal Trades Department, and the Carriage, Wagon, and Automobiles Workers' Union. But, wartime conditions made skilled and unskilled automobile workers restive. The small CWAWU gradually grew to threaten managerial efforts to dominate and to control workers and industrial processes. In 1916, a small group of veteran carriage and wagon unionists reestablished the Detroit local on the basis of militant industrial unionism. It rapidly mushroomed into the largest automobile workers' local. The national CWAWU's successful organizational campaigns resulted in repeated jurisdictional dispute with AFL craft unions. In 1918, the AFL revoked its charter. The socialist CWAWU leaders formed an independent union—the United Automobile, Aircraft, and Vehicle Workers' Union—with its headquarters in Detroit. In 1919, this Auto Workers' Union had 40,000 members in Detroit. (The International Association of Machinists, the next largest union attached to the automobile industry, had only 9,000 members in the city at the time.) Firmly committed to industrial unionism, the AWU Detroit local was a fiercely democratic rank-and-file organization. Shop committees elected a delegate to the local's board of administration for every ten members. A rank-and-file decision to strike committed the leadership to follow and to support that course of action. As the largest automobile manufacturer, the Ford Motor Company had the most to lose. And, the AWU ultimately, though indirectly, challenged the Ford enterprise.[7]

Underneath the veneer of paternalism and good-will, traditional forms of discipline and authority prevailed in the Ford shops. In 1914, H. L. Arnold reported that "a workman must show a very decided incapacity before he is finally discharged." Naturally, Ford managers made every effort to reduce turnover. "But wilful insubordination is, of course, absolutely intolerable," Arnold added, "and Ford workers must be, first of all, absolutely docile." Later, he suggested the reason for this docility: "Mutinous labor nullified, in large part, the gains which can be made by good management of willing labor." In 1915, O. J. Abell admitted that despite good intentions, some Ford employees got "drunk" or were "lazy or incompetent." But, these "offenses," Abell continued, indicated:

> a need for getting a new hold on the employee and a need for giving him some new help. This help is not likely to be of the parlor variety. The dirtiest, meanest job in the foundry is the probable lot of the man who has been too lazy to do a day's work at an easier task. The discipline is not vindictive but carefully chosen for its probable effect.[8]

Finally, George Brown, a Ford office worker, recalled an incident which revealed a combination of discipline and deep fear within the Ford shops. Despite a safety device, a foreign worker cut off his finger at his machine. Plant superintendent P. E. Martin and his assistant Sorenson wanted the worker to show them how it happened so the device could be corrected. The workman showed them and cut off another finger. "He understood," Brown related, "they actually wanted him to demonstrate how he cut the tip of his finger off." Obviously, the plant managers and the immigrant worker failed to communicate. Nevertheless, the docile worker did not refuse the wishes of his superiors.[9]

Industrial espionage was also an early activity in the Ford shops. As early as 1906, a Ford labor spy reported on the "industrial efficiency" of workers in the old Ford plant. Later, William Klann, the general foremen of motor assembly, indicated that espionage was an important feature in the day-to-day administration of the Highland Park plant. "We always had spies or agents," Klann recalled, "to get information on the union." He detailed an informal network of foremen, sub-foremen, and other loyal workers who reported to him. "I had," he remembered, "twenty-five fellows working for me." And, Klann sent his information to the watchman's department. "We didn't get written reports from these fellows," he added:

> They were all verbal . . . There were certain men who weren't going to do much work the next day; they were going to lay down so you had better put a man to watch them. . . . So we put a man there who would work fast and then we'd see what they would say to him. . . . They'd talk back to him and we'd trace the story down and fire the man.

Although hardly systematic, the system was effective. And, with such tactics, the company prevented the formation of personal and informal networks in the shop which could grow into the nucleus of a trade union organization.[10]

With the American entry into the European war in April 1917, Ford labor policies gradually began to change. Managerial attitudes towards workers became tougher. Until this time always in the background, more authoritarian and more repressive labor policies moved to the foreground. Two national laws, the Espionage Act and the Sedition Act, caused the shift in Ford labor policy. The Espionage Act of 1917 forbade the advocacy of "treason, insurrection, or forcible resistance to any law of the United States" and banned criticism of or interference with the military or naval forces or with their efforts at recruitment and enlistment. The Sedition Act of 1918 provided severe punishment for any person who

> shall willfully utter, print, write, or publish disloyal, profane, scurrilous, or abusive language about the government of the United States, or the Constitution of the United States, or the military or naval forces of the United States, or the flag of the United States, or the uniform of the Army or Navy. . . .

In addition the law forbade any language which brought these institutions "into contempt, scorn, contumely, or disrepute." Under extremely broad judicial interpretation, both of these laws were used to prosecute German, Austrian, and Hungarian immigrant workers, members of the IWW and the Socialist Party, and finally, any worker who voiced discontent or dissatisfaction with the war or American society.[11]

The American Protective League (APL) implemented and enforced the stringent national policies at the local and community level. Created as "a semiofficial auxilliary of the Justice Department," the APL was a nationwide voluntary organization of patriots who fought the World War on the domestic front. The organization rapidly grew to about 1,200 separate units with approximately 250,000 members. Indeed, a vast network of spies and informants reached down to the local level in American industrial communities.[12]

Emerson Hough, the official APL historian, detailed the wide range of the patriotic organization's activities. Its principal task, he wrote, was "the collection of evidence, and nothing else." In collaboration with the Department of Justice's Bureau of Investigation, Military Intelligence, and local law enforcement agencies, the APL collected information on diverse anti-patriotic and anti-American activities throughout the war. "Limited as its power was," Hough reported, "it really saved the day for our hard-pressed country." He noted that it captured thousands of draft evaders, assisted in the internment of enemy aliens, and apprehended numerous plotters and conspirators. "It kept down the danger of the disloyal element," Hough boasted:

> and held Germany in America safe. It is by no means too much to say that much of the Kaiser's disappointment over his German-American revolt was due not so much to loyalty to the American flag . . . as it was to fear of the silent and stern hand searching out in the dark and taking first one and then another German or pro-German away. . . . It was *fear* that held our enemy population down—*fear* and nothing else.

The APL was an early institutional expression of the same mass hysteria which culminated in the postwar "Red Scare." Throughout the United States, the APL and national, state, and local law enforcement officials instilled fear into and silenced dissident American and immigrant workers.[13]

In Detroit, the APL rapidly expanded into a substantial organization due to its industrial character, large foreign population, and numerous military contracts. F. M. Randall first directed the Detroit Division of the APL. Later, Frank H. Croul, a former police commissioner, succeeded him. Its offices, "adjacent to and intercommunicating with" those of the Bureau of Investigation, occupied the entire third floor of a downtown office building. In 1918, the Detroit APL Financial Committee detailed future plans:

... we expect to have 2500 in the organization, divided into Fifty Divisions of fifty men each. Each Division will be under the guidance of a Captain, with a Lieutenant for each ten men in each Division, in order to attain greater efficiency in the assignment of work.

In its first nine months, the Detroit APL conducted 90 percent of the total number of investigations handed to the Bureau of Investigation. At the end of the war, it had nearly 4,000 men and had conducted more than 30,000 investigations.[14]

In industrial Detroit, the "Plants Protection Department" performed the principal investigative work of the APL. This department stationed operatives in each important factory of the city. "A thorough covering of each plant was made," Hough noted, "and a captain of the APL was stationed in each factory, where he had entire supervision and reported to ... the League's main office." And, he added, "It was not unusual for a man to be brought in for an interview, and many such cases were turned over to the Department of Justice and the District Attorney's office." In addition, the Detroit Committee on Protective Measures planned to maintain a centralized file on foreign workers. "This Committee," the Financial Committee noted, "will also index and make an exhaustive record of foreign labor here, so that each manufacturer in addition to his own records, may be able to know and to check ... the loyalty and exact status of every employee."[15]

In the Highland Park plant, the Sociological Department served to coordinate and to centralize the Ford network. The Ford Motor Company was the Detroit APL's Eighth Industrial Division. A Sociological Department investigator, E. F. Clemett, noted as Captain 90, directed four Lieutenants in this Division. Two Lieutenants, Alex G. Spark, Lieutenant 38, with the Superintendent's Office, and Fred R. Gillen, Lieutenant 30, with the Sociological Department, were Ford employees. These three Ford managers, Clemett, Spark, and Gillen, supervised the Ford APL network which included about 100 operatives in forty-five different departments and shops of the Ford factory. These operatives reported on the activities of their fellow workers in the various shops and departments of the Ford factory.[16]

Some sections of the factory had more operatives than others. Since the Employment Department hired the unknown new workers, it had the most operatives—seventeen. Other shops or departments with more than one APL operative included transmission parts—six; main tool room—five; repair, shipping, motor assembly, maintenance, power station tools, foundry, and educational (i.e., sociological)—three each; and factory accounting, tool grinding, factory transportation, top department, machine repair, triple gears, stock, truck, tool stock, and photographic—two each. Indeed, Ford APL spies and agents kept their superiors well informed about conditions in the Highland Park factory.[17]

Members of the Sociological and Employment Departments had access to the thousands of individual "Records of Investigation" maintained since the inauguration of the Ford Profit-sharing Plan. When an APL operative reported on the suspicious statement or behavior of a Ford worker, his superior pulled the workman's file and started a new record with his background and an account of the incident. For example, the new record would contain the worker's name and badge number and then a list of information from his Sociological Department "Record of Investigation," such as the date hired, age, nationality, religion, marital status, dependents, how long the worker was in the United States and in Detroit, whether or not the worker spoke English or was naturalized, and a statement on the worker's thrift and habits. In addition, the new record contained a description of the statement or activity which resulted in the APL report. This new record on the worker often passed into the hands of the Department of Justice, military intelligence officers, and local law enforcement officers.[18]

Aside from E. F. Clemett and F. R. Gillin, a number of other sociological department investigators worked for the APL in the Ford factory. These included G. M. Rounds, who was in charge of special investigations, W. M. Purvis, an APL operative, J. S. Brooks, and H. E. Squier. Their names all appeared on APL reports. On one occasion, a report with information gleaned from a worker's Record of Investigation "was shown to Naval Intelligence at the request of Dr. Marquis." Naval Intelligence, said G. M. Rounds, requested that "the Ford Motor Co. place a trusted man on the job near him and advise them (Naval Intelligence) in case any evidence of pro-Germanism or sabotage be found." Most often, however, the information gathered in the new record circulated between the Ford Sociological Department and Detroit APL Chief F. M. Randall and Detroit Bureau of Investigation agent Herbert C. Cole.[19]

In the Ford APL records, the most common complaint against individual workers was their expression of "pro-German" and "Prussian" sentiments. For the most part, German and German-American workers publicly voiced their opinions on the progress of the war. With social, cultural, and other familial ties to Germany, many of these workers had divided loyalties on the outcome of the war and verbally expressed their sympathies for the Fatherland. In one case, "a very pro-German" worker simply boasted that he would return to Germany after the war ended. Another worker "habitually" brought "newspapers relating to any German success" into his workshop. He also stated that "he would not allow his son to fight for any damned country." Often the information was inaccurate. E. F. Clemett noted that a worker, who was "pro-German in his remarks," had a "burnt wood cut of the German flag in his room." A subsequent investigation noted that this German flag was really a Norwegian flag. S. S. Marquis reported an "ex-Austrian worth keeping under observation." The man, he noted, was a "rabid pro-German and a bad actor." Dr. J. E. Mead, the director of the Medical Department, and an APL operative wrote on a Ford worker: "This employee wears the Kaiser's photograph in his watch charm and is a rabid pro-German."[20]

Sometimes, the vindictive assessments followed Ford workers to other jobs. A foreman reported on one of his workers who refused to purchase a Liberty Bond. Six days later, Harry Sommers, an APL operative in the Employment Department, pulled his card as a "five day quit." "The spirit of Patriotism in the shop," Sommers commented, "was too much for him to stand, him being a German." Three months later H. E. Squier sent an employment reference for the worker at the request of a Standard Oil service station. The short reference read: "He left our employ June 28th, 1917. German sympathizer."[21]

Many other German workers expressed nationalistic sentiments and pride and often praised Germany and its institutions. One German worker asked a fellow worker, who he thought to be German, how he liked the job? When the worker replied that "he didn't like it because there was such a quantity of the same thing. . . ," the German worker then said, "Nobody likes this government work. I am just laying down on the job myself, and I know others around here that are doing the same thing." He later asked, "Why should we help this government kill our brothers over there? The Germans are good people. They have the best mechanics in this country. Germans made this country what it is."[22]

Another German worker criticized the "Michigan state troops" as a "wash woman affair." He boasted, "I belonged to a regular army, the Prussian army that walked through Belgium on time. I am proud of it. They will need you on the western front soon because Prussia is going to give America a d— good licking." This "strong German sympathizer," noted Lieutenant 2814, also criticized the American educational system. "The Germans," he also said, "have about 90 percent of the people educated while the United States has only about 30 percent educated." Another worker claimed that he would not send his children "to an American school because they learned to salute the flag." F. R. Gillen referred this case to Herbert Cole, the Detroit Bureau of Investigation agent.[23]

Many immigrant workers merely made negative comments about American citizenship or anti-patriotic statements. "The United States government," proclaimed one Romanian worker, "can hang me before I become a citizen." "To Hell with Liberty Bonds," said a Hungarian worker, "to Hell with the [naturalization] papers and the United States army. I would not belong to this country." Alex Spark noted that he laid off the worker and turned the case over to Herbert Cole. "I will f— the United States," said an Austrian sweeper. "This country has no business in the war." A German worker said, "For all my citizenship papers represent, I might as well wipe my a— with them." Moreover, he said that he "would like to see the German Kaiser on the job in the United States to run things in a German way." An informant reported that a German worker "has not taken out naturalization papers, is not an American citizen and claims that he would rather be shot in this country than go to France to fight."[24]

The Ford APL operatives also recorded critical statements or verbal threats made against President Wilson. Because Wilson campaigned for reelection under the slogan that he "kept America out of the war," many workers felt that he betrayed the close mandate of his election. In the cylinder department, a salaried employee, reported Captain 4, made the remark "that he would rather kiss the Kaiser's ass than take his hat off to Mr. Wilson." A native American die sinker in the tool room stated that "Germany ought to whip the United States and that President Wilson should be assassinated." Operative 831 reported on a German worker: "On one occasion he said that 'President Wilson ought to be shot.' His reason for so saying was because the United States sided with the allies and not with Germany."[25]

The Highland Park police reported to the company that a Ford worker "refused to rise during the Star Spangled Banner." In another case, an accuser stated that a Ford worker "wiped his shoes with an American flag." The record noted that the worker was "severely questioned and given release" by the Bureau of Investigation. Federal agent Johnson concluded that the "accusation" was an incident of "personal spite." G. M. Rounds, a Sociological Department investigator, noted: "Appears okay in regard to his loyalty."[26]

Additionally many immigrant workers came to the United States to earn money in order to establish a new and better life in the old country after several years of hard work and saving. When the war broke out in 1914 and closed the European borders, foreign workers found themselves trapped in America far from their homes and families. With the American declaration of war and the mass patriotic hysteria, they found themselves required to pledge their loyalty to America and to abandon their allegiances to their native lands. Naturally, many were resentful.

An Austrian worker refused to subscribe to Thrift Stamps. "To Hell with the United States," he proclaimed. "All that I am here for is what I can get out of it. When the war is over I am going back to the old country." On another occasion, the same worker said: "F— this country; I wouldn't fight for it anyway." Rounds noted that this worker undermined authority and discipline in his shop. The worker "assumed a jaunty defiant manner which has a very bad effect on his fellow workmen." Another workman also "came to the United States just to make a stake." He reportedly told a fellow worker, "You go to war before I do and you shoot bullets while I am making $5.00 a day here." The workman "always refused to subscribe to the various drives." He was "the cause of constant friction in his department and a wet blanket on government efforts to finance the war." Of course, he paid the economic consequences for the expression of his thoughts. "On the above data," G. M. Rounds noted, "I recommend that this man be at once removed from the Ford Motor Company payroll." In another case, Mr. Jas. A. Robinson, a local draft board director, reported an Austrian Pole to Ford officials. In a pre-induction questionnaire, the Ford worker expressed "unfriendly sentiments toward this country." Moreover, he refused "to aid or defend it." He claimed "to be in this country only to make money."[27]

Many Ford workers, native-born Americans and foreign-born immigrants, voiced anger and hostility toward the war-related fundraising drives in the Highland Park factory. American and immigrant workers forcefully protested the organized campaigns to finance the war through Liberty Loans and the similar drives to aid American soldiers through subscriptions for the Red Cross and YMCA. In one case, a Bulgarian worker, the foundry supervisor reported:

> made fun of and tried to discourage workmen working around him from buying Liberty Bonds, when the salesmen were in his department selling bonds. He told the other men that if they bought Liberty Bonds they all would lose their money and the only reason they were buying them was because they were afraid of losing their jobs.

Earlier, the report noted, "when subscriptions were being taken up for the Red Cross," the Bulgarian and another worker "did their utmost to discourage the other workmen from giving to the Red Cross." The foundry supervisor concluded, "This man seems to be the ring leader and believe he is a very undesirable alien and a traitor."[28] On the basis of this report, the Ford officials discharged the worker.

Moreover, the Ford supervisors constantly applied pressure to Ford workers so that they would purchase Liberty Bonds or donate to the YMCA or Red Cross. "After much controversy," the report on a strong-willed worker noted, "he purchased a bond and afterwards tore up the strips and threw them at the bond salesman." For this, the company transferred the worker to a "harder job." Some time later, the worker's foreman told Ford officials that he "absolutely refused to contribute a day's pay to the YMCA." The worker, the foreman reported, "again claims poverty." The foreman "offered Sunday overtime to earn the money to contribute" and the worker "eventually decided to sign the YMCA card." A German worker said that "he had a father and brothers in Germany and that he would not buy any [bonds]." He also claimed that "he is a socialist and would not buy any." Disciplinary foreman, William Klann, pressured the worker in his native language, but he still refused. The company fired him "on account of his pro-German attitude."[29]

On the YMCA fund, one worker said that "he would be damned if he would give a damned cent and anybody is a fool to give their money to such damned schemers." In another instance, an American foreman sided with the men in his shop. Operative 832 reported that the foreman was reluctant to ask his men to contribute to the

YMCA campaign. Asked about how the drive was coming among the men in his shop, the foreman replied:

> Oh, I did not keep cards and I will not ask my men to sign them because I will not sign under any circumstances. Even if it was a case of this card and my job, to hell with The Ford Motor Company and anything they are doing.[30]

A Russian Pole refused to make a contribution to the Red Cross. He stated that "he was going back to the old country and he did not care for this country." In the end, under pressure, he conceded that "he would give one dollar if we insisted on it." H. J. Emerson labeled the worker "undesirable." Another worker said, "To Hell with the Red Cross." He did not contribute "because they refused to help him 3 or 4 years ago when he was down and out." Moreover, "if they don't want me here," he said "they should ship him back to the old country. . . ."[31]

The APL reports also indicated that socialist ideals and principles frequently motivated Ford workers in their support for Germany, their anti-American attitudes and statements, and their opposition to the fund raising drives. A German worker told an informant that he "is a German socialist and has no use for the military clique; that the people of Germany will before long realize that they are misled and that socialism in Germany will overthrow militarism." A German tool-maker was "a most radical socialist and Prussian believer." Two Ford disciplinarians, Hartner and Klann, "harangued him for an hour to force him to buy a Liberty Bond." The worker responded that he "would take a more active part in socialistic work after the war."[32]

An American worker, H. J. Emerson reported, "absolutely refused to purchase a Liberty Bond," because "he did not think this country should be embroiled in this war." This American agitator, another informant reported, was

> altogether too loud and open in his speech against this country. . . . Whenever he can get someone to listen to him he is ready to denounce this country stating that he would not fight for it and he has contributed absolutely nothing to Liberty Bonds, Red Cross, or YMCA.

Alex Spark interviewed the worker and noted that he "admits that he is a regular reader of literature of a socialistic nature, but does not approve of the IWW method." Another informant concluded, "This man is an IWW or a socialist."[33]

The Ford officials and their informers maintained a special watch for workers who favored or advocated the ideas of the Industrial Workers of the World. One informant described a Ford worker as "a rank IWW and an agitator." He noted that this worker "is pretty sly when he has the least suspicion that a person is trying to lead him on." And, H. J. Emerson accused a native American worker of being "either an active or passive member of the I.W.W. or a Socialist, or both, as he has on many occasions upheld both against that of lawful government and society." Also, F. R. Gillen reported a toolmaker to federal agent H. J. Cole for "comments in praise of the IWW." "The IWW should go on with their work," stated the toolmaker, "and show that the men cannot be made to go to war. . . ." Another worker stated that he was "a friend of the IWW because they did more for the working men than anything else." Still another Ford worker, an American, commented on the impact of the wartime repression and on the relationship between American workers and the IWW. Operative 841 reported that the worker "said he was formerly an IWW but dropped on account of the war, as they dealt too hard with the members when arrested, but said he intended taking out another membership as soon as the war closed."[34]

A number of Ford workers also made critical comments and statements about capitalism. Lieutenant 2814 reported on an American worker who became involved in an "argument about capitalists." In a heated exchange, the informant stated, the worker "passed the remark that 'Mr. Ford Was a G— d— son of a b— ['] and further stated that he believed Germany and her allies were right and that if he were a young man he would refuse to don a uniform and fight." Another American refused to buy a Liberty Bond "on the grounds that he is not in sympathy with the government." According to Lieutenant 30, the worker claimed that "the bond issue is a scheme to enslave workmen and make them pay the debt of a capitalist war." He also stated that "he does not consider it necessary 'to purchase his liberty.' " Lieutenant 30 concluded that "this man belongs in the class that is attempting to hinder the government." In another case, Operative 30, dictated the statement of an English worker in the tool room. "This government," the worker said, "is not fighting for democracy but for capitalists." On another occasion, the same worker stated: "They ought to set J. Pierpont Morgan up in front of a wall with a ten-pound gun in front of him."[35]

G. M. Rounds, an investigator with the Sociological Department, reported on the subversive activities of an American worker and also suggested the appropriate discipline for him. The worker refused to purchase a Liberty Bond. Moreover, Rounds noted that the "man customarily lectured on Sunday to crowds at Riopelle and Davison streets during the past year." This street agitator, he wrote,

> is perfectly willing to work as an unskilled worker on one of our soft jobs, to grab off $5.00 per day, while the Ford Motor Company continues to manufacture the sinews of war for the United States but he is unwilling to loan the United States a small part of that $5.00 to help the United States in this war.

While the American citizen had "his constitutional privileges," he observed, "he is still an undesirable citizen of this country from any angle. Cooperation and wholehearted support on the part of each man is desirable in any nation or organization." Since the worker held an easy job, Rounds suggested the way to discipline the dissident worker. "If this company views a man refusing to cooperate but getting specially desirable work in the light of the bad example to those who do cooperate," Rounds concluded, "I recommend that the above employee be transferred to one of the less desirable jobs, and some loyal cooperating employee be given his place.[36]

Interestingly, Ford officials turned high rates of efficiency and productivity into the patriotic duty of Ford workers. Thus, they interpreted their workers' tendencies toward soldiering and output restriction as examples of treasonous behavior. Furthermore, they raised the specter of IWW sabotage. Hence, the "conscientious withdrawal of efficiency" made IWW sympathizers into agents of the German government. In this atmosphere, every suspicious activity which retarded productivity, from the individual workman who "laid down on the job" to the worker who encouraged others not to work overtime, became a conscious and treasonous act of sabotage.

For example, an American worker, who worked in the Ford shop which produced Liberty engines for military aircraft, had an "oiler's job in the Crankshaft Dept." "This man," L. B. Scofield reported to Alex Spark, "walked around at least two weeks without any oil in his can. Kindly advise if you would care to interview him." Within a week, the Sociological Department had a full report on the suspicious American worker. His foreman stated that he found the worker "on the job with an empty oil can [and] that he picked up the can twice, fifteen minutes apart, and found it empty both times." Other informants uncovered a wide range of suspicious behavior and statements. His wife visited a German woman who was in prison as a German spy. On the war, he said "that this was a rich man's war and it was a shame to see all these good people being killed." He formerly worked as a draftsman and he paid too much attention to the blueprints for the aircraft motors. He told a fellow worker "that he did not believe in war; that we had no right to fight; no business to kill each other" and that he "claimed to have worked in the mines in Colorado and Montana." These parts of the country were strongholds of IWW activity. With the exception of the statement from the foreman who lifted his oil can, most of the evidence against the worker was from second-hand sources or from casual conversations. Nevertheless, the American worker with the empty oil can was obviously a German spy or a radical Wobbly.[37]

The Ford APL reports also listed other instances of suspected sabotage or espionage for the Germans. One oiler, an informant reported, appeared "to spend a great deal of time sightseeing in the building." Another informant noted that another worker was "tampering with drills." H. J. Emerson reported on an Austrian worker, who was "chummy with radical Germans." The worker operated a machine that was "tampered with and [had] emery dust distributed among the bearings." A naturalized German foreman, a jealous informant who worked "next to a German fellow who does very little work" believed, "pads this fellow's work slip allowing him to hold his job."[38]

Two patriotic foremen in the tool room reported that a Hungarian worker "deliberately held up or tried to slow up work on U.S. aircraft machine repair work." This worker, they added, "has been talking or agitating the men to refuse to work overtime on government work saying that by so doing they will help Germany or words to that effect." An American worker "encouraged men in killing time by such remarks as, "Oh! H—, don't kill yourself and work yourself gray here." "This," the informants noted, "is while the Liberty motor work was being done." After a disciplinary session in the factory manager's office about the incident, the same worker remarked that "he must pretend to look busy, whether he has anything to do or not, until this thing blows over." One worker reported that his foreman "had told him . . . [that] they were working on a rush government job and that he should not hurry same, to look around and get something else to keep himself busy. . . ."[39]

Another workman devised an ingenious scheme to relieve his repetitive tasks at a lathe. "On several occasions," his foreman related, "he had the machine going at top speed and threw it into reverse—blowing out the fuse which necessitates an electrician and causing a loss of from 10 to 15 minutes." Since the worker refused to purchase a Liberty Bond, his motives were obviously unpatriotic. The foreman detailed his suspicious behavior: "This is always done on U.S.A. work. He also spends a lot of time looking at blueprints . . . much more than is necessary." Indeed, the boundary between diligent work habits and treason became blurred. "I think this man has shown us enough," the foreman concluded, "that he is against our government and our spirit at this time to warrant some action being taken at once."[40]

To be sure, nations required some degree of social and political conformity from citizens and others in wartime. But, in this instance, the national government reached down to the shop level to insure the national unity of Ford workers. Loyal American workers informed on their rebel American and immigrant shopmates. Ford officials used this information for their own ends. These spies and informants watched and recorded the statements and behavior of their fellow workers. And, they reported this information to the factory superiors. Factory managers, supervisors, and foremen frequently acted on this sometimes dubious information without any substantial basis in fact. They harangued and berated the dissident worker who refused to contribute to a Liberty Loan, who made an off-handed anticapitalist remark, or who did not produce at full capacity for the war effort. Sometimes the worker was disciplined, at other times he was discharged, and at still other times he was turned over to federal authorities for prosecution. An atmosphere of fear and intimidation most certainly pervaded the shops of the Highland Park plant. Only the boldest rebel dared to speak. Indeed, the mood of the Ford plant changed. The more repressive stick supplanted the paternalistic Five Dollar carrot.

The APL network operated in the Highland Park factory from April 1917 until the Armistice in November 1918. From this time until the spring of 1919, the activities of Ford spies and informants subsided. However, in the postwar period, the Detroit AWU conducted a series of strikes for union recognition and for improvements in wages, hours, and shop conditions. Many Detroit automobile workers contributed their wages and their labor to make the world "safe for democracy." Now, they sought to establish their vision of industrial democracy in the small shops and large factories of the automobile industry. Frustrated by new mechanized working conditions and by wartime inflation, thousands of skilled and unskilled automobile workers swarmed into the growing AWU in 1919. And, industrial espionage became means for the containment of militant labor.

In mid-April 1919, the AWU struck the Wadsworth Manufacturing Company, a major supplier of Ford bodies. For the 1,500 strikers, the principal issues included management's refusal to deal with existing AWU shop committees, the eight-hour day, and the shift from day-work to piece-work. Detroit workers, especially the automobile workers, greeted the strike with enthusiasm. In the first weeks, the AWU headquarters, the *Detroit Labor News* reported, was "a veritable beehive of activity." "The workers in the automobile industry," the paper reported,

are stirred as never before and hundreds are flocking to the union standard. . . . An average of 700 members are joining the union weekly and last week saw the high water mark when 987 signed their union cards.[41]

The Wadsworth strike had a serious impact on the productive operations of the Ford factory. Without the strength to tackle the nation's largest automobile manufacturer, the AWU directed its attack on one of Ford's principal body suppliers with poor wages and working conditions. Wadsworth and other strikes forced the Ford plant to curtail its production schedules. In the first week, the company attempted to intervene in the situation and send Ford workers as strikebreakers at Wadsworth.[42]

Ford foreman William Klann directed the strike-breaking operation. "The men who have been loaded into trucks at the Ford plant to be transported to the Wadsworth plant," the *Detroit Labor News* triumphantly reported, "have, upon their arrival at the strike-bound shop, refused to betray the striking workers. They would not become scabs." In one incident, a class-conscious sailor, a Ford worker who served in the war, expressed his vision of the postwar struggle for industrial democracy:

Boys, my uniform will indicate that I am one of Uncle Sam's fighters. I have risked my life in this war to make the world a better place to live and I would not besmirch this uniform by scabbing it on this job. I call upon you to be good Americans and refuse to help management to break this strike and aid them to establish the Prussianized method of dealing with labor.

The Navy veteran had transformed Wilsonian wartime rhetoric into his own vision of democracy in industry. The newspaper reported: "None of the men went to work."[43]

Ford strike-breaking activities, the *Detroit Labor News* ominously noted, raised discontent and tensions among the workers in other automobile shops. "The danger of the situation," it noted, "cannot be overestimated, because it will involve over 25,000 men and it may amount to a miniature revolution." Even the normally quiescent Ford workers moved to act against the provocative Ford policies in the Wadsworth strike. Thousands signed their cards and joined the AWU. Others circulated petitions in the factory which supported the Wadsworth strikers.[44]

Faced with the AWU's militant campaign for industrial unionism in the automobile industry, the Ford Motor Company reverted to its successful wartime experience in industrial espionage. Alex Spark, a manager with prior experience in the Ford APL organization, directed a formal network of factory spies and informants from the Superintendent's Office, which supervised the plant's productive operations. From surviving records, four operatives—numbers 8, 9, 11, and 15—reported directly to Spark. All four operatives made their reports in the midst of the Wadsworth strike in the spring and summer of 1919. Some of these and others were active into 1920 and later. The reports of Operative 15 also indicated that many other operatives and informants functioned both inside and outside the Ford plant.[45]

Operative 15 left the most extensive set of reports. He was B. J. Licardi, a professional industrial spy and investigator with years of experience. He worked for the Chicago Metal Trades Association during a machinist's strike and in New York during a patternmaker's strike. He also served as a Ford investigator in the Chicago *Tribune* trial. For spying and informing on his fellow workers, Licardi received $7.20 per day, the Ford wage rate for foremen and skilled mechanics. The company also paid his expenses, which included carefare, phone calls, union papers and magazines, typing paper and union dues. It classified his service as "special work."[46]

According to Licard's reports from June 13, 1919, to April 9, 1920, he worked with and spied on his shopmates in the generator department, the T. B. shed (sic), and the box factory. At times, the company assigned Licardi to investigate individual workmen and agitators inside and outside the factory. He made special reports on the meetings and activities of radical and trade union organizations. Usually each day or so, Licardi made two- or three-page reports on the activities and sentiments of the men in the shops. In his reports, Licardi identified the most active leaders and agitators. He also generally noted incidents of soldiering and output restriction, weak foremen and lapses of shop discipline, infractions of Ford rules (such as smoking, eating, or gambling during working hours), and workmen with sympathies toward Bolshevism, socialism, or even trade unionism.[47]

In June 1919, Licardi wrote a letter to Alex Spark and requested the payment of his expenses for the period from April 31 to May 13. In this letter, he detailed and characterized his work for the Ford Motor Company.

> I was advised by Mr. Perini [an assistant to Klann] the company would stand my exspences [sic], but nothing more has been said concerning same. I furnished daily reports on labor organizations and various men in the shop who proved to be undesirable to the concern.

He then itemized the money, which he spent on carfare, union papers and magazines, phone calls, typing paper, and donations to the union. "$6.00 is what I spent beside losing 1 days pay and a deduction for being late, and both times I was attending a union meeting of the Wadsworth strike, I made no charges for the report [sic]."[48]

Licardi's first reports concerned labor organizations and undesirable Ford workers. Until August 1919, he spent most of his time with the organizational campaign of the AWU. But, with the impending national steel strike at the end of the summer, he shifted his attention to the activities of radical workers in the shop, notably the members of the IWW and Socialist Party and "Bolsheviks." At this time, Ford officials even had an operative who reported local conditions in Ohio iron and steel communities. So, besides the daily reports on the activities in the shop, Licardi now made extensive reports on Detroit socialist, IWW, and union meetings. After early 1920, his reports usually concerned an individual worker who belonged to a radical organization or who engaged in some other undesirable activity.

In his reports, Operative 15 also made many references to other operatives and spies in the Ford factory and in Detroit. In his conversation with an associate from the Chicago *Tribune* case, Licardi discovered a "loyal Roumanian" who might serve as a potential recruit and interpreter. In a report on conditions in the box factory, he advised his superiors on the use of another informant: "I would suggest that when the Russian Operative be placed into this department that no one be told who he is except [Foreman] McCay as he is the only one who can be trusted. . . ." At another point, he advised Foreman McCay where to assign the "Russian Operative." And, in still another instance, he advised his superiors on the placement of an operative:

> The Operative you have assigned on D-3325 (Gruber) is a member of the K. of C. and that Gruber is well aware of the fact that Operative is with him for no good cause, as you cannot belong to the Bolshevic or I.W.W. and be the member of any religious order . . . I suggest that you pull Operative off Gruber and use some other method as I believe you are wasting time and money keeping him with Gruber.

Also, when a Ford worker asked Licardi whether he should attend the Russian speaking or the English-speaking section of the Socialist Party, Licardi reported to Spark, "I did not urge him to go to either as the other Operative could cover him if he went to the English branch." Apparently, the Ford network of spies was quite extensive and quite thorough.[49]

B. J. Licardi also had acquaintances and associates among Detroit law enforcement officials and among other professional industrial operatives. His connections provided him with information on an internal dispute within the Detroit Local 82 of the International Association of Machinists. He reported that "five men were suspended, the five were all charged with preaching I.W.W. Doctrines." Then he added: "They are all operatives, 2-Pinkertons, 2-O'Neill and 1-Burns." Other Detroit manufacturers also seemed to keep a watchful eye on trade union activities.[50]

After Operative 15 attended a Detroit celebration on the second anniversary of the Russian Revolution at Arena Hall, he wrote, "I called on Inspector O'Grady and showed him my credentials." O'Grady introduced him to Sergeant Fred Clark, "who is in charge of the Police Bolshevici Squad." Clark proceeded to outline a proposed plan for the formation of an organization similar to the wartime APL. He told Operative 15:

> that the Police Commissioner was organizing a Police Reserve
> . . . and that the reserve was not to be used on strike but to be
> used to run down organizations such as the Bolshevic. . . . The
> Reserve was to furnish the Mfg. with information free of charge
> and that the Mfg. would have to cooperate with the Reserve
> That is with the assistance of their operatives. . . . the Reserve
> would be similar to U.S. Military Intelligence.

Licardi concluded: "Sgt. Clark asked me 'Who would be the best man to see in regards to the Reserve at the Ford Motor Co. [?'] I told him I did not know, But I thought Mr. Alex G. Spark or Dean Marquis."[51]

In one report, B. J. Licardi told about a vigilante action which he and others performed against a Detroit IWW local.

> I called upon an operative who was with the bunch of us that
> wrecked the I.W.W. Hall . . . Monday night at Delray. The local
> was known as the Shipbuilders Industrial Union No. 325, its
> members were mostly from the Great Lakes and Ford's at River
> Rouge.

He stated that this group had similar plans for "Local 472 and 573" except "we have learnt that one of our men has been uncovered [and] we have postponed same until further date."[52]

From August 20 to November 25, 1919, the Ford Motor Company assigned B. J. Licardi to spy and to inform on shop mates in the box factory. This was a wood-working shop which constructed boxes for the shipment Model T components. The workers in the box factory were predominantly Romanian, Italian, and Polish. The Romanian workers openly expressed their sympathies for socialism and Bolshevism. Almost daily, Operative 15 wrote his reports on the activities and the attitudes of the workers in this Ford shop. Moreover, in a three-month period, he attended ten Socialist Party meetings, periodically stopped in meetings at the Detroit House of Masses, attended three IWW Metal and Machinery Worker's Industrial Union meetings, participated in two Auto Workers' Union meetings, visited two International Association of Machinist meetings, went to a Detroit celebration of the Russian Revolution, and checked on the Modern Brotherhood of America, a fraternal insurance organization. At these meetings he reported on the number who attended, their nationality, the number of Ford workers present, and the leaders and most radical members. He also provided summaries and outlines of the speeches. And, sometimes he stole documents and membership lists and sent them to his supervisor A. G. Spark.[53]

In early September, Licardi investigated a group of Romanian "Bolsheviks" in the box factory. His detailed reports revealed the tactics used against rebellious Ford workers. In his investigation, he paid particular attention to a Romanian worker, Ford badge number J-1681. "During the noon hour," an early report noted, "the following men gathered together and discussed the situation in Roumania and Boshevicism, J-1731, J-2486, J-2411, J-1829, J-1959, J-1681, and J-2630, they would talk a while in English and then in Roumanian." The report then singled out some leaders in the group. "J-1697 and J-2093," he wrote, "seem to be the speakers in the box factory [and] the others simply listen. . . ." One of these, J-1681, admitted to the Ford operative "that he belongs to the Red Wing Roumanian Branch No. 1 Detroit . . . and that he has attended meetings at the English Branch No. 1 at Fraternity Hall, also English speaking Branch No. 2 at the Hall of Masses."[54]

Operative 15 also commented on this Romanian socialist's work habits:

This man operates a nailing machine, and has been on the same shift with me since Monday, the amount of work that he turns out in eight hours could easily be done in three, he is actually the laziest man in the department, he does not only waste his time while working but wastes the time of others working with him. . . .

He also noted the misbehavior of two other noon-hour Bolsheviks: "J-1731 and J-2411 constantly through the day are throwing nails in and around the department at other workers."[55]

And Licardi continued to gather information on the Romanian workers in the shop. He cultivated a friendly relationship with J-1681. Along with another worker, the three "worked on a bench in the yard making magneto boards. J–1681 pursuaded us to take our time that we would get just as much as if we make 20 boards or 1000, he stated if a Foreman would ask him to turn out more work he would turn out less." As the days progressed, he continued to report the conversations which arose while they worked. "J–1681 told me that he was the one that advocated I.W.W. and Bolshevicism propaganda throughout the box factory 19 months ago, he said that he was the one that got J–2093 to join the Socialist Roumanian branch in Hamtramck, and between them, they got several to join out of their department. . . ."⁵⁶

Also, J–1681 related an incident from about two years earlier. He and other workers in the shop forced their subforemen to quit. When the new subforeman "came around ordering men to get a hustle on themselves or he would send them home," J–1681 decided that "he would take his time and lay down on the job. . . . " He "went to the toilet several times during the day and staying as long as twenty minutes at a time. . . . " As a result, he got into an argument with the subforeman who sent him to the Employment Office. A few days later, J–1681 and "several of the boys" told the new subforeman

> That if he didn't go to [department Foreman] Dan McCay, and tell Dan that he would have to quit because he was too nervous, they would catch him outside and kill him, so he did, he worked on the bench making small boxes by hand a while then he quit.

In this instance, the informal relationships among the men in the shop were stronger than the formal factory hierarchy.⁵⁷

Throughout the month of September, Operative 15 reported on the noon-hour clique of Romanian Bolsheviks. In the end, Ford officials developed effective tactics to disrupt the activities of the agitators in the box factory. It discharged some; it transferred others to different shifts and departments. Those who remained worked next to loyal and patriotic Americans. "With the assistance of the Foreman," Licardi noted, "J–1681 has been placed as a helper on a nailing machine with an American who is opposed to Socialism, Bolshevicism and Radicalism." Another Romanian worker, he mentioned, "has been placed as a helper with an American who is against organized labor and Bolsheviks." This worker used "to hold arguments with the Millwright and other agitators. . . ." Now, the worker claimed "that he is against the Bolshevic. . . ." Moreover, the Romanian workers suspected that this American worker was a Ford informant. Licardi concluded that "the bunch of agitators say this man is a *Spy* as some knew him while he worked on the elevators, tool crib, and for the Factory Service, they think he is working to catch some thief or Bolshevic." Licardi remained with the box factory for several more weeks. Later, he moved on to other shops and other investigations.[58]

As a result of these and similar employer activities, automobile unionism never had a chance in Detroit. In addition to the Wadsworth strike, automobile workers struck fifteen other automobile and automobile parts shops and factories in 1919. In the end, strike-breakers, factory spies, and intransigent employer attitudes broke the will of automobile unionists. In August 1919, Ford converted the River Rouge plant for the manufacture of Model T bodies and undercut the major thrust of the AWU's strike against his supplier. The AWU conducted no strikes in 1920, led six in 1921, and then rapidly lost members and faded into oblivion. Always in the forefront, Henry Ford, Detroit's "progressive" employer, carefully avoided public participation in the city's open-shop campaigns. He quietly adopted his own methods for the resolution of labor problems. He began with his dramatic effort to elevate the working-class standard of living and ended with his own version of the American plan.[59]

And, Americanism was a thread which ran through the different phases of Ford labor relations. Throughout this period, Ford and other employers coopted the very word American and gave it their own definition. In the Progressive Era, the Five Dollar Day sought to raise immigrant workers to Ford's positive vision of the good American life and to provide everyone with a decent "American" standard of living. Of course, material rewards and comforts were the product of hard work and reliable work habits. During the war, however, Ford and others gave Americanism a negative definition. Americans were not pro-German. They did not belong to the Socialist Party or the IWW. They did not criticize American social and economic institutions. And, they were not loafers or slackers. The World War and the Russian Revolution established a tougher atmosphere for industrial relations. In 1919, a nation-wide labor upsurge generated an hysterical fear of radicalism and Bolshevism. In Detroit, the Palmer raids indiscriminately rounded up hundreds of immigrant workers as part of the national Red Scare. The American Legion also harassed and intimidated the popular Detroit Labor Forum which offered controversial speakers on controversial topics. At the same time, Licardi and others went from shop to shop and from meeting to meeting, watched, and wrote their reports. Indeed, Ford and others connected radicalism to trade unionism. In fact, they were identical. And, above all, American workers were not union members.[60]

For all practical purposes, Ford paternalism ceased to exist. The Ford American plan, based upon militant anti-unionism, the open-shop, and a network of spies and informants, reigned in the Highland Park plant. Not until 1941, when the United Automobile Workers organized the recalcitrant Ford Motor Company, did Ford automobile workers come full circle to express their version of industrial democracy and to define their requirements for an American standard of living.

9. Conclusion

From 1908 to 1921, the Ford experience with technology, labor, and social control represents a microcosm of the experience of our modern industrial age. The labor problems which Ford first encountered with mass production have continued to plague manufacturers and managers throughout the twentieth century. The Ford experience also raises specific questions about modern industrial society. Why has paternalism failed in modern industry? Why did Ford abandon his welfare programs? How have workers accommodated themselves to monotonous and routinized work? What solution does industrial technology offer to the social and economic problem of degraded work in modern times?

Ultimately, Ford paternalism failed. It failed for a number of different reasons. Most important was the failure to achieve its principal objective—the control of workers. And, control was an essential element of the different phases of Ford labor policies. Initially, Ford officials struggled to meet the unprecedented consumer demand for the Model T Ford. This required the control of work processes. Ford engineers, factory managers, and others combined the most advanced features of existing industrial practice and developed the modern system of mass production. In the process, they wrested control over production from craftsmen and skilled workers. At the same time, work tasks and work routines were deskilled and degraded. So they devised technical and administrative forms of control for the unskilled workers at machines and assembly lines. Then, the massive influx of immigrant workers filled the unskilled jobs in the Highland Park plant. These workers did not have the traditional discipline and incentive for industrial work. The conventional means of control, which rested upon craft traditions, independent work groups, and trade union apprenticeship systems, no longer functioned after the reorganization of work processes. The Lee reforms strengthened administrative controls and experimented with methods to internalize discipline within the Ford workforce. But

195

these reforms did not solve the many labor problems in the Highland Park factory.

Indeed, the pervasive nature of the crisis of control required substantial efforts to reshape the attitudes and habits of Ford workers. Following the prevailing mood of the Progressive Era, Ford officials designed a sophisticated network of social controls for the workforce. Based upon the progressive notion that home environment, and not innate moral qualities, determined attitudes and habits, the Five Dollar (eight-hour) Day served as a powerful economic incentive to control the home life and factory efficiency of the unskilled workforce. But, some labor problems persisted; welfare programs were costly. Finally, the World War changed the national mood. Progressivism waned as the national climate became more rigid and repressive. And, paternalism gave way to more authoritarian patterns as a means to insure social conformity. The rise of the Auto Workers' Union signalled the ultimate failure of paternalistic labor policies. Confronted with an independent working-class culture of resistance, Ford officials shifted to tougher political forms of control. This political control was more effective. At least, it worked as well as the much more expensive Profit-sharing Plan.

Ford paternalism also failed because of the uncertain and precarious economic conditions of the postwar period. After all, the Ford enterprise was a profit-making institution and not a benevolent one. When welfare programs no longer had an economic logic, Ford officials ended them. In the first years, the Ford Motor Company held the technological advantage over its competitors and could afford to be generous with the distribution of its profits. Nonetheless, as the new industrial technology rapidly spread to other automobile manufacturers, the Ford Motor Company lost its competitive economic advantage. Additionally, the severe war-induced inflation destroyed the economic incentive of the Five Dollar Day. By 1919, the company simply could not afford to pay its greatly expanded workforce a Ten Dollar Day. Furthermore, the postwar recession strained Ford's financial resources. At the war's end, Ford borrowed heavily to finance an extensive expansion of the industrial plant at River Rouge. Automobile sales slumped and creditors called in their notes. The company underwent a phase of ruthless cost-cutting. Since the Sociological Department had no direct connection to productive operations, Ford officials drastically reduced its size and curtailed its functions.

Finally, Ford paternalism failed because it did not work in a mature industrial society. It was a managerial strategy for an earlier stage of social and economic development. Even unskilled and unschooled immigrant workers recognized that money talked in the modern industrial world. This they easily learned from their American and Americanized shopmates. As long as Ford paid a high price, they took the money and ran with it. To be sure, they suffered the indignities of the paternalistic welfare plan, but their economic insecurity conditioned their responses. On the surface, their attitudes and habits suited the requirements of the Ford program. Below the surface, discontent and resentment persisted until it eventually boiled over. When the opportunity arose, they asserted their autonomy and joined the Auto Workers' Union in droves. They forcefully, but unsuccessfully, resisted the imposition of managerial values. And, while they lost their battle, it was not due to their lack of will and initiative but to the superior forces and more sophisticated weapons of their opponents.[1]

In the recession of 1920–1921, Ford officials ended the Profit-sharing Plan and dismantled the Sociological Department. They began the gradual process when they announced the Six Dollar Day in January 1919. Later, they introduced a year-end bonus based upon skill and length of service to reward valuable and faithful workers. They abolished the premium for acceptable values and habits. The Six Dollar Day became the basic wage rate. They paid the first bonus and instituted an employees' investment plan in January 1920. And, Ford officials shut down the plant for one month in January 1921 to take inventory and to wait for cash payments from dealers. When the plant reopened, they rehired only 60 to 70 percent of the workforce and doubled Model T production for the year. The recession and ruthless discipline forced automobile workers to conform to the regimen of the Ford technological system. Ford workers faced "the Six Dollar speed-up."[2]

In 1921, a dispute between S. S. Marquis and Charles Sorensen underlined the harsh new realities. Marquis, the liberal clergyman, and Sorensen, the hard-nosed production manager, were protagonists in a policy debate which centered on how best to motivate Ford workers. Their differences revealed how central the question of production was to the Profit-sharing Plan and Sociological Department. Marquis wanted to save men and elevate their moral and social condition. Sorensen wanted to produce more and more au-

)

198 The Five Dollar Day

tomobiles. Each had their particular self-serving position on Ford labor policy. And each argued their case before the final arbiter of the dispute—Henry Ford.

In his account, Marquis lamented the end of the paternalistic welfare programs. "The old group of executives," he wrote:

> who at times set justice and humanity above profits and production, were gone. With them, so it seemed to me, had gone the era of cooperation and good-will in the company. There came to the front men whose theory was that men are more profitable to an industry when driven than led, that fear is a greater incentive to work than loyalty.

For Marquis, the demonstration of good intentions and sound leadership was the best way to motivate workers.[3]

In his account, Sorensen complained about the interference with productive operations. "So long as the [Sociological] department and Dean Marquis did not interfere with production," he wrote:

> it was none of my business what they did or how much they pried into employees' personal affairs. But when they began calling men away from their work during the day, plant foremen and superintendents became so annoyed that I had to call a halt.

Sorensen implicitly criticized the paternalism of the Ford welfare program.[4]

In the midst of the dispute, Marquis arranged for a showdown in Ford's Highland Park office. When he arrived for the meeting, Sorensen related, Marquis "sailed into me for 'interfering' with him and his staff." After the harangue, Marquis "got as big a surprise as I had. He was astonished to find that Mr. Ford supported me in everything I had said. Before he got through he discovered that both Mr. Ford and I were set on keeping his nose out of the plant." Marquis decried the end of "humane policies" and the rise of the "new influence." And, he recounted the Ford and Sorensen attitude on motivation:

> "Loyalty and good-will on the part of the employees toward the company were discounted. Men worked for money," I was informed. "Pay them well, and then see to it that you get your

money's worth out of them," seemed to be the new policy of the company.

For Ford and Sorensen, an adequate wage combined with a stern hand was the best method for the motivation of Ford workers.[5]

So, Marquis quit. Ford officials merged the Sociological Department into the Service Department, which later acquired notoriety under the infamous Harry Bennett. Here, it served as a purely charitable institution and dispensed largess to the truly needy Ford worker who met with misfortune. For all practical purposes, the Sociological Department ceased to function as an institution for the social control of the Ford workforce.[6]

And, Ford officials ruthlessly ruled with a stern hand. In 1924, Jonathon Norton Leonard drew "a sketch of what it meant" to work in the Ford factory. "No one who works for Ford," he suggested:

is safe from spies—from superintendents on down to the poor creature who must clean a certain number of toilets an hour. There are spies who ask embarrassing questions of visitor's guides, spies who worm their way into labor unions, spies who speak every language under the sun. The system does not stop at the factory gates. An anonymous letter accusing a man of stealing Ford parts is enough to bring him before the 'Service Department.' He is forced to sign a 'Permission for Search' which allows Ford detectives to ransack his home, turn out all his poor possessions in hopes of finding a Ford incandescent lamp or a generator armature. There are spies to watch these in turn.

The repressive policies, which emerged during the war, proved the most effective means to discipline the Ford workforce. They made economic sense. A small number of well-placed spies and informants actually kept tabs on the attitudes and the behavior of large numbers of Ford workers. And, a few spies and informers were much less expensive than a full-fledged welfare program. Since the labor market favored management and other plants had similar technical conditions, Ford managers no longer remade men: they replaced them.[7]

Nevertheless, workers made their accommodation to degraded work and demanded monetary incentives for their labor. For workers, the significant effect of the new industrial technology was their monotonous and routinized work tasks and routines. This became a general feature of the modern industrial age as other mass produc-

200 The Five Dollar Day

tion industries duplicated the Ford experience. Given the authoritarian social relations of industry and the managerial monopolization of technical skills and knowledge, workers could do little to change the conditions of their work processes. So, they made their tradeoff. Workers have endured the inhuman conditions in their shops and factories, but they have sought and have acquired a considerable degree of job security and off-the-job satisfaction. They have traded degrading work for shorter hours and higher wages, or for more leisure with more material comforts. If they have not improved the nature of their work, they have at least improved their standard of living. And, after all, this was precisely what Ford offered in 1914—the Five Dollar (eight-hour) Day. But, he included a demeaning veneer of paternalism.

For automobile workers, the tradeoff became a reality in the turbulent thirties. Industrial unionism came to the automobile plants after the General Motors sit-down strike at Flint, Michigan, in 1936–1937. The settlement between the United Automobile Workers and General Motors initiated a process which eventually regularized and rationalized labor relations in the automobile industry. Four years later, in 1941, the UAW organized the recalcitrant Ford Motor Company. Automobile workers received higher wages and the forty-hour week with time-and-a-half for overtime, even during periods of peak production. Grievance procedures, shop committees, seniority, rules for layoffs, and a limited voice on production speed curtailed much of management's arbitrary power and authority. Production was scheduled, jobs became steadier, and unemployment was minimized. A Flint striker, who initially opposed the sit-down, wrote:

> The inhuman high speed is *no more*. We now have a voice, and have slowed up the speed of the line. And [we] are now treated as human beings, and not as part of the machinery. The high pressure is taken off. . . . It proves clearly that united we stand, divided or alone we fall.

To be sure, the euphoria did not last. Gradually, the union and the companies have developed a special arrangement which never really has tackled the problem of degrading work and which has dissatisfied many rank-and-file workers. The union also has become an instrument to discipline and to control the workforce. Nonetheless, automobile workers have seen some improvements in shop conditions and have acquired greater and greater levels of material comforts.[8]

Still, the tradeoff never completely was satisfactory to workers or managers. The meaningless work never has received adequate compensation for its human costs. After World War II, sociologists uncovered the problems of alienation and of work and its discontents. Other social critics debunked the myth of the happy worker and decried the degradation of labor in the modern world. In the 1970s, the "Blue-collar Blues" have become the malaise of urban-industrial America. *Fortune* editor Judson Gooding discovered the "job revolution." As a human problem, jobs failed "to provide a reasonable measure of personal satisfaction for millions of Americans." As an economic problem:

> High absenteeism and quit rates, excessive rework and scrap, deliberate acts of soilage and vandalism, hostile resistance to supervision, and an increased willingness to strike are all symptoms of the problem and they all have a direct impact on plant efficiency.

Old, familiar problems, very similar to Ford labor problems, have persisted through the auto-industrial age.[9]

In the 1970s, the tradeoff grew into an economic liability for automobile manufacturers as the costs eroded their profits. Automobile assemblers received the five dollar hour in 1973. Also, other forms of financial compensation—shift premium pay, Saturday and Sunday pay, holiday pay, paid vacations, bereavement pay, relief-time pay, educational pay, moving allowances, insurance benefits, supplemental unemployment benefits, retirement benefits, and separation pay—all have amounted to considerable additional sums paid for human labor. As a result, contemporary automobile manufacturers face the same problem as Ford did in the early 1920s— the substantial cost of providing an appropriate incentive for their workers.[10]

So, technology comes full circle and offers its new fix for social and economic problems. Computer technology, which now can transform mental work in the same manner that machine tools transformed manual work, has come of age in the modern factory. Numeric control which directs the movements of machine tools, microprocessors which send information from machines to centralized computers, and programmable robots which have the physical capacities of men are producing substantial and profound changes at the workplace. For industrial engineers, robots provide a novel, solution to the problem of degrading work. They now have the technical sophistication to compete with men on the shop floor. "Robots," one reporter noted,

> bring to their work several special qualities. For one thing, they are perfect—they never make a mistake. For another, they never get bored.

At the same time, the "labor costs" for robots are much less than for men. Currently, a programmable robot would cost $4.50 per hour and an automobile worker costs $15 per hour in 1980 and may cost about $20 per hour in 1983. And, American automotive engineers project that in 1995, "50 percent of the direct assembly of an automobile would be accomplished by automated machines." Presently, Japanese engineers have automated 97 percent of the work in Datsun's Zama plant.[11]

Industrial engineers finally may have found their technical solution to the problem of the "human element in production." But, who, or what, will the labor historian of the future study?

Notes

Chapter 1

1. Allan L. Benson, *The New Henry Ford* (New York, 1923), p. 137 and David L. Lewis, *The Public Image of Henry Ford* (Detroit, 1976), pp. 75–6. The popular works on Henry Ford include his own publications, written in collaboration with others, *My Life and Work* (Garden City, N.Y., 1922), *Today and Tomorrow* (Garden City, N.Y., 1926), and *Moving Forward* (Garden City, N.Y., 1931). I have presumed that *My Life and Work* is the most important statement of Ford's ideas on the development of mass production. It contains information found in factory materials from the period. The most detailed and authoritative works for the period are Allan Nevins, *Ford: The Times, the Man, the Company* (New York, 1954) and Allan Nevins and Frank E. Hill, *Ford: Expansion and Challenge* (New York, 1957). For additional Ford literature, *see* Selected Bibliography.

2. John R. Commons, et al., "Henry Ford Miracle Maker," *Independent*, 102 (May 1, 1920), p. 160; R. M. Fox, "Fordism: A Critical Evaluation," *The Nineteenth Century and After*, 101 (February 1927), p. 234; and Nevins, *Ford: Expansion*, p. 296.

3. Nevins, *Ford: The Times*, pp. 648, 644, 647, and 488.

4. Keith Sward, *The Legend of Henry Ford* (New York, 1948); Nevins, *Ford: The Times*; Nevins and Hill, *Ford: Expansion*; Nevins and Hill, *Ford: Decline and Rebirth* (New York, 1963); Reynold M. Wik, *Henry Ford and Grass-roots America* (Ann Arbor, 1972); Lewis, *Public Image*; and Anne Jardim, *The First Henry Ford: A Study in Personality and Business Leadership* (Cambridge, Mass., 1970).

5. Merritt Roe Smith, *Harpers Ferry Armory and the New Technology: The Challenge of Change* (Ithaca, N.Y., 1977); David Noble, *America By Design: Science, Technology, and the Rise of Corporate Capitalism* (New York, 1979); and David F. Noble, "Social Choice and Machine Design: The Case of Automatically Controlled Machine Tools and the Challenge for Labor," *Politics and Society*, 8 (1978), pp. 313–47.

6. David Brody, "The Old Labor History and the New: In Search of an American Working Class," *Labor History*, 20 (Winter 1979), pp. 109–26; E. P. Thompson, *The Making of the English Working Class* (New York, 1963); Eric J. Hobsbawm, *Labouring Men: Studies in the History of Labour* (New York,

1964); David Brody, *Labor in Crisis: The Steel Strike of 1919* (Philadelphia, 1965); Herbert G. Gutman, *Work, Culture, and Society in Industrializing America: Essays in American Working-class and Social History* (New York, 1977); and David Montgomery, *Workers' Control in America: Studies in the History of Work, Technology, and Labor Struggles* (Cambridge, Mass., 1979).

7. Alfred D. Chandler, *The Visible Hand: The Managerial Revolution in American Business* (Cambridge, Mass., 1977); Daniel Nelson, *Managers and Workers: Origins of the New Factory System in the United States, 1880–1920* (Madison, 1975); and Montgomery, *Workers' Control in America*.

8. Henry Eilbert, "The Development of Personnel Management in the United States," *Business History Review*, 33 (Autumn 1959) pp. 345–64 and Loren Baritz, *The Servants of Power: A History of the Use of Social Science in American Industry* (Middletown, Conn., 1960).

Chapter 2

1. Henry Ford, *My Life and Work* (Garden City, N.Y., 1922), p. 78.

2. David Landes, *Prometheus Unbound: Technological Change and Industrial Development in Western Europe from 1750 to the Present* (New York, 1969); Melvin Kranzberg and Carroll W. Pursell, eds., *Technology in Western Civilization*, vol. 2 (New York, 1967); and Alfred D. Chandler, *The Visible Hand: The Managerial Revolution in American Business* (Cambridge, Mass., 1977). Recent works which develop new approaches to the social history of technology include Harry Braverman, *Labor and Monopoly Capital: The Degradation of Work in the Twentieth Century* (New York, 1974); Daniel Nelson, *Managers and Workers: The Origins of the New Factory System in the United States, 1880–1920* (Madison, 1975); Merritt Roe Smith, *Harpers Ferry Armory and the New Technology: The Challenge of Change* (Ithaca, N.Y., 1977); David Noble, *America By Design: Science, Technology, and the Rise of Corporate Capitalism* (New York, 1979); and David Montgomery, *Workers' Control in America: Studies in the History of Work, Technology and Labor Struggles* (Cambridge, Mass., 1979).

3. Chandler, *The Visible Hand*, p. 280. On the development of mass production, see John B. Rae, "Rationalization of Production" in Kranzberg and Pursell, *Technology*, vol. 2, pp. 37–52 and Siegfried Giedion, *Mechanization Takes Command* (New York, 1955), pp. 14–127.

4. On the expansion of the Ford workforce, see Allan Nevins, *Ford: The Times, the Man, the Company* (New York, 1954), p. 648. On the number of immigrant workers, see "Automobile Trade Notes," *New York Times*, November 15, 1914, sec. 7, p. 6.

5. John B. Rae, *The American Automobile: A Brief History* (Chicago, 1965), pp. 17–68; Ralph C. Epstein, *The Automobile Industry: Its Economic and Commercial Development* (Chicago, 1928), pp. 23–101; and Nevins, *Ford*, pp. 220–386.

6. Montgomery, *Workers' Control*, pp. 11 and 12–27 and Nelson, *Managers and Workers*, pp. 17–54. See also, John Buttrick, "The Inside Contract System," *Journal of Economic History*, 12 (Summer 1952), pp. 205–21; Benson Soffer, "A Theory of Trade Union Development: The Role of the 'Autonomous' Workman," *Labor History*, 1 (Spring 1960), pp. 141–63; Katherine Stone, "The Origins of Job Structures in the Steel Industry," *Review of Radical Political Economics*, 6 (Summer, 1974), pp. 113–73; R. R. Lutz, *The Metal Trades* (Philadelphia, 1916); and George E. Barnett, *Chapters on Machinery and Labor* (Cambridge, Mass., 1926).

7. O. J. Abell, "Making the Ford Motor Car," *Iron Age*, 89 (June 6, 1912), p. 1391; H. L. Arnold, "Ford Methods and the Ford Shops: Inspection and Assembling Methods and Practices," *Engineering Magazine*, 47 (July 1914), p. 510; and Fred H. Colvin, "Machining Ford Cylinders—II," *American Machinist*, 38 (June 12, 1913), p. 975.

8. H. L. Arnold and Fay L. Faurote, *Ford Methods and the Ford Shops* (New York, 1916), pp. 115–16.

9. "Glossary" in United States, Bureau of the Census, *Special Reports: Employees and Wages* (Washington, 1903), pp. 1182–3 and Ford, *Life and Work*, p. 87.

10. "Glossary," p. 1168 and "International Association of Machinists Agreement," Folder 3, Box 45, File A, Series 11, American Federation of Labor Papers, Wisconsin State Historical Society, Madison, Wisconsin.

11. Nelson, *Managers and Workers*, p. 41.

12. Ford, *Life and Work*, p. 77; Ford quoted in Alfred D. Chandler, *Giant Enterprise: Ford, General Motors, and the Automobile Industry* (New York, 1964), p. 28.

13. H. L. Arnold, "Ford Methods and the Ford Shops: The Stock System and Employment Methods," *Engineering Magazine*, 47 (May 1914), p. 179 and H. F. Porter, "Four Big Lessons from Ford's Factory," *System*, 31 (June 1917), pp. 640–1.

14. Porter, "Four Big Lessons," p. 640.

15. Porter, "Four Big Lessons," p. 640.

16. John R. Lee, "The So-called Profit Sharing System at the Ford Plant," *Annals AAPSS*, 65 (May 1916), p. 298 and Porter, "Four Big Lessons," p. 642.

17. Porter, "Four Big Lessons," p. 640.

18. American Society of Mechanical Engineers (Hereafter ASME), "The Present State of the Art of Industrial Management," *Transactions ASME*, 34 (1912), pp. 1133–9.

19. ASME, "Industrial Management," pp. 1133 and 1137.

20. ASME, "Developments in Machine Shop Practice in the Last Decade," *Transactions ASME*, 34 (1912), p. 851.

21. Taylor quoted in Nevins, *Ford*, p. 469.

22. Fred H. Colvin, "Making Rear Axles for the Ford Auto," *American Machinist*, 39 (July 24, 1913), p. 148.

23. H. L. Arnold, "Ford Methods and the Ford Shops: Machining and Assembling the Front Axle," *Engineering Magazine*, 47 (September 1914), p. 857 and Frederick W. Taylor, "Shop Management," *Transactions ASME*, 24 (1903), p. 1405.

24. Ford, *Life and Work*, p. 88.

25. Arnold and Faurote, *Ford Methods*, p. 245.

26. Ford Motor Company Archives, *The Reminiscences of Mr. William C. Klann* (September 1955), p. 7; O. J. Abell, "Making the Ford Motor Car," *Iron Age*, 89 (June 13, 1912), p. 1457; and Frederick Winslow Taylor, *The Principles of Scientific Management* (New York, 1967), pp. 120–2.

27. Robert S. Woodbury, *Studies in the History of Machine Tools* (Cambridge, Mass., 1972); Nathan Rosenberg, "Technological Change in the Machine Tool Industry, 1840–1910" in *Perspectives on Technology* (New York, 1976), pp. 9–31; Chandler, *The Visible Hand*, pp. 240–83; and David Allen Hounshell, "From the American System to Mass Production: The Development of Manufacturing Technology in the United States, 1850–1920." Ph.D. dissertation, University of Delaware, 1978.

28. ASME, "Machine Shop Practice," p. 847 and ASME, "Industrial Management," pp. 1133–4.

29. ASME, "Machine Shop Practice," passim.

30. Charles E. Sorensen, *My Forty Years with Ford* (New York, 1956), p. 126; H. L. Arnold, "Ford Methods and the Ford Shops," *Engineering Magazine*, 47 (April 1914), p. 23; and Nevins, *Ford*, pp. 456 and 648.

31. Arnold and Faurote, *Ford Methods*, p. 41.

32. Arnold and Faurote, *Ford Methods*, pp. 307–8, 8, 159, and 308.

33. Fred H. Colvin and Lucian L. Haas, *Jigs and Fixtures* (New York, 1943), p. 1; Franklin D. Jones, *Jig and Fixture Design* (New York, 1920), pp. 1–3; ASME, "Machine Shop Practice," p. 858; "The Importance of Holding Fixtures for Machines," *American Machinist*, 38 (January 23, 1913), p. 162; and "Making Fixtures to Go with Machines," *American Machinist*, 38 (February 13, 1913), p. 286.

34. Jones, *Jig and Fixture Design*, p. 2 and Sterling H. Bunnel, "Jigs and Fixtures as Substitutes for Skill," *Iron Age*, 93 (March 5, 1914), p. 610–11.

35. Abell, "Making the Ford Motor Car," p. 1389 and Fred H. Colvin, "Machining the Ford Cylinders—I," *American Machinist*, 38 (May 22, 1913), p. 846.

36. Arnold and Faurote, *Ford Methods*, p. 189–90.

37. Fred H. Colvin, "Special Machines for Making Pistons," *American Machinist*, 39 (August 28, 1913), p. 350–1.

38. Abell, "Making the Ford Motor Car," p. 1389 and Colvin, "Cylinders—I," pp. 843 and 844.

39. Fred H. Colvin, "Interesting Milling and Grinding Operations," *American Machinist*, 39 (August 14, 1913), pp. 289–80 and Arnold and Faurote, *Ford Methods*, pp. 208–9.

40. Arnold, "Assembling and Machining the Front Axle," p. 848; Oscar C. Bornholt, "Placing Machines for Sequence of Use," *Iron Age*, 92 (December 4, 1913), pp. 1276–7; and ASME, "Machine Shop Practice," pp. 853–4.

41. Arnold, "Stock System," p. 186; Nelson, *Managers and Workers*, pp. 20–3; and Charles Day, "The Machine Shop Problem," *Transactions ASME*, 24 (1903), p. 1308.

42. ASME, "Machine Shop Practice," pp. 853–4.

43. Sorensen, *Ford*, p. 125 and Abell, "Making the Ford Motor Car," pp. 1389, 1388, and 1390.

44. Fred H. Colvin, "Building an outomobile Every 40 Seconds," *American Machinist*, 38 (May 8, 1913), p. 759 and Ford, *Life and Work*, p. 83.

45. Bornholt, "Placing Machines," p. 1276.

46. H. L. Arnold, "Ford Methods and the Ford Shops: Conveyors, Workslides, and Roll Ways," *Engineering Magazine*, 48 (December 1914), pp. 339–41 and Fred H. Colvin, "Handling Work between Operations," *American Machinist*, 41 (December 17, 1914), pp. 1057–60.

47. Arnold, "Stock System," p. 185; Arnold and Faurote, *Ford Methods*, p. 26; and E. A. Rumley, "The Manufacturer of Tomorrow," *World's Work*, 28 (May 1914), p. 110.

48. Colvin, "Cylinders—II," p. 975; Fred H. Colvin, "Special Machines for Small Auto Parts," *American Machinist*, 39 (September 11, 1913), p. 442; and Colvin, "Building an Automobile," pp. 761–2.

49. Arnold, "Inspection and Assembling," pp. 522–3.

50. Sorensen, *Ford*, pp. 116 and 130.

51. H. L. Arnold, "Ford Methods and the Ford Shops: How the Work in the Ford Factory Is Actually Done," *Engineering Magazine*, 47 (June 1914), pp. 331–2; H. L. Arnold, "Ford Methods and the Ford Shops: Ford Motor-Test Blocks and Chassis Assembling Lines," *Engineering Magazine*, 47 (August 1914), pp. 672–3 and 677; and Colvin, "Building an Automobile," pp. 657–62.

52. Arnold, "Chassis Assembling Lines," p. 677–80.

53. Arnold, "Chassis Assembling Lines," p. 680.

54. Arnold, "Chassis Assembling Lines," p. 672.

Chapter 3

1. *Detroit Labor News*, April 24, 1914, p. 3.

2. H. F. Porter, "Four Big Lessons from Ford's Factory," *System*, 31 (June 1917), p. 643–4.

3. On the nature of and changes in skill for the period, see "Glossary" in United States, Bureau of the Census, *Special Reports: Employees and Wages* (Washington, 1903), pp. 1167–9; Anna Bezanson, "Skill," *Quarterly Journal of Economics*, 36 (August 1922), pp. 626–45; George E. Barrett, *Chapters on*

Machinery and Labor (Cambridge, Mass., 1926); and R. R. Lutz, *The Metal Trades* (Philadelphia, 1916).

4. *New York Times*, January 11, 1914, sec. 4, p. 1.

5. John A. Fitch, "Ford of Detroit," *Survey*, 31 (February 7, 1914), pp. 545−6.

6. Julian Street, "Detroit the Dynamic," *Collier's*, 53 (July 4, 1914), p. 24.

7. William A. Logan, "The Evolution of the Automobile Business," *Auto Worker*, 5 (August 1923), p. 7.

8. Adam Coaldigger, "Why I'm for Henry," *Auto Worker*, 5 (August 1923), p. 5 and Anonymous letter to *Ford Worker*, vol. 1, no. 3 (1926), p. 3.

9. Chen-nan Li, "A Summer in the Ford Works," *Personnel Journal*, 7 (June 1928), p. 23 and notes on Mimms, Cruden, and Zendt in Robert W. Dunn Papers, Archives of Labor and Urban History, Wayne State University, Detroit, Michigan.

10. Notes on Zendt and Mimms in Robert W. Dunn Papers.

11. Myron W. Watkins, "The Labor Situation in Detroit," *Journal of Political Economy*, 28 (December 1920), p. 847.

12. "Glossary," pp. 1167−9; Daniel Nelson, *Managers and Workers: Origins of the New Factory System in the United States, 1880−1920* (Madison, 1975), pp. 17−54 and David Montgomery, *Workers Control in America: Studies in the History of Work, Technology, and Labor Struggles* (Cambridge, Mass., 1979), pp. 11−27.

13. Frederick W. Taylor, "Shop Management," *Transactions of the American Society of Mechnical Engineers*, 24 (1903), pp. 1347 and 1346 and "Glossary," p. 1183.

14. Taylor, "Shop Management," p. 1346 and "Glossary," p. 1181.

15. Frederick Winslow Taylor, *The Principles of Scientific Management* (New York, 1967), p. 40 and "American vs. British Workmen," *Iron Age*, 65 (March 3, 1900), p. 19.

16. "Glossary," p. 1183 and Taylor, "Shop Management," p. 1346.

17. Mark Perlman, *The Machinists: A New Study in American Trade Unionism* (Cambridge, Mass., 1961), pp. 12 and 34.

18. Taylor, "Shop Management," p. 1347.

19. The table was constructed from a sample of the data in "A Canvass of the Agricultural Implement and Iron Working Industries in Detroit" in Michigan Bureau of Labor Statistics, *Eighth Annual Report* . . . (Lansing, 1891), pp. 1−151.

20. See an eight-page sample of occupations and wages from around 1910 in Box 18, Accession 940, Ford Motor Company Archives, Dearborn, Michigan.

21. *Official Journal of the Carriage, Wagon, and Automobile Workers' Union* (Hereafter *Official Journal CWAWU*), 3 (November 1914), p. 5.

22. Logan, "Automobile Business," p. 5.

23. See Charles Reitell, "Mechanical Evolution and Changing Labor Types," *Journal of Political Economy*, 24 (March 1918), pp. 274−90 and

Charles Reitell, "Machinery and Its Effects on the Automobile Industry," *Annals AAPSS*, 116 (November 1924), pp. 37–43. Quotes from "Machinery," pp. 38 and 37.

24. Reitell, "Machinery," p. 40.

25. O. J. Abell, "Labor Classified on a Skill-Wages Basis," *Iron Age*, 93 (January 1, 1914), p. 48.

26. Reitell outlined three classes of occupations to describe the new occupational structure of the automobile industry. First, "technical" employees planned, routed, and scheduled the work tasks and routines. Second, foremen and clerks recorded "all the miscellaneous activities of the shop," checked "the quality and quantity of production and kept watch on the flow of material." And, third, the production workers fell into six separate groups: (1) the machine tenders who operated the specialized machinery; (2) the assemblers, who performed similar, but "more physical," specialized work; (3) the skilled workers who still possessed a craft or trade; (4) the testers and inspectors who examined the work in progress and tested the finished component or product; (5) the helpers who assisted the skilled workers; and (6) the common laborers who carried or handled the work or who cleaned the plant.

The table classified Ford workers according to Reitell's six categories. It was constructed from information in "List of Trades and Occupations and Number of Men Employed in Same," Box 16, Accession 940, Ford Motor Company Archives, Dearborn, Michigan.

27. Reitell, "Machinery," pp. 39–40.

28. H. L. Arnold and F. L. Faurote, *Ford Methods and the Ford Shops* (New York, 1916), pp. 41–2.

29. Porter, "Four Big Lessons," p. 646.

30. Arnold and Faurote, *Ford Methods*, p. 182.

31. Alford quoted in Henry Eilbert, "The Development of Personnel Management in the United States," *Business History Review*, 33 (Autumn 1959), p. 359; Edwin D. Jones, *The Administration of Industrial Enterprises* (London, 1926), p. 392; and Taylor, "Shop Management," p. 1388.

32. O. J. Abell, "Making the Ford Motor Car," *Iron Age*, 89 (June 13, 1912), p. 1458.

33. Arnold and Faurote, *Ford Methods*, p. 46.

34. John W. Love, "Detroit a Sterile Field for Organized Labor," *Annalist*, 28 (November 12, 1926), p. 629 and Ford Motor Company Archives, *Reminiscences of Mr. William C. Klann* (September 1955), p. 85.

35. *Klann Reminiscences*, pp. 37 and 54 and Arnold and Faurote, *Ford Methods*, p. 46.

36. On the average number of workers for each month of each year, see "Model T Production Statistics," Accession 922, Ford Motor Company Archives, Dearborn, Michigan. Arnold said that there were 255 foremen in March 1914. "List of Trades and Occupations" noted 2,523 foremen in January 1917.

37. Abell, "Making the Ford Motor Car," p. 1458.

38. H. L. Arnold, "Ford Methods and the Ford Shops: How the Work in the Ford Factory Is Actually Done," *Engineering Magazine*, 47 (June 1914), p. 332.

39. Arnold, "How the Work," pp. 332–5.

40. H. L. Arnold, "Ford Methods and the Ford Shops: Inspection and Assembling Methods and Practices," *Engineering Magazine*, 47 (July 1914), p. 509 and Arnold and Faurote, *Ford Methods*, p. 99.

41. Sidney Pollard, "Factory Discipline in the Industrial Revolution," *Economic History Review*, 16 (December 1963), pp. 264–71; E. P. Thompson, "Time, Work-Discipline, and Industrial Capitalism," *Past and Present*, 38 (December 1967), pp. 56–97; David F. Noble, "Social Choice and Machine Design: The Case for Automatically Controlled Machine Tools, and the Challenge for Labor," *Politics and Society*, 8 (1978), pp. 313–47; and Richard Edwards, *Contested Terrain: The Transformation of the Workplace in the Twentieth Century* (New York, 1979), pp. 90–162.

42. Abell, "Making the Ford Motor Car," pp. 1457–8.

43. Abell, "Making the Ford Motor Car," p. 1457 and Fred H. Colvin, "Making Rear Axles for the Ford Auto," *American Machinist*, 39 (July 24, 1913), p. 148.

44. E. A. Rumley, "The Manufacturer of Tomorrow," *World's Work*, 28 (May 1914), p. 110.

45. Ralph C. Epstein, *The Automobile Industry: Its Economic and Commercial Development* (Chicago, 1928), pp. 32–3.

46. Oscar Bornholt, "Placing Machines for Sequence of Use," *Iron Age*, 93 (December 4, 1912), pp. 1276–7.

47. Notes on Cruden in Robert W. Dunn Papers and I. T. Martin, "The Melting Pot at Ford's," *Official Journal CWAWU*, 4 (August 1915), p. 8.

48. Porter, "Four Big Lessons," p. 644.

49. Arnold and Faurote, *Ford Methods*, pp. 151, 139–40, and 151–3.

50. Arnold and Faurote, *Ford Methods*, pp. 331–3.

51. Arnold and Faurote, *Ford Methods*, pp. 334–5 and Rumley, "Manufacturer," p. 110.

52. Porter, "Four Big Lessons," p. 642; Harold W. Slauson, "A Ten Million Dollar Efficiency Plan," *Machinery* (October 1914), p. 86; and Arnold and Faurote, *Ford Methods*, p. 119.

53. Nelson, *Managers and Workers*, pp. 55–78 and Montgomery, *Workers Control*, pp. 32–47 and 113–38.

54. Arnold and Faurote, *Ford Methods*, pp. 67–8 and 99.

55. Arnold and Faurote, *Ford Methods*, p. 76 and Porter, "Four Big Lessons," p. 646.

Chapter 4

1. Henry Ford, *My Life and Work* (Garden City, N.Y., 1922), p. 3.

2. Edgar S. Furniss, *Labor Problems* (Cambridge, Mass., 1925), p. 3.

3. Gordon S. Watkins, *Labor Problems* (New York, 1922), p. 361; Peter Roberts, *The New Immigration: A Study of the Industrial and Social Life of Southeastern Europeans in America* (New York, 1912), p. vii; William M. Leiserson, *Adjusting Immigrant and Industry* (New York, 1924), p. 332; and Jeremiah W. Jenks and W. Jett Lauck, *The Immigration Problem* (New York, 1912), pp. 1 and 6–8.

4. John R. Commons, et. al., *Industrial Government* (New York, 1921), p. 121; Furniss, *Labor Problems*, p. 4; and Sumner H. Slichter, *The Turnover of Factory Labor*, (New York, 1919), pp. vii–viii.

5. Watkins, *Labor Problems*, pp. 3–13.

6. E. P. Thompson, "Time, Work-Discipline, and Industrial Capitalism," *Past and Present*, 38 (December 1967), pp. 56–97; Sidney Pollard, "Factory Discipline in the Industrial Revolution," *Economic History Review*, 16 (December 1963), pp. 254–71; Herbert Gutman, "Work, Culture, and Society in Industrializing America, 1815–1915," *American Historical Review*, 78 (June 1973), pp. 531–87; David Montgomery, "Workers' Control of Production in the Nineteenth Century," *Labor History*, 17 (Fall 1976), pp. 486–509; and Daniel Rodgers, "Tradition, Modernity, and the American Industrial Worker," *Journal of Interdisciplinary History*, 7 (Spring 1977), pp. 655–81.

7. Alan Dawley and Paul Faler, "Workingclass Culture and Politics in the Industrial Revolution: Sources of Loyalism and Rebellion" in Milton Cantor, ed., *American Workingclass Culture: Explorations in American Labor and Social History* (Westport, Conn., 1979), pp. 61–75 and Raymond Williams, "Base and Superstructure in Marxist Cultural Theory," *New Left Review*, 82 (November-December 1973), pp. 3–16.

8. John R. Lee, "The So-Called Profit Sharing System at the Ford Plant," *Annals AAPSS*, 45 (May 1916), p. 299.

9. Lee, "Profit Sharing System," p. 299 and Ford Motor Company Archives, *The Reminiscences of Mr. George Brown* (May 1953), pp. 86–9.

10. Frederick Winslow Taylor, *The Principles of Scientific Management* (New York, 1967), p. 142.

11. The data for the table comes from "Model T Production Statistics," Accession 922, Ford Motor Company Archives, Dearborn, Michigan. The monthly statistics for "Men on Roll" and "Automobiles Manufactured during Period" were averaged for the different years.

12. *Ford Times*, 1 (May 15, 1908), p. 3.

13. *Ford Times*, 2 (December 15, 1908), p. 1.

14. *Ford Times*, 2 (February 15, 1909), p. 10; *Ford Times*, 2 (March 15, 1909), p. 2; and *Ford Times*, 2 (April 1, 1909), p. 2.

15. United States, Bureau of the Census, *Special Reports: Occupations of the Twelfth Census* (Washington, 1904), pp. 546–7.

16. W. Jett Lauck and Edgar Sydenstricker, *Conditions of Labor in American Industries* (New York, 1917), p. 125 and Lois Rankin, "Detroit Nationality Groups," *Michigan History*, 23 (Spring 1939), pp. 129–205.

17. *Detroit Tribune*, January 10, 1910 and *Detroit Free Press*, July 14, 1912 in "Automobile Industry History," Box 1, Edward Levinson Papers, Archives

of Labor History and Urban Affairs, Wayne State University, Detroit, Michigan.

18. Ford Motor Company Archives, *The Reminiscences of Mr. William C. Klann* (September 1955), p. 14.

19. O. J. Abell, "The Ford Plan for Employees' Betterment," *Iron Age*, 93 (January 29, 1914), p. 306 and H. L. Arnold and F. L. Faurote, *Ford Methods and the Ford Shops* (New York, 1916), p. 47.

20. "Model T Production Statistics" and "Automobile Trade Notes," *New York Times*, November 15, 1914, sec. 7, p. 6.

21. Ford quoted in Rose Wilder Lane, *Henry Ford's Own Story* (New York, 1917), p. 150 and Isaac A. Hourwich, *Immigration and Labor* (New York, 1912), p. 12. See also, John Mitchell, "Immigration and the American Laboring Classes," *Annals AAPSS*, 34 (1909), pp. 125–9 and Royal Meeker, "What Is the American Standard of Living?," *Monthly Labor Review*, 9 (July 1919), pp. 1–13.

22. Lauck and Sydenstricker, *Conditions of Labor*, pp. 305 and 310–1.

23. Roberts, *New Immigration*, pp. 99 and 95–9.

24. Lee, "Profit Sharing System," p. 308; O. J. Abell, "The Making of Men, Motor Cars, and Profits," *Iron Age*, 95 (January 7, 1915), p. 37; and Boyd Fisher, "Methods of Reducing Labor Turnover," *Bulletin of the Bureau of Labor Statistics*, 196 (1916), p. 15.

25. O. J. Abell, "Labor Classified on a Skill-Wages Basis," *Iron Age*, 93 (January 1, 1914), p. 48 and G. Demerest, "On the Failure of the Craft Unions to Organize in Detroit," *Official Journal of the Carriage, Wagon, and Automobile Workers' Union* (Hereafter *Official Journal CWAWU*), 3 (July 1914), p. 6.

26. Myron W. Watkins, "The Labor Situation in Detroit," *Journal of Political Economy*, 28 (December 1920), p. 851.

27. John W. Love, "Detroit a Sterile Field for Organized Labor," *Annalist*, 28 (November 12, 1926), p. 630 and Frank Marquart, *An Auto Worker's Journal* (University Park, Pa., 1975), pp. 13–4.

28. Lee, "Profit Sharing System," p. 308 and Abell, "Labor Classified," p. 37.

29. John S. Keir, "The Reduction of Absences and Lateness in Industry," *Annals AAPSS*, 71 (May 1917), pp. 141–2; Emil Frankel, "Labor Absenteeism," *Journal of Political Economy*, 29 (June 1921), pp. 487–99; Sumner H. Slichter, "The Management of Labor," *Journal of Political Economy*, 27 (December 1919), pp. 813–9; and Keir, "Absences and Lateness," pp. 143 and 145.

30. Slichter, "Management," p. 827; Boyd Fisher, "How to Reduce Labor Turnover," *Bulletin of the Bureau of Labor Statistics*, 227 (1917), p. 42; and Watkins, "Labor Situation," p. 851.

31. Thomas T. Read, "Shop Dividends Due to Personnel Work," *Iron Age*, 100 (November 1, 1917), p. 1059; Arthur E. Corbin, "Training Employees in

a Motor Car Plant," *Iron Age*, 94 (June 30, 1914), p. 261; and H. F. Porter, "Giving the Men a Share," *System*, 31 (March 1917), p. 263.

32. Porter, "Giving the Men a Share," p. 263 and United States, Senate, *Report of Commission on Industrial Relations*, vol. 8, (Washington, 1915), p. 7626.

33. E. A. Rumley, "Ford's Plan to Share Profits," *World's Work*, 27 (April 1914), p. 667.

34. Magnus W. Alexander, "Waste in Hiring and Discharging Men," *Iron Age*, 94 (October 29, 1914), pp. 1032−3 and Fisher, "Methods of Reducing Labor Turnover," p. 25.

35. Fisher, "How to Reduce Labor Turnover," pp. 16−9 and Fisher, "Methods of Reducing Labor Turnover," p. 19.

36. John R. Godfrey, "Keeping Men on the Job," *American Machinist*, 41 (November 11, 1914), pp. 901−2 and John R. Commons, *Labor and Administration* (New York, 1923), p. 365.

37. Frederick W. Taylor, "Shop Management," *Transactions of the American Society of Mechanical Engineers*, 24 (1903), p. 1349.

38. Taylor, "Shop Management," p. 1350.

39. United States, Department of Commerce and Labor, *Regulation and Restriction of Output* (Washington, 1904), pp. 29 and 18. See also "How the Union Limits Output," *Iron Age*, 70 (October 16, 1902), p. 45 and "Restriction of Output in the United States," *Iron Age*, 71 (January 1, 1903), pp. 77−8.

40. Stanley B. Mathewson, *Restriction of Output among Unorganized Workers* (Carbondale, Ill., 1969), pp. 146−8.

41. *Klann Reminiscences*, pp. 11 and 52.

42. Ford, *Life and Work*, pp. 258−9 and 80.

43. Watkins, "Labor Situation," pp. 850−1.

44. Marquart, *Auto Worker's Journal*, pp. 23−4.

45. W. E. Chalmers, "Labor in the Automobile Industry: A Study of Personnel Policies, Workers' Attitudes and Attempts at Unionism" (Ph.D. dissertation, University of Wisconsin, 1932), p. 188.

46. Ford, *Life and Work*, pp. 256 and 257.

47. Ford, *Life and Work*, p. 262.

48. Ford Motor Company Archives, *The Reminiscences of Mr. W. A. Walters* (November 1955), p. 38.

49. Melvyn Dubofsky, *We Shall Be All: A History of the IWW* (Chicago, 1969), pp. 285−7 and Philip S. Foner, *The Industrial Workers of the World* (New York, 1973), pp. 273−83.

50. *Detroit News*, April 30, 1913 and *Free Press*, April 30, 1913 in "Automobile Industry History;" Foner, *Industrial Workers of the World*, p. 285; Keith Sward, *The Legend of Henry Ford* (New York, 1972), p. 51; and *Detroit News, Journal, Times*, and *Free Press* from June 17 to 25, 1913 in "Automobile Industry History."

51. Foner, *Industrial Workers of the World*, p. 161.

52. Ralph Chaplin, *Wobbly: Rough-and-Tumble Story of an American Radical* (Chicago, 1948), p. 207; Foner, *Industrial Workers of the World*, pp. 157−67; and Mike Davis, "The Stop Watch and the Wooden Shoe," *Radical America*, 9 (January-February 1975), pp. 69−75.

53. Jack W. Skeels, "Early Carriage and Auto Unions," *Industrial and Labor Relations Review*, 17 (July 1964), pp. 566−83; William A. Logan, "Historical Sketch of the Automobile Workers' Union," *Detroit Labor News*, November 9, 1917; and Proceedings of Carriage, Wagon, and Automobile Workers' Union for 1913 in "Automobile Industry History."

54. Metal Trades Department, "Joint Organizing Campaign in the Automobile Industry" in American Federation of Labor, *Report of Proceedings . . . 1914* (Washington, 1914), p. 182 and American Federation of Labor, *Proceedings 1914*, p. 240.

55. Lee quoted in I. T. Martin, "The Melting Pot at Ford's," *Official Journal CWAWU*, 4 (August 1915), p. 7.

Chapter 5

1. Paul H. Douglas, "Plant Administration of Labor," *Journal of Political Economy*, 27 (July 1919), pp. 545−6.

2. Harold W. Slauson, "A Ten Million Dollar Efficiency Plan," *Machinery* (October 1914), p. 86.

3. Daniel Nelson, *Managers and Workers: Origins of the New Factory System in the United States, 1880−1920* (Madison, 1975), pp. 55−121; David Montgomery, *Workers' Control in America: Studies in the History of Work, Technology, and Labor Struggles* (Cambridge, Mass., 1979), pp. 32−47 and 113−38; Henry Eilbert, "The Development of Personnel Management in the United States," *Business History Review*, 33 (Autumn 1959), pp. 345−64; and Sumner H. Slichter, "The Management of Labor," *Journal of Political Economy*, 27 (December 1919), p. 814.

4. Stephen J. Scheinberg, "Progressivism in Industry: The Welfare Movement in the American Factory," *Canadian Historical Association: Historical Papers . . .* (1967), pp. 184−97; Stanley Buder, *Pullman: An Experiment in Industrial Order and Community Planning* (New York, 1967), pp. 28−117; Robert Ozanne, *A Century of Labor-Management Relations at McCormick and International Harvester* (Madison, 1967), pp. 71−95; Homer J. Hagedorn, "A Note on the Motivation of Personnel Management," *Explorations in Entrepreneurial History*, 10 (April 1958), pp. 134−9; Samuel Haber, *Efficiency and Uplift: Scientific Management in the Progressive Era, 1890−1920* (Chicago, 1964); and Stuart D. Brandes, *American Welfare Capitalism, 1880−1940* (Chicago, 1976).

5. Frederick W. Taylor, "Shop Management," *Transactions of the American Society of Mechanical Engineers*, 24 (1903), p. 1346.

6. Taylor, "Shop Management," p. 1404.

7. Tolman quoted in Eilbert, "Personnel Management," p. 346.

8. Josiah Strong, "What Social Service Means," *Craftsman*, 9 (February 1906), pp. 620–1 and Brandes, *Welfare Capitalism*, passim.

9. H. F. Porter, "Giving the Men a Share," *System*, 31 (March 1917), p. 263; Ford Motor Company, *Ford Factory Facts* (Detroit, 1915), p. 61; and Ford Motor Company, *Facts from Ford* (Detroit, 1920), passim.

10. "Employee Services of the Ford Motor Company," Box 15, Accession 940, Ford Motor Company Archives, Dearborn, Michigan; Ford Motor Company Archives, *The Reminiscences of Mr. George Brown* (May 1953), p. 84; *Free Press*, July 21, 1912 in "Automobile Industry History," Edward Levinson Papers, Archives of Labor History and Urban Affairs, Wayne State University, Detroit, Michigan; and "Welfare Work in the Ford Automobile Works" report to Commission on Industrial Relations, Record Group 174, National Archives, Washington, D.C.

11. Allan Nevins, *Ford: The Times, the Man, the Company* (New York, 1954), p. 531.

12. Samuel M. Levin, "Ford Profit Sharing, 1914–1920," *Personnel Journal*, 6 (August 1927), p. 76 and Nevins, *Ford*, p. 531.

13. Nevins, *Ford*, pp. 599, 459–61, and 529–33.

14. "Memorandum on Labor Dissatisfaction," Box 17, Accession 940, Ford Motor Company Archives, Dearborn, Michigan; "Reducing Labor Turnover," *Iron Age*, 102 (December 12, 1918), p. 1463; and Ford Motor Company, *A Brief Account of the Educational Work of the Ford Motor Company* (Detroit, 1916), p. 9.

15. Rose Wilder Lane, *Henry Ford's Own Story* (New York, 1917), p. 5; "Ford Auto Workers Get Raise in Pay," *Detroit Tribune*, October 12, 1913; and Ford Motor Company, *Educational Work*, p. 1.

16. O J. Abell, "Labor Classified on a Skill-Wages Basis," *Iron Age*, 93 (January 1, 1914), pp. 48–50; E. A. Rumley, "Ford's Plan to Share Profits," *World's Work*, 27 (April 1914), pp. 664–9; Porter, "Giving the Men a Share," pp. 262–70; John R. Lee, "The So-Called Profit Sharing System at the Ford Plant," *Annals AAPSS*, 65 (May 1916), pp. 297–310; and George Bundy, "Work of the Employment Department of the Ford Motor Company," *Bulletin of the Bureau of Labor Statistics*, 196 (1916), pp. 63–71.

17. Abell, "Labor Classified," p. 48. The table is adapted from the table in Abell, "Labor Classified," p. 48. The wage-rates for the different grades and skill levels are from Rumley, "Ford's Plan," pp. 665–6.

18. On the importance of a job ladder as a managerial form of control, see Katherine Stone, "The Origins of Job Structures in the Steel Industry," *Review of Radical Political Economics*, 6 (Summer 1924), 113–73.

19. Lee, "Profit Sharing System," p. 300; Porter, "Giving the Men a Share," p. 263; and Rumley, "Ford's Plan," p. 665.

20. Abell, "Labor Classified," p. 49; "Auto Workers Get Raise in Pay"; Lee, "Profit Sharing System," p. 300; and Rumley, "Ford's Plan," p. 665.

21. Abell, "Labor Classified," pp. 49 and 50 and Rumley, "Ford's Plan," pp. 665–6.

22. Abell, "Labor Classified," p. 50.

23. Ford Motor Company, *Ford Factory Facts*, p. 14; Rumley, "Ford's Plan," p. 666; and Bundy, "Employment Department," p. 67.

24. Porter, "Giving the Men a Share," p. 264; Abell, "Labor Classified," p. 50; Sarah T. Bushnell, *The Truth about Henry Ford* (Chicago, 1922), p. 210; and Rumley, "Ford's Plan," p. 666.

25. Lee, "Profit Sharing System," p. 300; Rumley, "Ford's Plan," p. 666; and Abell, "Labor Classified," p. 50.

26. Lee, "Profit Sharing System," p. 301.

27. "Ford Auto Workers Get Raise in Pay"; O. J. Abell, "The Ford Plan for Employees' Betterment," *Iron Age*, 93 (January 29, 1914), p. 306; Abell, "Labor Classified," p. 50; and Henry Ford quoted in *New York Times*, January 6, 1914.

28. Abell, "Labor Classified," pp. 48 and 50; H. L. Arnold and F. L. Faurote, *Ford Methods and the Ford Shops* (New York, 1916), p. 44.

29. Abell, "Labor Classified," p. 50.

30. Abell, "Labor Classified," p. 50.

31. Abell, "Labor Classified," p. 50.

32. Nevins, *Ford*, pp. 532–4.

33. Press release on the Five Dollar Day, Box 16, Accession 940, Ford Motor Company Archives, Dearborn, Michigan.

34. Press release on Five Dollar Day.

35. Nevins, *Ford*, p. 536; General letter, January 17, 1914, Box 1, Accession 683, Ford Motor Company Archives, Dearborn, Michigan; and "Welfare Work in the Ford Automobile Works."

36. Ford Motor Company, *Bonus, Investment, and Profit Sharing Plan: An Extension to Present Profit Sharing* (Highland Park, Michigan, 1919), passim.

37. John A. Fitch, "Making the Job Worthwhile," *Survey*, 40 (April 27, 1914), p. 88; Levin, "Ford Profit Sharing," p. 80; and Ford Motor Company, *Helpful Hints and Advice to Employees to Help Them Grasp the Opportunities which Are Presented to Them by the Ford Profit Sharing Plan* (Detroit, 1915), p. 9.

38. Letter to Omaha Branch, January 26, 1914, Box 1, Accession 683, Ford Motor Company Archives, Dearborn, Michigan.

39. Fitch, "Making the Job Worthwhile," p. 88; Abell, "Employees' Betterment," p. 306; and Arthur R. Barret, *Profit Sharing: Its Principles and Practice* (New York, 1918), pp. 181–2.

40. Levin, "Ford Profit Sharing," pp. 79–80. The monthly wage and profit rates were computed by multiplying the daily rates times six and then times four and one-third.

41. I. Paul Taylor, *Prosperity in Detroit* (Highland Park, Mich., 1920), pp. 123–4. On the economic security of a job, see Whiting Williams, *What's on the Worker's Mind* (New York, 1920), pp. 282–5.

42. Ford Motor Company, *Educational Work*, pp. 13 and 4.

43. Letter to Cleveland Branch, April 29, 1914, Box 1, Accession 683, Ford Motor Company Archives, Dearborn, Michigan.

44. *New York Times*, January 11, 1914, sec. 4, p. 3.

45. "Excerpts from pamphlet 'Ford Profit Sharing Plan . . .' (1914), 52–4," Box 17, Accession 940, Ford Motor Company Archives, Dearborn, Michigan; Ford Motor Company, *Educational Work*, p. 6; Ford Motor Company, *Helpful Hints and Advice*, p. 13; Ford quoted in Levin, "Ford Profit Sharing," pp. 79–89; Lee, "Profit Sharing System," p. 302; and General letter, January 17, 1914.

46. *New York Times*, April 19, 1914, sec. 3, p. 12.

47. General letter, January 17, 1914.

48. Instructions to investigators, Box 17, Accession 940, Ford Motor Company Archives, Dearborn, Michigan. Hereafter cited as "Sociological Department Instructions."

49. General letter, January 17, 1914 and Lee, "Profit Sharing System," p. 307.

50. *New York Times*, January 9, 1914 and *New York Times*, January 7, 1914.

51. "Excerpts 'Ford Profit Sharing Plan.' "

52. Letter to Omaha Branch, January 26, 1914.

53. "Lee's Talk, April 16, 1914."

54. Memoranda dated May 22, 1916, May 24, 1919, and July 1, 1919 and general letters dated November 15, 1914, October 17, 1916, October 20, 1917, November 30, 1917, July 10, 1918, January 4, 1919, and February 6, 1919 in Box 1 Accession 683, Ford Motor Company Archives, Dearborn, Michigan.

55. Arnold and Faurots, *Ford Methods*, p. 47 and Porter, "Giving the Men a Share," p. 265.

56. *New York Times*, January 11, 1914, sec. 5, p. 3; United States, Senate, *Report of the Commission on Industrial Relations*, vol. 8 (Washington, 1915), p. 7628; Lee quoted in I. T. Martin, "The Melting Pot at Ford's," *Official Journal of the Carriage, Wagon, and Automobile Workers' Union*, 4 (August 1915), p. 7; and Marquis quoted in Levin, "Ford Profit Sharing," p. 82.

57. Ford quoted in Levin, "Ford Profit Sharing," p. 77.

Chapter 6

1. "From the Reminiscences of William Pioch," Box 17, Accession 940, Ford Motor Company Archives, Dearborn, Michigan.

218   *The Five Dollar Day*

2. E. P. Thompson, "Time, Work Discipline, and Industrial Capitalism," *Past and Present*, 38 (December 1967), p. 57.

3. H. F. Porter, "Giving the Men a Share," *System* (March 1917), p. 268 and "Mr. Lee's Talk to Second Group of Investigators, April 16th, 1914," Box 17, Accession 940, Ford Motor Company Archives, Dearborn, Michigan.

4. S. S. Marquis, "The Ford Idea in Education" in National Education Association, *Addresses and Proceedings . . . 1916*, vol. 64, pp. 913−4 and 911 and "Ford Profit Sharing," Box 1, Accession 293, Ford Motor Company Archives, Dearborn, Michigan.

5. John A. Fitch, "Ford of Detroit and his Ten Million Dollar Profit Sharing Plan," *Survey*, 31 (February 1914), pp. 547−8.

6. Press release on Five Dollar Day, Box 17, Accession 940, Ford Motor Company Archives, Dearborn, Michigan and "Exerpts from pamphlet 'Ford Profit Sharing Plan . . . ,'" pp. 51−2, Box 17, Accession 940, Ford Motor Company Archives.

7. United States Senate, *Report of the Commission on Industrial Relations*, vol. 8, (Washington, D.C., 1915), p. 7626.

8. Boris Emmett, "Profit Sharing in the United States," *Bulletin of the Bureau of Labor Statistics*, 208 (1916), p. 105; Ford Motor Company, *Helpful Hints and Advice to Employees to Help Them Grasp the Opportunities which Are Presented to Them by the Ford Profit Sharing Plan* (Detroit, 1915), p. 34; and S. M. Levin, "Ford Profit Sharing, 1914−1920," *Personnel Journal*, 6 (August 1927), pp. 79−80.

9. Ford Motor Company, *A Brief Account of the Educational Work of the Ford Motor Company* (Detroit, 1916), p. 7; Letter to Omaha, January 26, 1914, Box 1, Accession 940, Ford Motor Company Archives, Dearborn, Michigan; John R. Lee, "The So-Called Profit Sharing System in the Ford Plant," *Annals AAPSS*, 65 (May 1916), p. 302.

10. O. J. Abell, "The Ford Plan for Employees' Betterment," *Iron Age*, 93 (January 29, 1914), p. 307; *New York Times*, April 19, 1914, sec. 3, p. 12; I. T. Martin, "The Melting Pot at Ford's," *Official Journal Carriage, Wagon, and Automobile Workers' Union*, 4 (August 1914), p. 6; and Emmett, "Profit Sharing," p. 104.

11. Ford Motor Company, *Ford Factory Facts* (Detroit, 1915), p. 43; Ford Motor Company, *Educational Work*, pp. 6−7; Letter to Omaha, January 26, 1914; and Lee, "Profit Sharing System," p. 305.

12. Report on Educational Department, July 1917, Box 30, Accession 572, Ford Motor Company Archives, Dearborn, Michigan and C. T. Shower, "Guiding the Workman's Personal Expenditures," *Automotive Industries*, 38 (May 14, 1918), p. 540.

13. Report on Educational Department.

14. Report on Educational Department.

15. Ford Motor Company, *Ford Factory Facts*, p. 43 and General letter,

January 17, 1914, Box 17, Accession 940, Ford Motor Company Archives, Dearborn, Michigan.

16. For a photographic copy of a Record of Investigation, see Porter, "Giving the Men a Share," p. 267. For others, see Emmett, "Profit Sharing," pp. 99–104.

17. "Sociological Department Instructions, Accounting for Share of Profits," Box 17, Accession 940, Ford Motor Company Archives, Dearborn, Michigan.

18. General letter, January 17, 1914 and Lee, "Profit Sharing System," p. 307.

19. "Sociological Department Instructions, Habits."

20. Porter, "Giving the Men a Share," p. 267. The "v" means verified.

21. Emmett, "Profit Sharing," pp. 99–100.

22. "Sociological Department Instructions, Accounting for Share of Profits."

23. Emmett, "Profit Sharing," pp. 101–2.

24. Emmett, "Profit Sharing," pp. 103–4.

25. "Human Interest Stories," Box 17, Accession 940, Ford Motor Company Archives. The Ford investigators seem to have been instructed to search their memories and records for those cases which best reflected the objectives and successes of Ford sociological work. Only fourteen of these stories have survived. But, the ones which exist are numbered from 1 through 38. See "Human Interest Stories" numbered 4, 14, 22, and 37.

26. "Human Interest Story, Number 4."

27. "Human Interest Story, Number 14."

28. "Human Interest Story, Number 22."

29. "Human Interest Story, Number 27."

30. H. L. Arnold and F. L. Faurote, *Ford Methods and the Ford Shops* (New York, 1916), p. 58 and *New York Times*, January 7, 1914.

31. "Sociological Department Instructions, Domestic Trouble" and "General Discussion, Educational Department, Detroit," Box 17, Accession 940, Ford Motor Company Archives, Dearborn, Michigan.

32. "Mr. Lee's Talk to Investigators on July 7th, 1914," Box 17, Accession 940, Ford Motor Company Archives, Dearborn, Michigan.

33. "Lee's Talk, July 7th, 1914."

34. "Lee's Talk, July 7th, 1914."

35. W. M. Purves, "The Investigators' Standing with Employees and Others, June 21, 1915," Box 17, Accession 940, Ford Motor Company Archives, Dearborn, Michigan.

36. Letter to Cleveland, April 29, 1914, Box 1, Accession 683, Ford Motor Company Archives, Dearborn, Michigan.

37. Letter to Cleveland, April 29, 1914.

38. General letter, November 30, 1917, Box 1, Accession 683, Ford Motor Company Archives, Dearborn, Michigan.

39. "Sociological Department Instructions, Honor Roll."

40. "Sociological Department Instructions, Honor Roll;" "Star Employees," Box 27, Accession 572, Ford Motor Company Archives, Dearborn, Michigan; and Ford Motor Company Archives, *The Reminiscences of Mr. William C. Klann* (September 1955), pp. 108–9.

Chapter 7

1. Robert E. Park and Herbert A. Miller, *Old World Traits Transplanted* (New York, 1921), p. 280.

2. Edward G. Hartman, *The Movement to Americanize the Immigrant* (New York, 1948), p. 7. Other important works on Americanization include: Gerd Korman, *Industrialization, Immigrants, and Americanizers* (Madison, 1967); Herbert Gutman, "Work, Culture, and Society in Industrializing America, 1815–1915," *American Historical Review*, 78 (June 1973), pp. 531–87; and John Higham, *Strangers in the Land: Patterns of American Nativism* (New York, 1973).

3. Sidney Pollard, "Factory Discipline in the Industrial Revolution," *Economic History Review*, 16 (December 1963), p. 254; E. P. Thompson, "Time, Work Discipline, and Industrial Capitalism," *Past and Present*, 38 (December 1967), p. 57; Gutman, "Work, Culture, and Society," pp. 541 and 543; David Montgomery, "Workers' Control of Machine Production in the Nineteenth Century," *Labor History*, 17 (Fall 1976), pp. 486–7; and Daniel Rodgers, "Tradition, Modernity, and the American Industrial Worker," *Journal of Interdisciplinary History*, 7 (Spring 1977), p. 680.

4. John R. Commons, "Henry Ford: Miracle Maker," *Independent*, 102 (May 1, 1920), p. 161.

5. Letter to Omaha, January 29, 1914, Accession 683, Ford Motor Company Archives, Dearborn, Michigan; Henry Ford quoted in *New York Times*, April 19, 1914, sec. 3, p. 12; and "Progress among Foreigners," Box 17, Accession 940, Ford Motor Company Archives, Dearborn, Michigan.

6. Ford Motor Company, *Helpful Hints and Advice to Employees to Help Them Grasp the Opportunities which Are Presented to Them by the Ford Profit Sharing Plan* (Detroit, 1915), p. 13.

7. Ford Motor Company, *Helpful Hints and Advice*, p. 15.

8. S. S. Marquis, *Henry Ford: An Interpretation* (Boston, 1923), p. 151.

9. Ford Motor Company, *Helpful Hints and Advice*, p. 13.

10. Boris Emmett, "Profit Sharing in the United States," *Bulletin of the Bureau of Labor Statistics*, 208 (1916), p. 106.

11. "Sociological Department Instructions, Verifying Marriage," Box 17, Accession 940, Ford Motor Company Archives, Dearborn, Michigan.

12. "Human Interest Stories," Box 17, Accession 940, Ford Motor Company Archives, Dearborn, Michigan.

13. "Human Interest Story, Number 9."

14. "Human Interest Story, Number 38."

15. *New York Times*, January 10, 1914, sec. 4, p. 6.

16. S. S. Marquis, "The Ford Idea in Education" in National Education Association, *Addresses and Proceedings . . . 1916*, vol. 64 (1916), pp. 911, 915, and 916.

17. Peter Roberts, *English for Comingmericans* (New York, 1909); Peter Roberts, "The Y.M.C.A. Teaching Foreign Speaking Men," *Immigrants in America Review*, 1 (June 1915), pp. 18–23; and Peter Roberts, "The Y.M.C.A. Among the Immigrants," *Survey*, 29 (February 1915), pp. 697–700.

18. Roberts, *English for Coming Americans*, p. 20.

19. Roberts, *English for Coming Americans*, pp. 22–3.

20. Roberts, *English for Coming Americans*, pp. 20–1.

21. "Ford Profit Sharing Plan," Accession 293, Ford Motor Company Archives, Dearborn, Michigan; Marquis, "Ford Idea in Education," p. 912; and "Preliminary Report of Work Done Teaching the English Language to Employees of the Ford Motor Company, at Stevens School, Highland Park, Mich., June 12, 1914," Box 17, Accession 940, Ford Motor Company Archives, Dearborn, Michigan.

22. Clinton C. DeWitt, "Industrial Teachers" in United States Bureau of Education, *Proceedings: Americanization Conference . . . 1919*, p. 116.

23. O. J. Abell, "The Making of Men, Motor Cars, and Profits," *Iron Age*, 95 (January 7, 1915), p. 39.

24. "Ford Profit Sharing Plan." See also, Marquis, "Ford Idea in Education," pp. 911–2.

25. Gregory Mason, "Americans First: How the People of Detroit Are Making Americans of Foreigners in their City," *Outlook*, 114 (September 27, 1915), p. 200; Marquis, "Ford Idea in Education," p. 915; DeWitt, "Industrial Teachers," p. 118; and Ford Motor Company, *Facts from Ford* (Highland Park, Mich., 1920), p. 33.

26. DeWitt, "Industrial Teachers," p. 119 and "Ford Profit Sharing Plan."

27. DeWitt, "Industrial Teachers," p. 119.

28. Ford Motor Company, *Facts from Ford,* p. 32 and "Ford Sociological Statistics" (My title), January 12, 1917, pp. 1–6, Box 31, Accession 572, Ford Motor Company Archives, Dearborn, Michigan.

29. Mason, "Americans First," pp. 193–201 and Esther Everett Lape, "The English First Movement in Detroit," *Immigrants in America Review*, 1 (September 1915), pp. 46–50.

30. George Qimby in *Proceedings of the National Conference on Americanization in Industries . . . 1919* (n.p., n.d.), pp. 4–5 and Peter Roberts, *Problems of Americanization* (New York, 1920), pp. 226–7.

31. Ford Motor Company, *A Brief Account of the Educational Work of the Ford Motor Company* (Detroit, 1916), pp. 2 and 7 and Abell, "Men, Motor Cars, and Profits," p. 37.

32. Ford Motor Company, *Educational Work*, p. 9.

33. Abell, "Men, Motor Cars, and Profits," pp. 33, 36, and 37.

34. "Ford Sociological Statistics," January 12, 1916 and January 12, 1917.

35. Harold Whiting Slauson, "A Ten Million Dollar Efficiency Plan," *Machinery* (October 1914), p. 86; H. F. Porter, "Giving the Men a Share," *System*, 31 (March 1917), p. 268; and Tarbell quoted in Boyd Fisher, "How to Reduce Labor Turnover," *Bulletin of the Bureau of Labor Statistics*, 227 (1917), p. 33.

36. "Welfare Work in the Ford Automobile Works," Record Group 174, National Archives, Washington, D.C.; W. M. Purves, "The Investigators' Standing with Employees and Others," Box 17, Accession 940, Ford Motor Company Archives, Dearborn, Michigan; and on the testimonials see reports scattered through Box 17, Accession 940.

37. "Mr. Lee's Talk to First Group of Investigators, April 15th, 1914," "Mr. Lee's Talk to Second Group of Investigators, April 16th, 1914," "Mr. Lee's Talk to Third Group of Investigators, April 17th, 1914," "Mr. Lee's Talk to Investigators on July 7th, 1914," and "Meeting of Sociological Department Held on Fourth Floor of Office Building, May 12th, 1915," Box 17, Ford Motor Company Archives, Dearborn, Michigan; General letter, November 30, 1917, Box 1, Accession 683, Ford Motor Company Archives, Dearborn, Michigan; Ford Motor Company Archives, *The Reminiscences of Mr. William C. Klann* (September 1955), p. 107; and William A. Logan, "Has Henry Ford Solved the Labor Problem," *Official Journal of the Carriage, Wagon and Automobile Workers' Union*, 3 (April 1914), p. 7.

38. "Disgruntled Writers Criticize Ford Plant Employing System," Detroit *Journal*, September 20, 1915, p. 8.

39. "Profit Sharing," *Official Journal CWAWU*, 4 (March 1915), p. 5; W. E. Schneeberg, Letter to *Official Journal CWAWU*, 3 (June 1914), p. 8; and Logan, "Henry Ford," p. 6.

40. "Ford Profit Sharing" and "Shares of Profits Distributed among Employees," Box 27, Accession 572, Ford Motor Company Archives, Dearborn, Michigan.

41. General letters, October 17, 1916, October 20, 1917, November 30, 1917, July 10, 1918, and January 4, 1919, Box 1, Accession 683, Ford Motor Company Archives, Dearborn, Michigan.

Chapter 8

1. "APL Reports," Rouston, n.d., Box 29, Accession 572, Ford Motor Company Archives, Dearborn, Michigan. In this record box, two looseleaf notebooks list the names of workers, biographical information from their Record of Investigation, and dated reports on their "illicit" activities in the Ford plant. Some of the Ford interdepartmental communications which

served as the basis for the reports were scattered throughout this box. For the citations in this chapter, I used the title "APL Reports" and give the last name of the worker and the date of the report.

2. Henry F. May, *The End of American Innocence: A Study of the First Years of Our Own Time, 1912–1917* (New York, 1979); Arthur S. Link, *Woodrow Wilson and the Progressive Era, 1910–1917* (New York, 1963); James Weinstein, *The Corporate Ideal and the Liberal State, 1900–1918* (Boston, 1971); Seward W. Livermore, *Woodrow Wilson and the War Congress, 1916–1918* (Seattle, 1966); Harold U. Faulkner, *The Decline of Laissez Faire, 1897–1917* (New York, 1951); and George Soule, *Prosperity Decade: From War to Depression, 1917–1929* (New York, 1964).

3. Daniel Nelson, *Managers and Workers: Origins of the New Factory System in the United States, 1880–1920* (Madison, 1975), pp. 140–62; David Montgomery, *Workers' Control in America: Studies in the History of Work, Technology, and Labor Struggles* (Cambridge, Mass., 1979), pp. 91–138; Samuel Haber, *Efficiency and Uplift: Scientific Management in the Progressive Era, 1890–1920* (Chicago, 1964), pp. 117–133; and Soule, *Prosperity Decade*, pp. 7–80.

4. John Higham, *Strangers in the Land: Patterns of American Nativism* (New York, 1973); Edward G. Hartman, *The Movement to Americanize the Immigrant* (New York, 1948); Gerd Korman, *Industrialization, Immigrants, and Americanizers: The View from Milwaukee, 1866–1921* (Madison, 1967); and William Preston, *Aliens and Dissenters: Federal Suppression of Radicals, 1903–1933* (New York, 1963).

5. Soule, *Prosperity Decade*, pp. 7–63; Weinstein, *Corporate Ideal*, pp. 214–54; and H. C. Peterson and Gilbert C. Fite, *Opponents of War, 1917–1918* (Seattle, 1957).

6. Ford Motor Company, *A Brief Account of the Educational Work of the Ford Motor Company* (Detroit, 1916), p. 2. Although dated 1916, this pamphlet contains statistics for the war period.

7. Jack W. Skeels, "Early Carriage and Auto Unions: The Impact of Industrialization and Rival Unionism," *Industrial and Labor Relations Review*, 17 (July 1964), pp. 566–83 and William A. Logan, "Historical Sketch of the Auto Workers' Union, Local 123," *Detroit Labor News*, November 9, 1917, p. 3.

8. H. L. Arnold and F. L. Faurote, *Ford Methods and the Ford Shops* (New York, 1916), pp. 329 and 331 and O. J. Abell, "The Making of Men, Motor Cars, and Profits," *Iron Age*, 95 (January 7, 1915), p. 37.

9. Ford Motor Company Archives, *The Reminiscences of Mr. George Brown* (May 1953), p. 101.

10. Allan Nevins, *Ford: The Times, the Man, the Company* (New York, 1954), pp. 381–4 and Ford Motor Company Archives, *The Reminiscences of Mr. William C. Klann* (September 1955) pp. 138 and 142.

11. Peterson and Fite, *Opponents*, pp. 16–7 and 215.

12. On the APL, see Higham, *Strangers in the Land*, pp. 211–2; Joan M. Jensen, *The Price of Vigilance* (Chicago, 1968); and Emerson Hough, *The Web* (Chicago, 1919). Hough was the official historian for the APL.

13. Hough, *The Web*, p. 459.

14. Detroit APL to Ford Motor Company, March 2, 1917, Box 28, Accession 572, Ford Motor Company Archives, Dearborn, Michigan.

15. Detroit APL to Ford Motor Company, March 2, 1917 and Hough, *The Web*, p. 286.

16. "Eight [sic] Industrial Division, Detroit, Mich., 10–5–17," Box 29, Accession 572, Ford Motor Company Archives, Dearborn, Michigan. This two-page document lists the officers and the operatives of the APL in the Ford Motor Company. In addition to the name and rank of each individual, it also lists the name, address, and Ford shop or department of each worker.

17. "Eight Industrial Division."

18. Samples of the various reports are scattered throughout Box 29, Accession 572, Ford Motor Company Archives, Dearborn, Michigan.

19. Memorandum, G. M. Rounds to S. S. Marquis, September 9, 1918, Box 29, Accession 572, Ford Motor Company Archives, Dearborn, Michigan.

20. "APL Reports," Manzner, June 11, 1917, Hoffrichter, November 3, 1918, Unser, February 28, 1918, Harder, June 1, 1917, and Soltys, November 15, 1917.

21. "APL Reports," Froch, June 21, 1917, June 27, 1917, and September 26, 1917.

22. "APL Reports," Wegner, July 9, 1918.

23. "APL Reports," Freiss, October 17, 1918 and Hennig, May 24, 1917.

24. "APL Reports," Nikoroi, December 15, 1917, Gose, June 8, 1917, Descou, n.d., Schlicker, January 1, 1918, and Schmidt, June 13, 1917.

25. "APL Reports," Media, March 5, 1917, Huntington, n.d., and Steihs, November 9, 1917.

26. "APL Reports," Ross, August 8, 1918 and Rodriguez, September 9, 1918.

27. "APL Reports," Kostuck, n.d., Negro, October 3, 1918, n.d., and Bereta, n.d.

28. "APL Reports," Angeloff, October 22, 1917.

29. "APL Reports," Milna, November 19, 1917, Pierce, June 9, 1917, Wolf, June 14, 1917, and Somner, June 20, 1917.

30. "APL Reports," Wurmlinger, November 21, 1917 and Naeyaert, November 11, 1917.

31. "APL Reports," Stetzuk, June 26, 1917 and Wanke, June 26, 1917.

32. "APL Reports," Zoch, September 11, 1918 and Oberhoffer, November 11, 1917.

33. "APL Reports," Van Buren, October 24, 1917, November 6, 1917, November 10, 1917, and November 19, 1917.

34. "APL Reports," Bortonezuk, n.d., Lettich, November 16, 1917, Frisch, August 27, 1917, Turner, September 25, 1918, Meeker, n.d., and Wilson, November 23, 1917.

35. "APL Reports," Slusser, June 8, 1917 and Bakewell, December 22, 1917.

36. "APL Reports," Bodia, April 15, 1918.

37. Memorandum, L. B. Scofield to A. G. Spark, August 21, 1918 and Memorandum, G. M. Rounds to A. G. Spark, August 28, 1918, Box 29, Accession 572, Ford Motor Company Archives, Dearborn, Michigan.

38. "APL Reports," Baunert, September 23, 1918 and Schreiber, n.d.

39. "APL Reports," Lorenz, n.d. and Oswald, November 6, 1917 and November 21, 1917.

40. "APL Reports," Schury, May 7, 1918 and May 8, 1918.

41. *Detroit Labor News*, April 25, 1919, May 2, 1919, and May 9, 1919 and *Auto Workers' News*, May 15, 1919.

42. *Auto Workers' News*, July 24, 1919 and *Detroit Labor News*, April 25, 1919.

43. *Detroit Labor News*, May 2, 1919.

44. *Detroit Labor News*, May 2, 19191 and May 9, 1919 and Memorandum, n.d., Box 29, Accession 572, Ford Motor Company Archives, Dearborn, Michigan.

45. Letters to A. G. Spark from Operative 8, May 30, 1919, Operative 9, May 25, 1919, Operative 11, June 30, 1919, and the extensive reports from Operative 15 from May 1919 to April 1920, Box 29, Accession 572 Ford Motor Company Archives, Dearborn, Michigan.

46. Report, Operative 15 to A. G. Spark, October 30, 1919, November 18, 1919, October 13, 1919, and June 13, 1919 and Letter, B. J. Licardi to A. G. Spark, June 16, 1919, Box 29, Accession 572, Ford Motor Company Archives, Dearborn, Michigan.

47. Reports, Operative 15, August 20 to November 25, 1919, passim.

48. Licardi to A. G. Spark, June 16, 1919.

49. Report, Operative 15, November 18, 1919, November 15, 1919, and November 24, 1919.

50. Report, Operative 15, November 4, 1919.

51. Report, Operative 15, November 9, 1919.

52. Report, Operative 15, November 4, 1919.

53. Reports, Operative 15, August 20, 1919 to November 25, 1919, passim.

54. Report, Operative 15, September 4, 1919.

55. Report, Operative 15, September 4, 1919.

56. Report, Operative 15, September 5, 1919.

57. Report, Operative 15, September 9, 1919.

58. Report, Operative 15, November 20, 1919.

59. "Auto Industry Strikes—Strikes and Lockouts," folder 1, Joe Brown

Papers, Archives of Labor History and Urban Affairs, Wayne State University, Detroit, Michigan and Allan Nevins and Frank E. Hill, *Ford: Expansion and Challenge* (New York, 1957), pp. 200–10.

60. John R. Commons, et al., *History of Labor in the United States, 1896–1932* (New York, 1966), pp. 489–514; James Weinstein, *The Decline of Socialism in America, 1912–1925* (New York, 1969) pp. 234–57; Robert K. Murray, *Red Scare: A Study in National Hysteria, 1919–1920* (New York, 1964), pp. 215–6; and Richard S. Jones, *A History of the American Legion* (Indianapolis, 1946), pp. 191–8.

Chapter 9

1. On paternalism, see E. P. Thompson, "Patrician Society, Plebian Culture," *Journal of Social History*, 7 (Summer 1974), pp. 382–505; David Roberts, *Paternalism in Early Victorian England* (New Brunswick, N.J., 1979); Stanley Buder, *Pullman: An Experiment in Industrial Order and Community Planning, 1880–1930* (New York, 1979); Eugene D. Genovese, *Roll, Jordan, Roll: The World the Slaves Made* (New York, 1974); and Richard Sennett, *Authority* (New York, 1980).

2. Allan Nevins and Frank E. Hill, *Ford: Expansion and Challenge* (New York, 1957), pp. 324–54 and Keith Sward, *The Legend of Henry Ford* (New York, 1972) pp. 74–80.

3. S. S. Marquis, *Henry Ford: An Interpretation* (Boston, 1923), p. 155.

4. Charles E. Sorensen, *My Forty Years with Ford* (New York, 1956), p. 145.

5. Marquis, *Ford*, p. 155 and Sorensen, *Ford*, p. 145.

6. Nevins, *Ford*, 324–55.

7. Jonathan Norton Leonard in John B. Rae, ed., *Henry Ford* (Englewood Cliffs, N.J., 1969), pp. 109 and 111.

8. Irving Bernstein, *Turbulent Years: A History of the American Worker, 1933–1941* (Boston, 1971), pp. 499–571 and 734–51; Sidney Fine, *The Automobile under the Blue Eagle: Labor, Management, and the Automobile Manufacturing Code* (Ann Arbor, 1963), pp. 410–30; Sidney Fine, *Sit-down: The General Motors Strike of 1936–1937* (Ann Arbor, 1969), pp. 313–41; and William Serrin, *The Company and the Union* (New York, 1974).

9. Ely Chinoy, *Automobile Workers and the American Dream* (Garden City, N.Y., 1955); Daniel Bell, "Work and Its Discontents" in *The End of Ideology* (New York, 1962), pp. 227–72; Robert Blauner, *Alienation and Freedom: The Factory Worker and his Industry* (Chicago, 1964); B. J. Widick, ed., *Auto Work and Its Discontents* (Baltimore, 1976); Harvey Swados, "The Myth of the Happy Worker" in Herbert G. Gutman and Gregory S. Kealey, *Many Pasts* (Englewood Cliffs, N.J., 1973), pp. 424–30; Harry Braverman, *Labor and Monopoly Capital: The Degradation of Work in the Twentieth Century* (New York,

1974); *Work in America: Report of a Special Task Force to the Secretary of Health, Education, and Welfare* (Cambridge, Mass., n.d.); Emma Rothschild, *Paradise Lost: The Decline of the Auto-Industrial Age* (New York, 1974); Barbara Garson, *All the Livelong Day: The Meaning and Demeaning of Work* (New York, 1979); Judson Gooding, "Blue-Collar Blues on the Assembly Line," *Fortune* (July 1970), pp. 68–71, 112–3, and 116–7; and Judson Gooding, *The Job Revolution* (New York, 1972), p. ix.

10. United States Bureau of Labor Statistics, *Wage Chronology: The Ford Motor Company, June 1941–September 1973, Bulletin 1787* (Washington, D.C., 1973) and *Wage Chronology: The Ford Motor Company, October 1973–September 1976* (Washington, D.C., 1975).

11. William Serrin, "New Auto Industry Technology a Source of Wonder and Anxiety," *New York Times*, November 5, 1979, p. 1; Peter J. Schuyten, "Technology: Light Industry Adding Robots," *New York Times*, October 25, 1979; and William H. Chapman, "Robots Do the Work on Datsuns," *Milwaukee Journal*, April 23, 1980, p. 10.

Selected Bibliography

Archives

The Ford Motor Company Archives in Dearborn, Michigan was a most invaluable source of information on the Ford Motor Company and its labor relations policies. Two accessions brought together useful information and documents from the numerous Ford collections: Accession 572, Selected Research Papers, a collection of the principal documents in the Archives and Accession 940, the Frank Hill Research Papers, a compilation of copies of documents from different parts of the Archives.

Some accessions contained specific information of the Ford Five Dollar Day, Profit-sharing Plan, and Sociological Department. Accession 63, the Samuel S. Marquis Papers, had Marquis' addresses and other materials relating to Ford sociological and educational programs. Accession 293, the Sociological Department: S. S. Marquis, included manuscripts, speeches, and press clippings on the Ford-profit sharing plan. Accession 683, the Five Dollar Day, contained memoranda, letters, and directives on the implementation and administration of the plan. Other important accessions were Accession 922, Early Model T Production, Accession 1, the Fairlane Papers, Accession 958, George Heliker Papers, and Accession 890, Old Highland Park Plant Payroll Records. Finally, the Oral History Section of the Archives had interviews with leading Ford personalities. Most useful were the interviews with William C. Klann, George Brown, and W. A. Walters.

The Archives of Labor History and Urban Affairs at Wayne State University provided a wealth of materials and information on the early labor movement and automobile industry in Detroit. The Edward Levinson Papers contained newspaper clippings and notes on the early years of the automobile industry. The Robert W. Dunn Papers had his research notes for his work on labor and the automobile industry. The Joe Brown Papers included a wide range of information on Detroit unionism and the automobile industry. In addition, the oral history interviews with Larry Davidov, Lester Johnson, John Panzner, Philip Raymond, and I. Paul Taylor provided important background information on the Auto Workers' Union in the 1910s and 1920s.

Finally, the Ford film collection of the National Archives added a most useful visual dimension on Ford workers, their work tasks and routines, and the Highland Park plant in the 1910s and 1920s.

Journals

Two groups of periodical literature provided general and detailed information of industrial technology and work for the period. First, national technical journals included *Engineering Magazine, Iron Age, Transactions of the American Society of Mechanical Engineers, Journal of the American Society of Mechanical Engineers, Transactions of the Society of Automotive Engineers, Journal of the Society of Automotive Engineers, American Machinist, Annals of the American Academy of Political and Social Sciences,* and *Journal of Political Economy.* Second, labor periodicals included *Detroit Labor News, Official Journal of the Carriage, Wagon, and Automobile Workers' Union, Auto Worker,* and *Auto Workers' News.* All added a technical, social, and economic dimension to the transformation of industrial technology in the period.

The Ford Motor Company was particularly open about the technical and social innovations in the Highland Park plant. As a result, several technical and industrial journalists visited the Ford factory and provided remarkably detailed accounts of its internal operations. Oliver J. Abell, the mid-Western correspondent for *Iron Age*, reported on the Highland Park plant at different times from 1912 to 1915. Fred H. Colvin, a writer for *American Machinist* and later a prominent mechnical engineer, spent several months at the Ford plant for his investigations of technical improvements in the summer and fall of 1913. Horace L. Arnold, a veteran industrial journalist for *Engineering Magazine*, spent almost a year at Highland Park and detailed developments throughout 1914 and 1915. He died before his series was completed and Fay L. Faurote did the last article. Their series of articles was published as the book, *Ford Methods and the Ford Shops*. Edward A. Rumley wrote two articles for *World's Work* in 1914. And, Harry F. Porter, a proponent of modern management, wrote three articles for the English journal *System* in 1916 and 1917. All have been extensively used for a description of the technical innovations and social programs in the Ford Motor Company.

Books and Pamphlets

Arnold, Horace L. and Fay L. Faurote. *Ford Methods and the Ford Shops*. New York, 1916.

Baker, Ray Stanndard, *The New Industrial Unrest: Reasons and Remedies*. Garden City, N.Y., 1920.

Baritz, Loren. *The Servants of Power: A History of the Use of Social Science in American Industry*. Middletown, Conn., 1960.

Barnett, George E. *Chapters on Machinery and Labor*. Cambridge, Mass., 1926.

Barrett, Arthur R., et. al. *Profit Sharing: Its Principles and Practice*. New York, 1918.

Barton, Josef J. *Peasants and Strangers: Italians, Roumanians, and Slovaks in an American City, 1890–1950*. Cambridge, Mass., 1975.

Bendix, Reinhard. *Work and Authority in Industry: Ideologies of Management in the Course of Industrialization*. New York, 1963.

Benson, Allan L. *The New Henry Ford*. New York, 1923.

Bernstein, Irving. *The Lean Years: A History of the American Worker, 1920–1933*. Boston, 1972.

———. *The Turbulent Years: A History of the American Worker, 1933–1941*. Boston, 1971.

Beynon, Huw. *Working for Ford*. London, 1973.

Bing, Alexander M. *War-Time Strikes and their Adjustment*. New York, 1921.

Blauner, Robert. *Alienation and Freedom: The Factory Worker and his Industry*. Chicago, 1964.

Bloomfield, Daniel, ed. *Selected Articles on the Problems of Labor*. New York, 1920.

Bodnar, John. *Immigration and Industrialization: Ethnicity in an American Mill Town, 1870–1940*. Pittsburgh, 1977.

Bonnett, Clarence E. *Employers' Associations in the United States: A Study of Typical Associations*. New York, 1922.

Boyer, Paul. *Urban Masses and Moral Order in America, 1820–1920*. Cambridge, Mass., 1978.

Brandes, Stuart D. *American Welfare Capitalism, 1880–1940*. Chicago, 1976.

Braverman, Harry. *Labor and Monopoly Capital: The Degradation of Work in the Twentieth Century*. New York, 1974.

Bremner, Robert H. *From the Depths: The Discovery of Poverty in the United States*. New York, 1956.

Bright, James R. *Automation and Management*. Boston, 1958.

Brody, David. *Labor in Crisis: The Steel Strike of 1919*. Philadelphia, 1965.

Buder, Stanley. *Pullman: An Experiment in Industrial Order and Community Planning, 1880–1930*. New York, 1979.

Bushnell, Sarah T. *The Truth about Henry Ford*. Chicago, 1922.

Burawoy, Michael, *Manufacturing Consent: Changes in the Labor Process under Monopoly Capitalism*. Chicago, 1979.

Byington, Margaret F. *Homestead: The Households of a Mill Town*. New York, 1910.

Calvert, Monte A. *The Mechnical Engineer in America, 1830–1910*.

Catlin, Warren B. *The Labor Problem in the United States and Great Britain*. New York, 1926.

Chandler, Alfred D. *The Visible Hand: The Managerial Revolution in American Business*. Cambridge, Mass., 1977.

Chaplin, Ralph. *Wobbly: The Rough-and-Tumble Story of an American Radical*. Chicago, 1948.

Chinoy, Ely. *Automobile Workers and the American Dream*. Garden City, N.Y., 1955.

Colvin, Fred H. *Labor Turnover, Loyalty, and Output.* New York, 1919.

Colvin, Fred H. and Lucian L. Haas. *Jigs and Fixtures.* New York, 1943.

Commons, John R. *Industrial Goodwill.* New York, 1919.

_____ . *Labor and Administration.* New York, 1923.

_____ . *Races and Immigrants in America.* New York, 1907.

Commons, John R., et. al. *History of Labor Movements in the States,* vol. 4. New York, 1966.

_____ . *Industrial Government.* New York, 1921.

Conot, Robert. *American Odyssey.* New York, 1975.

Crowther, Samuel. *Why Men Strike.* Garden City, N.Y., 1920.

Daugherty, Carroll R. *Labor Problems in American Industry.* New York, 1933.

Davis, Allen F. *Spearheads for Reform: The Social Settlements and the Progressive Movement, 1890–1914.* New York, 1967.

Dennison, Merrill. *The Power to Go.* New York, 1956.

Detroit Board of Commerce. *Information for Immigrants in Detroit, Michigan, Preparing to Be American Citizens.* Detroit, 1915.

Douglas, Paul H., et. al., eds. *The Worker in Modern Economic Society.* Chicago, 1923.

Dubofsky, Melvyn. *Industrialism and the American Worker, 1865–1920.* New York, 1975.

_____ . *We Shall Be All: A History of the IWW.* Chicago, 1969.

Dubreul, H. *Roberts or Men? A French Workman's Experience in American Industry.* New York, 1930.

Dunn, Robert W. *The Americanization of Labor: The Employers' Offensive against the Trade Unions.* New York, 1927.

_____ . *Company Unions: Employers' Industrial Democracy.* New York, 1927.

_____ . *Labor and Automobiles.* New York, 1929.

Edwards, Charles E. *Dynamics of the United States Automobile Industry.* Columbia, S.C., 1965.

Edwards, Richard. *Contested Terrain: The Transformation of the Workplace in the Twentieth Century.* New York, 1979.

Ehrlich, Richard L., ed. *Immigrants in Industrial America, 1850–1920* Charlottesville, Va., 1977.

Epstein, Ralph C. *The Automobile Industry: Its Economic and Commercial Development.* Chicago, 1928.

Estey, J. A. *The Labor Problem.* New York, 1928.

Ewen, Stuart. *Captains of Consciousness: Advertising and the Social Roots of the Consumer Culture.* New York, 1976.

Faulkner, Harold U. *The Decline of Laissez Faire, 1897–1917.* New York, 1951.

Fine, Sidney. *The Automobile under the Blue Eagle.* Ann Arbor, 1963.

_____ . *Sit-down: The General Motors Strike of 1936–1937.* Ann Arbor, 1969.

Fitch, John A. *The Causes of Industrial Unrest.* New York, 1924.

Flink, James J. *The Car Culture.* Cambridge, Mass., 1977.

Floud, Roderick. *The British Machine Tool Industry.* New York, 1976.

Foner, Philip S. *The Industrial Workers of the World, 1905–1917*. New York, 1973.

Ford, Henry, in collaboration with Samuel Crowther. *Moving Forward*. Garden City, N.Y., 1931.

———. *My Life and Work*. Garden City, New York, 1922.

———. *Today and Tomorrow*. Garden City, N.Y., 1926.

Ford Motor Company. *Bonus, Investment, and Profit Sharing Plan: An Extension to Present Profit Sharing*. Highland Park, Mich., (1919).

———. *A Brief Account of the Educational Work of the Ford Motor Company*. Detroit, 1916.

———. *Facts from Ford*. Highland Park, Mich., 1920.

———. *Ford at Fifty, 1903–1953*. New York, 1953.

———. *Ford Factory Facts*. Detroit, 1915.

———. *Ford Factory Facts*. Detroit, 1917.

———. *The Ford Idea in Education*. Detroit, 1917.

———. *The Ford Industries: Facts about the Ford Motor Company and Its Subsidiaries*. Detroit, 1924.

———. *Helpful Hints and Advice to Employees to Help Them to Grasp the Opportunities which Are Presented to Them by the Ford Profit Sharing Plan*. Detroit, 1915.

Friedheim, Robert. *The Seattle General Strike*. Seattle, 1964.

Friedman, Georges. *The Anatomy of Work: Labor, Leisure, and the Implications of Automation*. New York, 1964.

Fruniss, Edgar S. *Labor Problems*. Cambridge, Mass., 1925.

Garson, Barbara. *All the Livelong Day: The Meaning and Demeaning of Work*. New York, 1979.

Giedion, Siegfried. *Mechanization Takes Command: A Contribution to Anonymous History*. New York, 1955.

Gilbert, James B. *Work without Salvation: America's Intellectuals and Industrial Alienation, 1880–1910*. Baltimore, 1977.

Gooding, Judson. *The Job Revolution*. New York, 1972.

Goodrich, Carter. *The Frontier of Control*. New York, 1921.

Green, Marguerite. *The National Civic Federation and the American Labor Movement, 1900–1925*. Westport, Conn., 1973.

Gutman, Herbert G. *Work, Culture and Society in Industrializing America: Essays in American Working-class and Social History*. New York, 1977.

Haber, Samuel. *Efficiency and Uplift: Scientific Management in the Progressive Era*. Chicago, 1964.

Hamilton, J. G. deRoulhac. *Henry Ford: The Man, the Worker, the Citizen*. New York, 1927.

Hartman, Edward G. *The Movement to Americanize the Immigrant*. New York, 1948.

Herndon, Booton. *Ford: An Unconventional Biography of the Men and their Times*. New York, 1969.

Higham, John. *Strangers in the Land: Patterns of American Nativism,*

1880–1925. New York, 1973.

Hildebrand, Grant. *Designing for Industry: The Architecture of Albert Kahn*. Cambridge, Mass., 1974.

Hobsbawm, Eric J. *Labouring Men: Studies in the History of Labour*. New York, 1964.

Hopkins, Charles H. *The Rise of the Social Gospel in American Protestantism, 1865–1915*. New Haven, 1940.

Hough, Emerson. *The Web: The Authorized History of the American Protective League*. Chicago, 1919.

Hourwich, Isaac A. *Immigration and Labor: The Economic Aspects of European Immigration to the United States*. New York, 1912.

Hoxie, Robert F. *Scientific Management and Labor*. New York, 1916.

Interracial Council. *Proceedings: National Conference on Immigration*. New York, 1920.

James, Marquis. *History of the American Legion*. New York, 1923.

Jardim, Anne. *The First Henry Ford: A Study in Personality and Business Leadership*. Cambridge, Mass., 1970.

Jenks, Jeremiah W. and W. Jett Lauck. *The Immigration Problem*. New York, 1912.

Jensen, Joan M. *The Price of Vigilance*. Chicago, 1968.

Jones, Edward D. *The Administration of Industrial Enterprise*. New York, 1925.

Jones, Franklin D. *Jig and Fixture Design*. New York, 1920.

Jones, Gareth Stedman. *Outcast London: A Study of the Relationship between Classes in Victorian Society*. New York, 1971.

Kakar, Sudhir. *Frederick Taylor: A Study in Personality and Innovation*. Cambridge, Mass., 1970.

Kennedy, Edward D. *The Automobile Industry*. New York, 1941.

Kipnis, Ira. *The American Socialist Movement, 1897–1912*. New York, 1972.

Korman, Gerd. *Industrialization, Immigrants, and Americanizers: A View from Milwaukee, 1866–1921*. Madison, 1967.

Landes, David S. *The Unbound Prometheus: Technological Change and Industrial Development in Western Europe from 1750 to the Present*. New York, 1969.

Lane, Rose Wilder. *Henry Ford's Own Story*. New York, 1917.

Laub, Kenneth D. *An Investigation of Ford Profit Sharing*. Detroit, 1914.

Lauck, W. Jett and Edgar Sydenstricker, *Conditions of Labor in American Industries: A Summarization of the Results of Recent Investigations*. New York, 1917.

Ledenev, S. G. *Za stankom u Forda* (At the Ford Machine). Moscow, 1927.

Leiserson, William. *Adjusting Immigrant and Industry*. New York, 1924.

Lewis, David. *The Public Image of Henry Ford: An American Folk Hero and his Company*. Detroit, 1976.

Lubove, Roy. *The Professional Altruist: The Emergence of Social Work as a Career*. Cambridge, Mass., 1965.

Lutz, R. R. *The Metal Trades*. Philadelphia, 1916.

MacKenzie, Gavin. *The Aristocracy of Labor: The Position of Skilled Craftsmen in the American Class Structure*. New York, 1973.

Marquart, Frank. *An Auto Workers Journal: The UAW from Crusade to One-Party Union*. University Park, Pa., 1975.

Marquis, Samuel S. *Henry Ford: An Interpretation*. Boston, 1923.

Mathewson, Stanley B. *Restriction of Output among Unorganized Workers*. Carbondale, Ill., 1969.

May, Henry F. *Protestant Churches and Industrial America*. New York, 1969.

Mayo, Elton. *The Human Problems of Industrial Civilization*. New York, 1960.

Merz, Charles. *And Then Came Ford*. Garden City, N.Y., 1929.

Miller, James M. *The Amazing Story of Henry Ford*. Chicago, 1922.

Montgomery, David. *Workers' Control in America: Studies in the History of Work, Technology, and Labor Struggles*. Cambridge, Mass., 1979.

Munsterberg, Hugo. *Psychology and Industrial Efficiency*. Boston, 1913.

Murray, Robert K. *Red Scare: A Study of National Hyseria, 1919–1920*. New York, 1964.

National Americanization Committee. *Americanizing a City: The Campaign for the Detroit Night Schools*. Detroit, 1915.

National Civic Federation. *Profit Sharing Report*. New York, 1920.

National Conference on Americanization in Industries. *Proceedings . . . June 22–24, 1919*. New York, 1919.

Nelson, Daniel, *Managers and Workers: Origins of the New Factory System in the United States, 1880–1920*. Madison, 1975.

Nevins, Allan. *Ford: The Times, the Man, the Company*. New York, 1954.

Nevins, Allan and Frank E. Hill, *Ford: Decline and Rebirth*. New York, 1963.

———. *Ford: Expansion and Challenge*. New York, 1957.

Noble, David F. *America By Design: Science, Technology, and the Rise of Corporate Capitalism*. New York, 1979.

Norwood, Edwin. *Ford Men and Methods*. Garden City, N.Y., 1931.

Ozanne, Robert. *A Century of Labor-Management Relations at McCormick and International Harvester*. Madison, 1967.

Park, Robert. *The Immigrant Press and its Control*. New York, 1922.

Park, Robert E. and Herbert A. Miller. *Old World Traits Transplanted*. New York, 1921.

Parker, Carlton H. *The Casual Laborer and Other Essays*. New York, 1920.

Perlman, Mark. *The Machinists: A New Study in American Trade Unionism*. Cambridge, Mass., 1961.

Petersen, H. C. and Gilbert C. Fite, *Opponents of War, 1917–1918*. Seattle, 1957.

Pollard, Sidney. *The Genesis of Modern Management: A Study of the Industrial Revolution in Great Britain*. Baltimore, 1968.

Preston, William, Jr. *Aliens and Dissenters: Federal Suppression of Radicals, 1903–1933*. New York, 1966.

Rae, John B. *The American Automobile: A Brief History*. Chicago, 1965.

236   *The Five Dollar Day*

Rae, John B., ed. *Henry Ford*. Englewood Cliffs, N.J., 1969.
Roberts, Peter. *English for Coming Americans*. New York, 1909.
———. *The New Immigration: A Study in the Industrial and Social Life of South-eastern Europeans in America*. New York, 1912.
Rodgers, Daniel T. *The Work Ethic in Industrial America*. Chicago, 1978.
Roethlisberger, F. J. and W. J. Dickson. *Management and Morale*. Cambridge, Mass., 1939.
Rosenberg, Nathan. *Perspectives on Technology*. New York, 1976.
Rosenblum, Gerald. *Immigrant Workers: Their Impact on American Labor Radicalism*. New York, 1973.
Rothschild, Emma. *Paradise Lost: The Decline of the Auto-industrial Age*. New York, 1974.
Savage, Marion D. *Industrial Unionism in America*. New York, 1922.
Seltzer, Lawrence H. *A Financial History of the Automobile Industry*. New York, 1928.
Serrin, William. *The Company and the Union: The "Civilized Relationship" of the General Motors Corporation and the United Automobile Workers*. New York, 1974.
Sennett, Richard. *Authority*. New York, 1980.
Sennet, Richard and Jonathon Cobb. *The Hidden Injuries of Class*. New York, 1973.
Shannon, David. *The Socialist Party of America: A History*. Chicago, 1967.
Shorter, Edward, ed. *Work and Community in the West*. New York, 1973.
Sinclair, Upton. *The Flivver King: A Story of Ford America*. Pasadena, Calif., 1973.
Slichter, Sumner H. *The Turnover of Factory Labor*. New York, 1919.
Sloan, Alfred P. *Adventures of a White Collar Man*. New York, 1941.
Smith, Merritt Roe. *Harpers Ferry Armory and the New Technology: The Challenge of Change*. Ithaca, N.Y., 1977.
Sorensen, Charles E. *My Forty Years with Ford*. New York, 1956.
Soule, George. *Prosperity Decade: From War to Depression*. New York, 1964.
Stearns, Peter N. and Daniel J. Walkowitz, eds. *Workers in the Industrial Revolution: Recent Studies of Labor in the United States and Europe*. New Brunswick, N.J., 1974.
Stephenson, George M. *A History of Immigration, 1820–1924*. Boston, 1926.
Stidger, William L. *Henry Ford: The Man and his Motives*. New York, 1923.
Sward, Keith. *The Legend of Henry Ford*. New York, 1972.
Taylor, Frederick Winslow. *The Principles of Scientific Management*. New York, 1967.
Taylor, I. Paul. *Prosperity in Detroit*. Highland Park, Mich., 1920.
Tead, Ordway. *Instincts in Industry: A Study of Working-class Psychology*. Boston, 1918.
Thompson, Edward P. *The Making of the English Working Class*. New York, 1963.

Tolman, William H. *Social Engineering: A Record of Things Done by American Industrialists*. New York, 1909.

United States. Bureau of the Census. *Manufactures, 1905: Part 4. Special Reports on Selected Industries*. Washington, 1908.

———. *Special Reports: Occupations of the Twelfth Census*. Washington, 1904.

———. *Twelfth Census of the United States. Special Reports: Employees and Wages*. Washington, 1903.

United States, Bureau of Education. *Proceedings Americanization Conference*. Washington, 1919.

United States. Commissioner of Labor. *Eleventh Report of the Commissioner of Labor. Regulation and Restriction of Output*. Washington, 1904.

United States. Senate. *Report of the Commission on Industrial Relations*, vol. 8. Washington, 1915.

Vasil'ev, V. *Sto dnei u Forda* (One Hundred Days at Ford). Moscow, 1927.

Warne, Frank J. *The Workers at War*. New York, 1920.

Watkins, Gordon S. *Labor Problems*. New York, 1922.

Weinstein, James. *The Corporate Ideal in the Liberal State, 1900–1918*. Boston, 1969.

———. *The Decline of Socialism in America, 1912–1925*. New York, 1969.

White, Lawrence J. *The Automobile Industry since 1945*. Cambridge, Mass., 1971.

Widick, B. J., ed. *Auto Work and its Discontents*. Baltimore, 1976.

Wik, Reynold M. *Henry Ford and Grass-roots America*. Ann Arbor, 1972.

Williams, Raymond. *Keywords: A Vocabulary of Culture and Society*. New Ysrk, 1976.

———. *The Long Revolution*. New York, 1966.

———. *Marxism and Literature*. New York, 1977.

Williams, Whiting. *What's on the Worker's Mind: By One who Put on Overalls to Find out*. New York, 1920.

Woodbury, Robert S. *Studies in the History of Machine Tools*. Cambridge, Mass., 1972.

Zimand, Savel. *The Open Shop Drive: Who Is Behind it and Where Is it Going?* New York, 1921.

Articles

Abell, Oliver J. "The Ford Plan for Employees' Betterment." *Iron Age*, 93 (January 29, 1914), pp. 306–9.

———. "Labor Classified on a Skill-Wages Basis." *Iron Age*, 93 (January 1, 1914), pp. 48–51.

———. "The Making of Men, Motor Cars, and Profits." *Iron Age*, 95 (January 7, 1915), pp. 33–41 and 56.

_____ . "Making the Ford Motor Car." *Iron Age*, 89 (June 6, 1912), pp. 1383–90 and (June 13, 1912), pp. 1454–60.

_____ . "A Six Story Continuous Foundry Building." *Iron Age*, 92 (July 3, 1913), pp. 2–3.

Alexander, Magnus. "Waste in Hiring and Discharging Men." *Iron Age*, 94 (October 24, 1914), pp. 1032–3.

American Society of Mechanical Engineers. "Developments in Machine Shop Practice During the Last Decade." *Transactions ASME*, 34 (1912), pp. 847–65.

_____ . "The Present State of the Art of Industrial Management." *Transactions ASME*, 34 (1912), pp. 1131–1229.

Ardzoomi, Leon. "The Philosophy of Restriction of Output." *Annals AAPSS*, 91 (September 1920), pp. 69–75.

Arnold, Horace L. "Ford Methods and the Ford Shops." *Engineering Magazine*, 47–48 (April 1914-February 1915). This is a monthly series on Ford.

"Assembling Motor Cars in Packard Plant." *Iron Age*, 96 (October 14, 1916), pp. 873–6.

Babcock, George D. "Production Control." *Transactions ASME*, 46 (1925), pp. 667–90.

Baker, A. J. "Selection of Machine Tools." *Transactions ASME*, 17 (1922), pp. 682–97.

Bezanson, Anna. "Skill." *Quarterly Journal of Economics*, 36 (August 1922), pp. 626–45.

Bornholt, Oscar. "Placing Machines for Sequence of Use." *Iron Age*, 92 (December 4, 1912), pp. 1276–7.

Bundy, George. "Work of the Employment Department of the Ford Motor Co." *Bulletin of the Bureau of Labor Statistics*, 196 (1916), pp. 63–73.

Bunnel, Sterling H. "Jigs and Fixtures as Substitutes for Skill." *Iron Age*, 93 (March 5, 1914), pp. 610–1.

Buttrick, John. "The Inside Contract System." *Journal of Economic History* (Summer 1952), pp. 205–21.

"A Canvass of Agricultural Implement and Iron Working Industries in Detroit" in Michigan Bureau of Labor and Industrial Statistics. *Eighth Annual Report* . . . Lansing, Michigan, 1891.

Colvin, Fred H. A series of fourteen articles on Ford production methods. *American Machinist*, 38–39 (May 8-September 18, 1913).

_____ . "Handling Work between Operations." *American Machinist*, 41 (December 17, 1914), pp. 1057–60.

Commons, John R., et al, "Henry Ford, Miracle Maker." *Independent*, 102 (May 1, 1920), pp. 160–1 and 189–91.

"Continuous Pouring in the Ford Foundry." *American Machinist*, 39 (November 27, 1913), pp. 910–12.

Corbin, Arthur E. "Training Employees in a Motor Car Plant." *Iron Age*, 94 (July 30, 1914), pp. 259–61.

Day, Charles. "The Machine Shop Problem." *Transactions ASME*, 24 (1903), pp. 1302–21.

DeWitt, Clinton C. "Industrial Teachers" in *Proceedings Americanization Conference . . . 1919*. Washington, 1919.

Douglas, Paul H. "Plant Administration of Labor." *Journal of Political Economy*, 27 (July 1919), pp. 544–60.

Emmett, Boris. "Profit Sharing in the United States." *Bulletin of the Bureau of Labor Statistics*, 208 (1916), pp. 94–122.

Faurote, Fay L. "Ford Methods and the Ford Shops." *Engineering Magazine*, 48 (March 1915), pp. 859–76.

Fisher, Boyd. "Determining Cost of Labor Turnover." *Annals AAPSS*, 71 (May 1917), pp. 44–50.

———. "How to Reduce Labor Turnover." *Bulletin of the Bureau of Labor Statistics*, 227 (1917), pp. 29–47.

———. "Methods of Reducing Labor Turnover." *Bulletin of the Bureau of Labor Statistics*, 196 (1916), pp. 15–25.

Fitch, John A. "The Clash Over Industrial Unionism: Exhibit A—The Automobile Industry." *Survey Graphic* (January 1936), pp. 39–42 and 64.

———. "Ford of Detroit: And His Ten Million Profit Sharing Plan." *Survey*, 31 (February 7, 1914), pp. 545–50.

———. "Making the Job Worthwhile." *Survey*, 47 (April 27, 1918), pp. 87–9.

———. "Organized Industry in Action." *Official Journal CWAWU*, 3 (June 1914), pp. 7–8.

Flanders, Ralph E. "Design, Manufacture and Production Control of a Standard Machine." *Transactions ASME*, 46 (1925), pp. 691–738.

Ford, Henry. "How I Made a Success of My Business." *System*, 30 (November 1916), pp. 447–52.

"Foundry Economies in the Ford Motor Plant." *Iron Age*, 96 (September 23, 1915), pp. 680–3.

Frankel, Emil. "Labor Absenteeism." *Journal of Political Economy*, 29 (June 1921), pp. 487–99.

Gantt, H. L. "Training Workmen." *Transactions ASME*, 30 (1908), pp. 1037–64.

Glazer, Sidney. "The Michigan Labor Movement." *Michigan History*, 29 (January-March 1945), pp. 73–83.

Godfrey, John R. "Keeping Men on the Job." *American Machinist*, 41 (November 19, 1914), pp. 901–3.

Keeran, Roger R. "Communist Influence in the Automobile Industry, 1920–1933: Paving the Way for an Industrial Union." *Labor History*, 20 (Spring 1979), pp. 189–225.

Keir, John S. "The Reduction of Absences and Lateness in Industry." *Annals AAPSS*, 71 (May 1917), pp. 140–55.

Lape, Esther Everett. "The 'English First' Movement in Detroit." *Immigrants in American Review*, 1 (September 1915), pp. 46–50.

LaFever, Mortimer W. "Workers, Machinery, and Production in the Automobile Industry." *Monthly Labor Review*, 29 (October 1924), pp. 1–26.

Lee, John R. "The So-Called Profit Sharing System in the Ford Plant." *Annals AAPSS*, 65 (May 1916), pp. 297–310.

Leland, Henry M. "The Ideal Automobile Plant." *Transactions SAE*, 8 (1913), pp. 297–301.

Levin, Samuel M. "The End of Ford Profit Sharing." *Personnel Journal*, 6 (October 1927), pp. 161–70.

_____. "Ford Profit Sharing, 1914–1920." *Personnel Journal*, 6 (August 1927), pp. 75–86.

Logan, William A. "The Evolution of the Automobile Business." *Auto Worker*, 5 (August 1923), pp. 5 and 7.

_____. "Has Henry Ford Solved the Labor Problem." *Official Journal CWAWU*, 3 (April 1914), pp. 6–7.

_____. "Historical Sketch of Automobile Workers Union." *Detroit Labor News*, November 9, 1917.

Lord, Chester B. "Fundamentals of Interchangeable Manufacture." *Transactions ASME*, 43 (1921), pp. 421–7.

Love, John W. "Detroit a Sterile Field for Organized Labor." *Annalist*, 28 (November 12, 1926), pp. 629–31.

Marglin, Stephen A. "What Do Bosses Do? Origins and Functions of Hierarchy in Capitalist Production." *Review of Radical Political Economics*, 6 (Summer 1974), pp. 60–112.

Marquis, Samuel S. "Ford Idea in Education" in National Education Association. *Addresses and Proceedings . . . 1916*, vol. 64, pp. 910–17.

Martin, I. T. "The Melting Pot at Ford's: Conditions of Employees under the New Profit Sharing System." *Official Journal CWAWU*, 4 (August 1915), pp. 5–8.

Mason, Gregory. " 'American First': How the People of Detroit Are Making Americans of the Foreigners in their City." *Outlook*, 114 (September 27, 1916), pp. 193–201.

Mead, J. E. "Rehabilitating Cripples at Ford Plant." *Iron Age*, 102 (September 26, 1918), pp. 739–42.

Meeker, Royal. "What Is the American Standard of Living?" *Monthly Labor Review*, 9 (July 1919), pp. 1–13.

Mitchell, John. "Immigration and the American Laboring Classes." *Annals AAPSS*, 34 (July-December 1909), pp. 125–9.

Noble, David F. "Social Choice and Machine Design: The Case of Automatically Controlled Machine Tools, and the Challenge for Labor." *Politics and Society*, 8 (1978) 313–47.

"Occupations in the Automobile Industry." *Bulletin of the Bureau of Labor Statistics*, 348 (1921), pp. 63–70.

Parker, Carlton H. "The Technique of American Industry." *Atlantic Monthly*, 125 (January 1920), pp. 12–22.

Porter, Harry Franklin. "Four Big Lessons from Ford's Factory." *System*, 31 (June 1917), pp. 639–46.

———. "Giving the Men a Share: What It's Doing for Ford." *System*, 31 (March 1917), pp. 262–70.

———. "What's Behind Ford's $1,000,000 a Week." *System*, 30 (December 1916), pp. 598–605.

Pollard, Sidney. "Factory Discipline in the Industrial Revolution." *Economic History Review*, 16 (December 1963), pp. 254–71.

Rankin, Lois. "Detroit Nationality Groups." *Michigan History*, 23 (Spring 1939), pp. 129–205.

Reitell, Charles. "Machinery and its Effect upon the Workers in the Automobile Industry." *Annals AAPSS*, 116 (November 1924), pp. 37–43.

———. "Mechanical Evolution and Changing Labor Types." *Journal of Political Economy*, 26 (March 1918), pp. 274–90.

Rodgers, Daniel. "Tradition, Modernity, and the American Industrial Worker." *Journal of Interdisciplinary History*, 7 (Spring 1977), pp. 655–81.

Rumley, Edward A. "Ford's Plan to Share Profits." *World's Work*, 27 (April 1914), pp. 664–9.

———. "The Manufacturer of Tomorrow." *World's Work*, 28 (May 1914), pp. 106–112.

Shower, C. T. "Guiding the Workman's Personal Expenditures: Ford Reduced Turnover 350 Per Cent." *Automotive Industries*, 38 (March 14, 1918), pp. 539–41 and 547.

Skeels, Jack W. "Early Carriage and Auto Unions: The Impact of Industrialization and Rival Unionism." *Industrial and Labor Relations Review*, 17 (July 1964), pp. 566–83.

Slauson, Harold Whiting. "A Ten Million Dollar Efficiency Plan." *Machinery* (October 1914), pp. 83–7.

Soffer, Benson. "A Theory of Trade Union Development: The Role of the 'Autonomous' Workman." *Labor History*, 1 (Spring 1960), pp. 141–63.

Speek, Peter A. "The Psychology of Floating Workers." *Annals AAPSS*, 69 (January 1917), pp. 72–8.

Stone, Katherine. "The Origins of Job Structures in the Steel Industry." *Review of Radical Political Economics*, 6 (Summer 1974), pp. 113–73.

Strong, Josiah. "What Social Service Means." *Craftsman*, 9 (February 1906), pp. 620–33.

Taylor, Frederick W. "A Piece-Rate System, Being a Step Toward Partial Solution to the Labor Problem." *Transactions ASME*, 16 (1895), pp. 856–903.

———. "Shop Management." *Transactions ASME*, 24 (1903), pp. 1337–1480.

Thompson, Edward P. "Time, Work-discipline, and Industrial Capitalism." *Past and Present*, 38 (December 1967), pp. 56–97.

Van Vlissinger, A. "Safeguarding Your Plant from the Enemy." *Factory*, 20

(June 1918), pp. 1061–5.

Watkins, Myron W. "The Labor Situation in Detroit." *Journal of Political Economy*, 28 (December 1920), pp. 840–52.

"Weeding Out the Inefficient at the Ford Plant." *Automobile*, 30 (May 21, 1914), p. 1082.

Weinstock, Harris. "Immigration and American Labor." *Annals AAPSS*, 69 (January 1917), pp. 66–71.

Wild, Ray. "The Origins and Development of Flow Line Production." *Industrial Archaeology*, 11 (February 1974), pp. 42–55.

Index

DATE DUE